Modular Electrocution System, Operation and Instruction Manual

1. Determine that the main disconnect is off and the input circuit breaker to the power supply is off. Do not proceed unless electric chair energized light is off.
2. Prepare subject for electrocution: Shave approximately a three-inch diameter spot on the top of the executee's head. Cut off pants to knees, slit pants to knees or supply subject with short pants.
3. Mix a saturated saline (saltwater) solution (add salt until it will no longer mix to lukewarm water).
4. Wet sponge in helmet (saturate).
5. Wet ankle sponges if a determination is made that they are to be utilized. Use of sponges is recommended in most cases.
6. Loosen all adjustments in restraint system and move backrest all the way back.
7. Sedate subject either orally or by injection if permissible. A 5cc injection of Verset (Midazolam HCL) 1 mg/ml has been used in the past for sedating executees. Another alternative would be 1.5 ounces of eighty-proof whiskey. This should be done one half hour prior to the execution.
8. Curtain on witness window should be opened.
9. Subject must walk into execution chamber and speak (demonstrating he's alive).

DEATH ROW
CONFIDENTIAL

**Bob Weinstein and
Jim Bessent**

HarperPaperbacks
A Division of HarperCollins*Publishers*

HarperPaperbacks *A Division of* HarperCollins*Publishers*
          10 East 53rd Street, New York, N.Y. 10022

Cover photographs by AP/Worldwide and FPG International

First printing: May 1996

Printed in the United States of America

HarperPaperbacks and colophon are trademarks of HarperCollins*Publishers*

❖ 10 9 8 7 6 5 4 3 2 1

To Bonnie, Jenny, and Josh
To Tommie and James Bessent

ACKNOWLEDGMENTS

This project wouldn't have been possible if it weren't for the hundreds of sources who willingly provided information and leads. Special thanks to William J. Bowers, principal researcher in criminal justice at Northeastern University; death row survivors A. J. Bannister, Lawrence Hayes, Cornelius Butler, Muneer Deeb, Andrew Goldman; Don Cabana, former warden at Mississippi State Penitentiary at Parchman; attorneys Millard Farmer, Stephen Bright, Bryan Stevenson; Karen M. Kirk, public information specialist at the Georgia Department of Corrections; the New York, Florida, California, and Missouri Department of Corrections; researchers Tom Popp, Jenny and Enrique Ball; Jim Crisman of Dobisky Associates; Ricardo Villalobos of the National Coalition to Abolish the Death Penalty; Linda Thurston of Amnesty International; Damaris "Demmy" McGuire, New Yorkers Against the Death Penlaty; James Cameron, founder of the American Black Holocaust Museum in Milwaukee; and special correspondent T. Pete Bonner.

Special thanks also to David Nunnelee, Larry Fitzgerald, and the folks at the Texas Department of Corrections Public Information Office, and those at Ellis Unit; to Kica Matos of the Legal Defense and Educational Fund; to Lieutenant Joy Macfarlane, San Quentin, and the

California Department of Corrections; Debbie Buchanan and the Florida Department of Corrections; Pam Gehman and the Tennessee Department of Corrections; Colleen Williams and the Kentucky Department of Corrections; Alan Abels and the Arkansas Department of Corrections; Rex Tomb and the folks at the FBI's National Press Office; Judy Secondino of the American Correctional Association; and Steve Mundie of Amnesty International. Special assistance was also provided by Cynthia Lewis, Dick Hartzell, Allyson Arias, Danielle Munley, Harriet Weitzner, Ennise Williams, and Nancy Tortellini. Thank you all.

CONTENTS

INTRODUCTION

THE PEOPLE VS. . . .

*"Whatsoever a man soweth,
that shall he also reap."*
— MATTHEW 5: 38–39

- Joe Burrows spent six and a half years on Illinois's death row. He received the death sentence for the farmhouse killing of an eighty-eight-year-old man.
- Muneer Deeb received the death sentence for the brutal killings of three teenagers. He spent nine years at Texas's infamous death row at Huntsville.
- Andrew Golden spent twenty-six months on Florida's death row. He was convicted of killing his wife.
- Walter McMillian spent six years in Alabama's Holman Prison, only yards away from "Yellow Mama," as the state's electric chair is called. McMillian was arrested for killing an eighteen-year-old woman.
- Former Black Panther Lawrence Hayes spent two and a half years on death row in addition to an eighteen-year life sentence for killing an undercover cop.

The above men have one thing in common: they got off death row and lived to talk about their experiences. But more than three thousand men and women on death row throughout the United States won't fare as well. Most will shrivel and atrophy in prison; a small minority will be executed by either electrocution, cyanide gas, or lethal injection.

The prison population is increasing at a frightening rate. The numbers are staggering. Since 1980, the number of prisoners nationwide has grown by over 619,000—approximately 65,208 per year. That translates into an average of more than 1,254 additional prisoners each week. Twenty-two states have reported prisoner increases of 100 percent or higher. By the year 2000, these figures could triple if prisons continue to fill at the current rate. When it comes to incarceration rates, the United States ranks second in the world, behind only Russia. Based on the number of people in prisons, awaiting trial or serving short sentences for misdemeanors in local jails, the United States has an incarceration rate more than four times that of Canada, five times that of England, and fourteen times that of Japan.

As the prison population swells, so does the number of prisoners on death row, that terrifying purgatory where death is just a short walk away. Despite persistent cries by do-gooders, liberals, and the deeply religious, America is hell-bent on exacting revenge on the bad guys. No longer content to put them in jail and throw away the key, U.S. citizens are demanding an "eye for an eye." Vengeance, plain and simple. If you take a life, you pay with your own.

In 1980, only five hundred men and five women were awaiting execution in the United States. Today, that number has jumped to 2,928 men and 48 women. Since 1976, 285 executions have taken place. And, that's nothing compared with what lies ahead.

We are at the dawn of the era of the greatest number of executions in our history. In the pages ahead, you'll meet many of America's most notorious death row prisoners, plus get answers to the questions you've been afraid to ask. You'll discover death row is not like it's portrayed in the movies. It's far worse.

Take a look at your house, car, belongings. Open the window and take a breath of fresh air while sunlight splashes into the room. It feels good all right. Yet these are the things we take for granted. For death row prisoners, these simple pleasures have become unreachable fantasies. They live in a world that is dank, airless, and devoid of sunlight.

It's hard to imagine what it's like living within spitting distance of the gas chamber, the electric chair, or an antiseptic hospital-like room where lethal injections are administered with machinelike efficiency.

Death row prisoners have compared their numbing horror to that of soldiers facing death on the battlefield. But soldiers at least stand a fighting chance of survival. For many death row inmates, the most likely escape is in a cheap wooden box.

Who are the men and women on death row? How did they wind up there? Many are psychopaths, lunatics, mental defectives—society's throwaways who deserve to be locked up. A large number are bright, articulate, even sensitive people who, in a moment of madness, permanently altered the direction of their lives. Some have poignantly written about their death row experiences. The most eloquent of these writings describe the daily agony of coming to terms with death. Every minute of life is a brief respite from death, at the same time as it is a painful lash from a psychological bullwhip.

"Unlike other prisoners, death row inmates are not 'doing time,'" says Mumia Abu-Jamal (a.k.a. Wesley Cook) in *Live on Death Row,* his book about life at Pennsylvania's Huntingdon State Prison. "Freedom does not shine at the end of the tunnel. Rather, the end of the tunnel brings extinction. Bodies are kept alive to be killed."

Death row may be a morbid subject, yet it's also haunting and fascinating. In addition, death row is fertile ground for entrepreneurial ambitions—books, films, souvenirs, magazines, and collectibles, which plenty of vultures have become rich marketing. In all this horror lies a powerful niche industry. Although sickening, it exemplifies the American way.

But when all is said and done, every American citizen is entitled to know how America houses and kills society's menaces, as well as imprisons and sometimes executes innocent people. After all, he or she is footing the bill.

Justice is served in odd ways. Sometimes, it's slow and fair; other times it's swift, cruel, and unjust. There are trends in everything, even in meting out justice. At the moment, conservative thinking dominates America. The majority thinks it makes more sense to kill rather than warehouse prisoners who have committed capital crimes. Yet who's to say what the thinking will be five or ten years from now. Will we have had our fill of executions, realizing they're futile attempts at thwarting crime?

At the moment, the appeals process amounts to a crippling logjam of paperwork that can stall an execution for years. Yet we may be close to expediting the process to just a couple of months. Daily executions may only be a couple of years off. Imagine being so desensitized to the execution process that we'll hardly care.

Who's to say gurneys of condemned men and women with shunts in their arms ready for lethal intravenous injection hookups won't line the halls of execution chambers, waiting for their turn? These doomed prisoners will have showered, eaten their last meal, said last good-byes to family, made their final statements, and been blessed by clergy before clocking out forever. For most, a last-minute reprieve is hardly a remote possibility.

That futuristic image of assembly-line executions is frightening yet plausible. As any death row prisoner will tell you, waiting to die, especially in those last hours, is a slow torture. Spending thirteen years on Missouri's death row, A. J. Bannister achieved the awesome distinction of cheating the executioner only an hour and a half before   deadly poison was scheduled to be injected into his veins. It's no wonder many death row prisoners can't wait to get it over with.

After fifteen years on Virginia's death row and five stays of execution—one just four hours before the death sentence was to be carried out—forty-nine-year-old Willie Lloyd Turner gave up the fight and asked to be executed. On May 25, 1995, he got his wish. Turner had been convicted of shooting a jewelry store owner to death in 1978. Turner's last words, after the intravenous lines were inserted in his arms for his deadly lethal injection, were, "Even a cat has only nine lives. Enough is enough. This is psychological torture."

Because this is a heated issue, we've tried to stick to major issues. *Death Row Confidential* is not just about condemned prisoners facing execution, it's also about ambitious politicians, incompetent attorneys, a tangled legal system, racism, apathy, ruthless entrepreneurs as well as selfless and principled humanitarians. In short, we've covered the major players in this real-life drama.

If we accomplish anything at all, we will open minds and hearts to what's going on out there. We're not presenting fiction. This is a book about real people staring the Grim Reaper right in the eye.

DEATH ROW
CONFIDENTIAL

PART 1

Welcome to Death Row—
THE LAST STOP

*"From my cell you could smell the stench of
burning flesh. The smell of someone you
know burning to death is the most painful and
nauseating experience on this earth."*
—FORMER DEATH ROW PRISONER
WALTER MCMILLIAN DESCRIBING
AN ELECTROCUTION AT HOLMAN PRISON
IN ATMORE, ALABAMA

"All hope abandon, ye who enter here."
—SIGN AT THE GATE TO HELL, DANTE'S *INFERNO*

FORGET THE HOLLYWOOD VERSION OF DEATH
row. No matter what happens on the big screen, an element of hope is always present. The bad are punished, while the good are vindicated and set free. The horror, violence, and insanity are temporary. Predictably, the nightmare ends short of two hours and everyone lives happily ever after.

The real men and women who live on death row offer a more foreboding picture. Many death row prisoners have said waiting to die is little different than actually dying. The isolation, loneliness, boredom, numbing tension, and fear, combined with a loss of hope, have been labeled the "death row syndrome."

Death row is like an antechamber to hell, a surrealistic world. Typically, the appeals process drags on for years. If a prisoner is lucky, the case is reopened and there is a chance of a reversal. Otherwise, the inmate can expect to be wheeled off the row in a cheap pine box, the body burned and mutilated by electric shock or poisoned by cyanide gas or lethal chemicals.

Home for death row prisoners is a tiny closetlike cage containing the most basic amenities—bed, toilet, tiny sink, and cabinet to stow personal belongings. The fortunate get access to a black-and-white television, which helps while away the endless hours. In these windowless, poorly ventilated cells, time stops as days bleed into night.

It's never quiet on death row. Twenty-four hours a day, remote-controlled locks clang open and shut, giant electric gates groan and whir, and floor-to-ceiling metal doors bang shut. Uninterrupted sleep is as rare as it is welcome.

Privacy is nonexistent. Everything from masturbation to self-mutilation becomes a public spectacle. Prisoners can't even go to the bathroom without someone watching.

The moment these men and women are sentenced to death, their lives virtually end. From then on, they wait in limbo, praying for miracles, yet knowing their prayers are futile. "The reality of this waiting place for death is difficult to grasp," writes Sister Helen Prejean in *Dead Man Walking,* a beautifully etched account of her relationships as spiritual adviser to death row prisoners in Louisiana's Angola Prison. "It's not a ward in a hospital where the sick wait to die. People here wait to be taken out of their cells and killed."

The contrast to the freedom of the outside world is

shattering. Most prisons aren't located in ghettos or run-down crumbling neighborhoods. They're in serene, rural settings. That's exactly where law-abiding citizens want them. They certainly don't want rapists and killers caged in their own backyard. Potosi Correctional Center, Missouri's newest maximum security prison, can be found in an economically depressed mining center a day's drive from Kansas City, almost three hours from Jefferson City and an hour from St. Louis.

Maximum-security Huntsville Prison in Texas—which holds the dubious distinction of executing more people than any other state since the death penalty was reinstated in 1976—lies in quiet countryside seventy miles from Houston. Huntsville runs like an efficient bureaucracy. Seven days a week, white-uniformed prisoners trim and clean its well-groomed grounds. Like most country towns containing institutions, Huntsville's population of thirty thousand depends upon the prison. Housing, feeding, and executing criminals amounts to a multibillion-dollar industry. In many state budgets, prisons are now a priority item. The cost of building and operating such places has grown from $6.8 billion in 1980 to more than $30 billion a year.

Pull up to these sprawling fortresses spread out over acres of land and you're dumbstruck by the landscaped entrance, painstakingly manicured by prisoners. But what you see on the outside bears no likeness to what goes on behind the electronically controlled gates, gun towers, and razor wire. Sister Helen describes the red and yellow zinnias and neatly trimmed grass along the winding entrance to Angola Prison as if she were writing about the approach to a park or museum. Presentable on the outside, prison architecture ranges from high-tech modern to medieval fortress.

Inside, it's a different story. Typically, death row is a prison within a prison, a segregated section for the baddest of the bad, those earmarked for "execution" or "termination."

The Bureau of Prisons has sanitized and legitimized a process guaranteed to make the ordinary person sick to the stomach. The officials who run the prisons, wardens to guards, are mechanics of death. Their job is to carry out the death sentence by executing the condemned at the appointed hour. They're expected to do it coolly and professionally. But off the record, the very same bureaucrats who have made a career of housing the living dead occasionally use words like *butcher* or *torture* to describe execution methods gone awry. Even when all goes according to protocol, it's a painful procedure. When botched—and this happens more often than you'd think—it's a nightmare beyond anyone's wildest imagination.

Because of this grisly mission, prisons with death row facilities—thirty-eight states have capital punishment laws on the books—must be orderly places, run with the precision of a Swiss watch. The processing, housing, feeding, and control of hundreds of prisoners is done according to a military model so the work gets done and there's no rebellion in the ranks.

Like high-school janitorial squads swabbing halls, inmates keep prison corridors immaculately clean. No matter where you go, the stomach-turning odor of ammonia mixed with sweat and stale food follows you.

At its best, death row is functional and tolerable. At its worst, it can be likened to a concentration camp. Jefferson City Correctional Facility, home to Missouri's death row before it moved to the modern Potosi, was legendary for its deplorable conditions. Prisoners were locked down twenty-three hours a day with no contact with other prisoners. They were fed only twice a day, at 8:00 A.M. and 2:30 P.M. They went seventeen hours before they were served cold meals on Styrofoam trays.

Conditions were so bad, prisoners filed a class-action suit in federal court, eventually prompting the move to Potosi.

A. J. Bannister, a strapping thirty-seven-year-old death row veteran, spent six years at Jefferson City before he was moved to Potosi in 1989. His court records say he's a contract killer, rapist, and child molester. Bannister denies all charges. Belying his menacing appearance, he is an articulate spokesman for prisoners' rights and, needless to say, vehemently opposes capital punishment.

Bannister and the other death row prisoners at Jefferson City were housed in a subbasement with no natural light. Each cell had a low-wattage bulb that barely gave enough light to read, write, or even tell the time of day. Roach- and rodent-infested, the dank cells often flooded. During the hot summer months, it was so humid, overhead pipes perspired and dripped all day and night. "It was so cold during the winter that the first thing we did before urinating was make sure no ice had formed on top of the toilet," Bannister recalled. "It's a very unpleasant feeling peeing into a toilet and having it splash back up in your face because of a sheet of ice."

Yet many college-trained corrections managers say the days of barbaric prison conditions are over. More and more states are building state-of-the-art facilities, like Oklahoma State Penitentiary's H-Unit. A cleaner version of Jefferson City Correctional, this five-year-old unit is a super-maximum-security facility at ground level, covered by an earth bank on all sides except the entrance. With vaultlike steel doors, thick white concrete walls, and a double chain-link fence with sharp coils of razor wire, H-unit is escape-proof. Prisoners live virtually underground, with no natural light. An Amnesty International delegation inspected the unit and found the conditions to be "cruel, inhuman, and degrading." Confined twenty-four hours a day in windowless cells, prisoners call the H-Unit a tomb. There, Thomas J. Grasso, who holds the distinction of being the first New York resident to get the death penalty in thirty-two years, was strapped to a gurney and executed by lethal injection on March 19, 1995. Convicted in both New York and Oklahoma, he was executed in Oklahoma because New York didn't restore the death penalty until September 1995. Grasso strangled an eighty-seven-year-old woman in Tulsa with her own Christmas tree lights on Christmas Eve 1990 while stealing a cheap television set and twelve dollars. He preferred death to the excruciating boredom of prison life. He fought New York Governor Mario Cuomo's attempts to extradite him.

Despite the daily terror of waiting to die, many prisoners have undergone astounding transformations as their execution date drew near. Joe Ingle, a Church of Christ minister, has seen it repeatedly over his twenty years of counseling death row prisoners. Ingle has been to every death row in the South. Wardens call him by his first name; death row prisoners consider him one step removed from Jesus Christ himself.

Ingle estimates he's worked with more than two hundred death row prisoners, twenty of whom have been executed. He's watched some of them practically transcend the ordeal, mustering the courage to walk calmly to their death. Like Socrates, who spent hours prior to his execution by hemlock in 399 B.C. examining his life and discussing the immortality of the soul, many prisoners awaiting death become intensely philosophical. What better time to sort out all the ambiguities in life than during its last moments.

In a rhythmic North Carolina drawl, Ingle makes a point of saying that many of his relationships with death row prisoners turned into decade-long friendships. His cardinal rule is never to witness an execution. "You can't work closely with people and then watch them be exterminated," he said. "It's just inhuman."

He made an exception to this rule when Willie Jasper Darden asked him to witness his electrocution at Starke's Florida State Prison in March 1988. The men were good friends, having spent countless hours together over an eleven-year period. After seven execution stays, both Darden and Ingle knew Darden's card was finally going to be punched. The night before the execution, Ingle talked with Darden, helping him answer letters that had poured in from supporters all over the world. Darden's case had received a good deal of attention, largely due to people who were convinced he was innocent. But the question of innocence didn't count for much in his final hours. By 5:00 A.M., the appointed hour for Darden to be prepped (shaving of his head and calves) and driven to the execution chamber at the far end of the prison, death row had turned surreal.

At the crack of dawn of a new day on God's earth, Ingle could not understand how a human being could be quietly taken away and executed. At 6:30 A.M., a half hour before the scheduled event, witnesses were fed a breakfast of scrambled eggs, bacon, biscuits, and coffee in a small dining room with the Florida state flag propped prominently in a corner. His stomach churning, Ingle could barely sip black coffee.

At 7:00 A.M., witnesses took their seats in the observation booth of the execution chamber and watched as Darden marched in, his legs and hands shackled. Unflinching, without the slightest hint of fear, he sat in the sturdy oak electric chair as guards secured his chest and legs with thick leather straps. Ingle was awed by Darden's composure. "He was downright regal, like an

African king," he recalls, the event burned into his consciousness. "His posture was erect, his shiny head held up proudly."

When asked if he had a last statement, Darden spoke eloquently for five minutes, reiterating his claims of innocence and thanking everyone around him by name. When he finished, Darden winced as a guard shoved his head back so a chin strap could be fastened to the headpiece. Once his head was securely in place, Darden winked at Ingle, standing in the back of the witness room. After that, the curtain on Darden's life was brought down quickly and violently. A black shroud was dropped over his head just before 2,400 volts of electricity were run through his body. Darden was officially pronounced dead at 7:12 A.M.

Margaret Vandiver, a paralegal who assisted Darden's attorneys, as well as an opponent of capital punishment and all-around angel of mercy, also knew the prisoner well. She spent countless hours with him over a nine-year period during which he miraculously survived seven death warrants. A kind of Mother Teresa with legal training, she worked on about fifty death row cases throughout the South, over a twelve-year period. In the process, she got to know twenty-five prisoners well. Like Ingle, Vandiver was awed by Darden's composure each time he faced death. "Guilty or innocent, Willie was remarkable for his extraordinary courage," she recalled. "He was a role model and mentor to every person on death row." When, through some legal loophole, he managed to get a last-minute stay of execution from the Supreme Court, thunderous applause and cries of joy greeted him as he returned to his cell.

It wasn't hard to understand why everyone, including his captors, looked up to Darden. He was "an inspiration to everyone facing death," Vandiver remembered. His unspoken message rang loud and clear throughout death row. This is how you face death and not give up your dignity. This is how you live on death row and not demean yourself in front of your keepers. This is how you act like a man in the most degrading situation imaginable.

As upsetting as Willie Darden's execution was, Ingle says his behavior prior to the execution was not atypical. "Prisoners within hours of being killed reach out not only to me but to their families and to people around them in loving and supportive ways that are just astonishing," he said. He couldn't explain why it happens, yet candidly admitted that he doubts he would be able to do so if he were in their shoes.

Often, the transformation begins several months after they arrive on the row. Once they start coping with their fear and boredom, and learn how to get through the day, they reach out to other prisoners, forming tightly knit communities. Ingle debunks the myth that convicted felons cannot change. "The state doesn't accomplish that feat, they do it by themselves," he said. "I've known guys who have killed three people and mature into fine human beings." An outspoken opponent of capital punishment, Ingle says the problem is that prisoners are judged by their worst moments, "desperate seconds which bring their life to an untimely end."

Whether there is an actual transformation, a total rehabilitation of a once-tormented human being, countless men facing death become almost heroic in their final hours. Whether their defenses break down, or for the first time in their lives, they see vividly the results of their actions, they become legitimately worried about the effects of the death row drama on family and friends. Gary Gilmore, executed by firing squad in 1977 and the first person to be executed in the United States in a decade, seemed a pillar of strength right until the very end. His journalist brother, Mikal Gilmore, wrote countless stories of how Gary tried to ease the pain for his family. In a 1977 *Rolling Stone* article, Mikal remembered his brother's last words to him: "Give my love to Mom. . . . And put on some weight. You're still too skinny." And as Mikal left his brother and the gates closed behind him for the last time, Gary called out, "Take it easy, fella."

Ironically, despite the numbing tension accompanying the wait to die, many death row prisoners enjoy awesome celebrity status within the prison subculture. Whether due to the notoriety of their crime, efforts to foil the legal system, or the media attention they receive, they manage to capture star status and keep the executioner at bay. Unless the crime is as detestable as child molestation or cannibalism, death row prisoners capture immediate respect in the prison hierarchy.

Some prisoners admittedly enjoy being in the spotlight. For some, it's the only fame they'll ever enjoy. What does it matter if many are getting the attention for the wrong reasons? Serial killers head the list for marketing their crimes. Ted Bundy, David "Son of Sam" Berkowitz, Henry Lee Lucas, John Wayne Gacy, Richard Speck, and many others captured front-page headlines.

Caryl Chessman could have written the official death row handbook for stalling the execution machinery. A Los Angeles hood with a long criminal record, Chessman was found guilty and sent to death row in 1948 on seventeen counts, which included kidnapping, robbery, and sexual perversion. Bright, articulate, and belligerent, Chessman had secured eight stays before he was finally executed on March 10, 1960. He proved that by filing endless appeals, execution could be delayed almost indefinitely. Up to the last minute, Chessman scoffed at death. He walked proudly into San Quentin's gas chamber, known as the "Green Room," and defiantly held his breath for one minute before sucking in the deadly fumes.

More significant, Chessman quickly discovered public support could help keep him alive. In his twelve years on death row, a record at that time for an American prisoner, he became a symbol of what was wrong with capital punishment. In 1948, he held a news conference from his cell and stated, "I don't feel there is anything equitable, fair, sensible, or valid about capital punishment."

He also became a prolific writer, turning out several books, including the best-seller *Cell 2455*, in which he eloquently pleaded his case. A charismatic figure, he not only rallied "abolitionist" and prominent civil-rights attorneys like the late William Kunstler to his side, but the rich and famous as well. His case was followed all over the world. Two million supporters around the world—including Albert Schweitzer, Eleanor Roosevelt, Pablo Casals, Marlon Brando, and Shirley MacLaine—signed a petition calling for clemency.

More recently, serial killer Leslie Allen Williams cleverly manipulated the Detroit media after his 1992 killing of four women. Instead of randomly granting interviews, Williams created a contest, of which he would be the sole judge, to award one television station an exclusive interview. He also gave the *Detroit News* the right to publish a lengthy open letter to the public explaining his philosophy and expressing his opinions. In the recent book *Overkill: Mass Murder and Serial Killing Exposed,* criminologists James Alan Fox and Jack Levin tell the story of how serial killer Donald Harvey, who reputedly murdered several patients while working as an orderly in a Cincinnati-area hospital, landed a taped interview on Oprah Winfrey's TV show. Since the show was appropriately titled "Nurses Who Kill," what better expert than a confessed serial killer who had worked in a hospital. However, Winfrey and her producers got more than they bargained for. Throughout the lengthy interview, Harvey described how he suffocated some victims and injected others with poison in gory detail and with unbridled pleasure. As a result, the show's producers decided it would be unethical, not to mention in bad taste, to air the program.

Practically speaking, media attention does more than feed warped egos, it keeps the execution-bound alive. Nobody knows that better than Potosi's A. J. Bannister, who achieved the awesome distinction of cheating the executioner on December 7, 1994, just an hour and a half before they were planning to shoot deadly poison through his veins. He made sure the world knew about every lurid detail of the event, showering the media with lengthy, articulate letters describing his treatment on that traumatic day and what it felt like to be knocking on death's door. He had eaten his last meal (T-bone steak, french fries, salad, and low-calorie cheesecake), was given an antihistamine shot (the first part of the execution procedure), and said his last good-byes to his wife and family. "The incredible irony of the situation," quipped Bannister, "is they give an antihistamine to relax the lungs so you don't have an adverse reaction to the second drug. I'm thinking to myself, 'How much more adverse can it be than dying?'"

In the two hours preceding the execution, the machinery Bannister had set in motion kicked into high gear, saving his life. Waiting in the holding cell just prior to the execution, Bannister said Potosi's telephone lines were jammed by six hundred calls from supporters around the world protesting the execution. One of the callers was actor Ed Asner, an ardent and outspoken abolitionist, who had phoned with some kind words to help Bannister through the ordeal.

Even prior to the last-minute reprieve, Bannister had commandeered a small army of advocates. Worldwide support began in earnest after he and other Potosi death row prisoners were prominently featured in filmmaker Stephen Trombley's hard-hitting documentary *The Execution Protocol*. Filmed in Potosi in 1992, the documentary shows Bannister and fellow death row prisoner Doyle Williams describing what it's like waiting to die, plus every minute detail of the execution process. Within five weeks of airing, Bannister received seven hundred letters from all over the world. To date, he has received letters from four thousand supporters, including Mother Teresa. He's been interviewed (from prison) by Phil Donahue and Geraldo Rivera. Most recently, his life received national attention in Trombley's latest documentary, *Raising Hell: The Life of A. J. Bannister*. The documentary tells the story of how Bannister, the eldest of six children and an above-average student, screwed up his life and wound up on death row.

Like Chessman, Bannister devotes every waking hour to staying alive. Most of his time is spent answering his mail, especially to journalists, and making collect phone calls. His letters are sensitively and thoughtfully written, notable for their philosophical and often humorous insights about the daily art of living on death row. In a recent letter, Bannister mused that he's spent thirteen years on death row, one year more than Chessman, better than one third of his life.

It doesn't really matter whether Bannister got a raw deal or exactly what he deserves. The fact is, he's aroused public sympathy. After seeing thirteen friends

executed, Bannister pours all his energy into getting the
word out. His ultimate goal—if he can stay alive—is to
self-publish a book he has written about the American
justice system. He figures he's already got a waiting
audience.

Mumia Abu-Jamal already accomplished this feat. He
wrote a book in his prison cell, appropriately titled *Live
from Death Row,* arousing national public support for
his case, not to mention the plight of death row prisoners throughout the United States. The book focuses on
the prison system, corrupt politicians, and the psychological and physical torment of waiting to die.

Abu-Jamal was convicted of killing Philadelphia
police officer Daniel Faulkner in 1982 and sent to
Huntingdon Prison where he spent thirteen years until
his recent transfer to Pennsylvania's spanking-new
super-maximum SCI Greene County Prison. He is
locked in an almost soundproof eight-by-ten-foot cell
for twenty-three to twenty-four hours a day.

Abu-Jamal's story has all the makings of a
Hollywood epic and a TV miniseries rolled into one. At
its nucleus is Abu-Jamal, bright, educated, controversial, street-smart, an articulate speaker and masterful
media manipulator. He's surrounded by a supporting
cast that includes Judge Albert F. Sabo, better known
as the "hanging judge," with the distinction of sending
thirty-one people to death row, more than any other
judge in Pennsylvania. Also involved is Maureen
Faulkner, the widow of the police officer Abu-Jamal is
accused of killing, and the entire Philadelphia police
squad, all of whom are convinced Abu-Jamal is a cold-
blooded killer who ought to be executed. Last, but by
no means least, is Abu-Jamal's upscale and affluent
army of supporters, which includes authors Alice
Walker and Norman Mailer; poet Maya Angelou;
actors Paul Newman, Joanne Woodward, Tim Robbins,

and Danny Glover; and filmmakers Spike Lee and
Oliver Stone. A powerful entourage like that carries so
much clout even Judge Sabo saw fit to grant Abu-Jamal
a stay ten days before his scheduled execution date of
August 17, 1995.

The former Black Panther and radio reporter unflag-
gingly maintains his innocence. According to court
records, early on December 9, 1981, Faulkner stopped
Abu-Jamal's brother for driving the wrong way on a
downtown city street. The police contend Abu-Jamal,
who was driving a cab, stumbled on the scene and
came up and shot Faulkner in the back and face. The
wounded officer shot Abu-Jamal in the chest, then died
an hour later at a hospital. Abu-Jamal presents a different story. Abu-Jamal says he purposely drove down the
one-way street to come to the aid of his brother, who
was being beaten by Faulkner. After that, the facts get
muddy. Eyewitnesses say someone fired on the officer
and then fled and that Abu-Jamal was beaten at the
scene, shot, and left bleeding on the curb for forty-five
minutes before he was taken to a hospital. Oddly, no
one could determine why Abu-Jamal's younger brother
never came forward to testify on his sibling's behalf.

Guilty or innocent, Abu-Jamal has become a cause
célèbre among the abolitionist and intellectual/artistic
community, spearheaded by his book, which is selling
briskly thanks to rave reviews. A *Boston Globe*
reviewer said his "brief essays resonate with the moral
force of Martin Luther King Jr.'s 'Letter from
Birmingham Jail.'"

Thanks to a swirl of controversy, publisher Addison-
Wesley didn't have to work hard to arouse media interest in Abu-Jamal's book. He has been elevated to icon
status among civil libertarians, political leaders, and
abolitionists. Actor Ossie Davis led the campaign to
have Abu-Jamal's death sentence commuted and writers

like E. L. Doctorow and Cornell West have published scathing essays and articles attacking the legal system for condemning Abu-Jamal to death. In the midst of a national campaign driven by a star-studded cast of thousands, anti–death penalty resource group Equal Justice USA/Quixote Center, of Hyattsville, Maryland, is raising money to cover Abu-Jamal's court expenses. Meanwhile, Faulkner's widow launched a boycott of Addison-Wesley, saying the book perpetuates the nightmare of her husband's murder.

While the abolitionists are delighted with the attention Abu-Jamal is getting, it amounts to a bittersweet victory. It points up the fact that only death row superstars get the attention. Caryl Chessman, Bannister, and Abu-Jamal were fortunate because they were good writers as well as masterful promoters who enlist powerful intellectuals in their fight. But sometimes this tactic can backfire in the prisoner's face. Norman Mailer would like to forget how he rallied an influential group of writers to secure an early release for prison author Jack Henry Abbott. Hardly out of prison two weeks, Abbott stabbed a waiter to death because he refused to let him use an off-limits bathroom. The *New York Times* described the support of highly visible intellectual criminals as "radical chic," a powerful force that often altered the course of justice. But once the rich and famous tire of the cause, the hoopla dies and the once-popular prisoner becomes another forgotten statistic.

Beyond the occasional criminal media star, there are three thousand other death row prisoners about whom few people know or care. On every death row throughout the United States, there are tales of men and women relentlessly stalling the death row machinery. Outside of Potosi, few people know how cleverly and persistently Bannister's buddy Doyle Williams, forty-seven, managed to escape ten execution dates, two of which were down to the wire. A jailhouse lawyer with the polished intellectual dexterity of F. Lee Bailey in his prime, Williams doesn't rely solely on court-appointed lawyers to defend him. He's taken on the criminal justice system himself, playing a major role in his own defense. So far, his articulate appeals have kept him alive. That's no small feat when you consider he's been sitting on death row for fifteen years. The prosecutor claimed Doyle killed a man who knew Doyle had burglarized a doctor's office. The state said he handcuffed, beat, and pistol-whipped the man, who ran into a river and drowned trying to flee. Doyle insists this is sheer fabrication. In the process of bucking the legal system, he's become a walking encyclopedia of information about the criminal justice system and a master at delaying his death row sentence. This is especially impressive considering his court-appointed attorney specializes in representing savings-and-loan organizations. Defending death row prisoners is his lawyer's low-paying sideline.

While Bannister manages to snare headlines and be the star in his own real-life drama, Williams's days are spent poring over law books and teaching fellow prisoners how the legal system works; his nights are devoted to writing legal briefs on a portable typewriter he keeps underneath his bed.

Yet Williams's philosophy can be likened to the Alcoholics Anonymous "one day at a time" ritual. Knowing there may not be a tomorrow, he's thankful to get through each day. The speed-talking North Carolinian compares himself to a foot soldier engaged in trench warfare. "All a soldier can do is hope for the best and pray a bullet doesn't hit him," he said matter-of-factly. "My situation isn't much different. In fighting the judicial process, there will be casualties. It takes skill, but there is a lot of luck involved, too."

Whether it's skill, luck or a healthy combination of the two, Williams has cheated the executioner thus far. But who's to say what tomorrow will bring?

No matter how much media attention they capture or how many crowbars they jam into the legal machinery, the best that most death row prisoners can hope for is to stall the inevitable. Even startling transformations count for little. For most, they come too late. It's only a matter of time before the death warrant is carried out and they're ritualistically taken away to be killed in either the serene postdawn hours or at the ominous one minute past midnight.

The secret to staying sane on death row is finding a way to kill time. Jack Nordgaard, a Lutheran pastor who has worked with countless prisoners at Illinois's two maximum-security prisons, said, "It makes it a whole lot easier to survive with dignity when you can find something to fill the days. Most guys find ways to deal with it. The human spirit, even in the worst conditions, is resilient. If they don't do something, it becomes a long and depressing stay. Remarkably, many tap into their creative core, drawing upon abilities they never knew they had. They paint, write, crochet, knit. Some do amazing stuff with no tools to help them."

For many, that's easier said than done. Trying to cope with a hostile, meaningless existence drives many prisoners over the edge. Alvin Ford, convicted of killing a police officer, is one example. Before the Supreme Court barred the execution of the incompetent, Ford had lost his mind after receiving several last-minute stays. By the time his life was spared by the Supreme Court, he was a babbling, broken, and emaciated wisp of a man who spoke in code. Ford died in 1991 in Florida State Prison.

More pathetic are the subintelligent and feeble-minded who walk to their deaths having only a vague idea they're going to be killed. The execution of Arthur Frederick Goode is notable in this respect. Convicted in 1976 and executed in Florida in 1984 at the age of thirty, Goode stands out among death row's most pitiful and warped lunatics, despised by practically everyone who knew him. A product of a poor Washington, D.C., working-class neighborhood with the IQ of an eight-year-old, Goode was an obsessive and dangerous pedophile. Ever since puberty, he had a consuming fixation on little boys. It was the only thing he could think and talk about. By the time his parents tried to get him help, Goode had already molested countless little boys. No sooner did a psychiatrist at a Maryland mental hospital recommend that he be committed to a hospital for the criminally insane than Goode hopped on a bus headed to Cape Coral, Florida. When he got there, he wasted no time raping and strangling to death a nine-year-old boy.

Feeling some remorse, Goode headed back to the Maryland hospital and tried to check himself in. When a busy receptionist asked him to wait his turn and take a seat, he skipped again, this time getting on a bus to Virginia. As soon as he got off, he raped and strangled an eleven-year-old. Instead of heading back home, he bused to Florida, where he was finally arrested. It was bad enough he slipped through the cracks and wasn't tossed in a padded cell, the ultimate farce was he was allowed to defend himself, like insane Colin Ferguson, a psychopath who killed six passengers on a Long Island commuter train. To the disgust of jurors, attorneys, and horrified spectators, Goode turned the trial into a public forum on the joys of pedophilia. He stood up in the courtroom, candidly telling jurors what he'd do to their children if he were alone with them. After that, the jury came to a speedy verdict. When Goode begged for the death penalty, the judge gladly gave it to him. Yet the simple truth was, feebleminded Goode didn't have the foggiest idea what he was doing. Not only did he not know the difference between right and wrong, he didn't know the prison actually planned to execute him. Sadder still, this hopelessly infantile man naively befriended the one person he should have avoided. Goode had become attached to his executioner, Richard Dugger, then superintendent at the Florida State Prison. Goode was convinced Dugger would keep him out of harm's way. But it was Dugger who gave the electrician the signal to throw the switch.

Margaret Vandiver also worked on Goode's case, holding the dubious distinction of knowing him better than anyone else. Vandiver spent the last moments with Goode before he was strapped into the chair, and recalls that Goode barely had a clue as to what was happening. "Of all the people executed in Florida, he was probably the most pitiful," said Vandiver.

Even Vandiver, who, along with Goode's parents and attorneys, were his only allies, found him difficult beyond words. "After reading about his case, I went out to visit him with a lot of misgivings," she recalled.

Goode didn't disappoint her. "He was without a doubt the most difficult person I had ever dealt with, on or off death row. Give him a moment and he'd start talking about little boys," said Vandiver. "The only way to stop him was to treat him as if he were a three- or four-year-old child."

Vandiver would take a deep breath and stare him straight in the eyes and say, "I didn't come here to talk about little boys. I'm here to talk about your case, Arthur. We're going to file appeal papers."

Within a few minutes, he'd be back to the pleasures of tormenting little boys or would go off on an endless tirade about not having enough toilet paper or not getting certain channels on his TV.

Throughout his prison stay, Goode couldn't understand why everyone hated him. Vandiver remembered him stalking out of his cell one day like a hurt child, wailing that a certain guard was mean to him. "Did you do anything to the officer, Arthur?" she asked. "I told him what I'd like to do with his little boy," Goode replied.

For Goode's own protection, the superintendent kept him locked in his cell practically twenty-four hours a day on Q Wing, the confinement cell block reserved for the worst offenders, who can't be around other prisoners. He stayed there until he was executed. Allowing this tortured soul a mere hour in the yard would have meant sure death.

If Goode felt any remorse for his crime, it was more like a repentant child sent to his room for stealing candy than an adult who had committed rape and murder. At the prodding of Superintendent Dugger and Vandiver, Goode's final words were an apology to his parents and an expression of remorse for killing the two boys. Yet it was more than clear that Goode went to his death barely understanding the depth or the repercussions of his actions. Maybe it was a good thing. If he had experienced intense fear about his pending execution, he may have attempted to bolt from the execution chamber, screaming like an outraged adolescent. It would have meant forcibly strapping him into the chair. But, like a recalcitrant child who misbehaved once too often, Goode sheepishly sat in the chair awaiting punishment.

After the tragic event, outraged journalists and abolitionists rocked the nation with stories of gross moral and ethical wrongdoing by the state of Florida. What's remarkable about Goode's case is the combined incompetence of the criminal justice and mental health systems. What did it matter that the governor of Maryland ordered a full-scale investigation of the mental health facilities and that Florida's judicial system was given a firm slap on the wrist? The deed was done. Everyone asked the same questions. Is this what capital punishment is all about? How is the execution of a hapless, borderline retarded lunatic with a documented history of mental illness dating back to age three a deterrent to crime? Only after the event did anyone admit that a gross wrong had been done. Even Superintendent Dugger acknowledged that of all the executions he had to carry out, Goode's was the hardest because he was so sick. Harder still was the knowledge that Goode walked to his death thinking Dugger was his friend.

By then, it was too late. Goode had already been executed. Somehow, the system found a way to prosecute and kill a demented and tortured man who should have been locked away in a mental institution. Goode was snuffed with the same icy detachment as Hitler's henchmen, attempting to rid Germany of non-Aryan blood.

The 1992 execution of pitiful Ricky Ray Rector in Arkansas, Bill Clinton's home state, was similar. Severely learning-disabled, Rector grew up in the black section of the tiny town of Conway. The sixth of seven children, he was an odd and lost loner who lived on society's fringes until he got into trouble. He was expelled from school before he completed the tenth grade. He loved children and animals but couldn't get along with adults. At night, he aimlessly prowled the streets. He managed to hold down a series of jobs that included asphalt layer and roofer and to get married and have children. But no matter what Rector did, he remained disconnected from everything around him. On a clear and chilly early spring evening in 1980, Rector's life took a fatal turn. Twenty-nine years old at the time, Rector and two friends drove into town to attend a dance in a rented hall. Rector got into an argument over the three-dollar admission charge, insisting that one of his friends be admitted even though he had only one dollar. It ended badly when Rector pulled out a .38 pistol and began randomly firing. Two men were wounded and a third was killed immediately after being hit in the forehead and throat. Rector fled into the country, wandering in a daze for two days and eventually winding up at the home of his sister. She insisted he give himself up to sympathetic local policeman Bob Martin, who had known Rector since he was a child. Rector agreed.

Martin arrived at Rector's sister's house first. Rector followed shortly after. Proceeding cautiously, Martin had the good sense to never mention taking Rector in, for all the good it did him. Suddenly, without warning, Rector fired two shots at Martin, catching him in the jaw and neck. Martin slid from a chair to the floor in a pool of blood. The fatal bullet opened his cartoid artery, shattering his neck vertebrae. While his mother and sister screamed in horror, Rector slipped out the back door into the yard and shot himself in his left temple. When the police found him moments later, Rector was still breathing. He had botched the job. He was rushed to the hospital and underwent surgery, during which three inches of frontal brain tissue were removed. When it was over, Rector had undergone a prefrontal lobotomy, leaving him severely impaired and totally incompetent. He had no concept of past or future and had the mental age of a six-year-old child. Not only did he not remember what he did, he twisted the events. One of Rector's versions of what happened was that the police killed the policeman and then shot him in the head. Asked again, he said he ran from the house because he was afraid of being beaten in jail and thus, shot himself in the head. Rector's mental condition, however, didn't count for much. Despite his obvious incompetence, which was proven countless times by neuropsychologists, the citizens of Conway, as well as the majority of Arkansas, demanded revenge. Even though the Sixth Amendment says the accused must be capable of meaningfully assisting his counsel in his defense, Rector underwent two trials, the first for killing Arthur Criswell at the dance, the second for killing Officer Martin. The first trial sentenced him to life without parole. But in the second trial, all it took was fifteen minutes for an all-white jury to deliver the death sentence. When the judge told Rector he was going to be executed, Rector turned to his attorney and asked, "Does this mean I'll get a television in my cell?"

Rector was sent to death row at Cummins Prison and eventually transferred to the maximum-security unit at Tucker Prison in 1986. Six years later, he was executed by lethal injection. After his last meal of steak, fried chicken in heavy gravy, brown beans, three rolls, and cherry Kool-Aid, Rector put aside a plump helping of pecan pie for later, as was his habit. He was convinced he'd return to his cell after the execution. Over his ten-year prison stay, Rector was somewhat of a legend for gorging himself with food all day and uncontrollably dancing around his cell, howling and barking like a dog. When he was strapped onto the gurney in the death chamber, Rector weighed in at 298 pounds. Even urgent pleas to spare his life on moral and humanitarian grounds from Jesse Jackson and chaplains all over the country didn't count for much. A fellow prisoner who knew Rector well said, "It was like leading a lamb to slaughter. They might as well have executed a child."

Governor Clinton didn't lift a finger to halt the execution. He had other things on his mind. He was hot on the campaign trail and preoccupied with rebutting tabloid allegations over the Gennifer Flowers affair. What's more, Clinton was rebutting any claims that he was soft on crime. The night prior to the execution, Clinton barricaded himself in the governor's mansion, turning a deaf ear to last-minute pleas to save Rector's life. Ironically, just prior to being escorted to the execution chamber, Rector insisted he'd vote for Clinton in the upcoming presidential race.

More recently, the execution of thirty-seven-year-old Girvies L. Davis at Illinois's Menard Correctional Center by lethal injection tweaked the public's conscience about executing a mentally disabled person. What's more, it's still hotly contended that he was innocent. Davis was sent to death row for killing Charles Diebel, an eighty-nine-year-old retired farmer, on December 22, 1978. Diebel was found slumped in his wheelchair, his chest shredded by two bullet wounds.

A fourth-grade dropout who suffered brain damage from a childhood bicycle accident, Davis had an IQ bordering on mental retardation. With an arrest record dating back to age ten, Davis was raised by alcoholic parents and was taught how to steal by his mother. Despite the checkered past, Davis received the death sentence based on a signed confession, which Davis maintained was coerced. At the time he supposedly penned his confession, he was illiterate, a claim later supported by a doctor's report. Yet by the time he was executed, Davis had learned to read, thanks to prisoners who prepared flash cards. Eventually, he earned a high-school equivalency diploma and became an ordained minister. When asked if he had read the confession before signing it, Davis said, "Naw, I couldn't even read back then. I could barely sign my name." Nevertheless, Davis, who is black, was sentenced to death by an all-white jury.

Even many high-placed death penalty proponents felt Davis was innocent. If nothing else, he deserved life imprisonment due to all the unanswered questions surrounding his case. A hard-nosed former police chief, a former prosecutor, plus a long list of literati headed by author Studs Terkel tried in vain to rescue Davis from execution. Davis's final words: "I ain't never killed nobody."

There aren't many happy endings on death row, but a lucky few have escaped death and walked out of prison free citizens. Since 1970, about fifty people have been freed from death row after their convictions were reversed or thrown out. Joe Burrows is among them. Prior to that, like the eighty-eight other men on death row in Illinois's Menard Penitentiary, Burrows, forty, was doomed to die by lethal injection.

In 1989, he was sentenced to death for the farmhouse murder of an eighty-eight-year-old man. Like many other condemned men, he swore he was innocent. Burrows, however, was telling the truth. In 1994, he was vindicated when the prosecution's two chief witnesses recanted their testimony that they had seen Burrows commit the murder. One of the witnesses confessed to the killing. Perjured testimony almost sent Burrows to a premature death.

It's a miracle Burrows wasn't executed. During his almost six years and ten months on death row, he survived three death dates, all of which were stayed within weeks of the execution. Since 1991, there have been four executions at Menard, two of which occurred in one night in 1995. Not a day went by when Burrows didn't wonder whether he would be next to be prepped for lethal injection.

Today, Burrows lives with his wife and four children in Homer, Illinois, a tiny town 140 miles south of Chicago. Fearing his newfound freedom was only a dream, the former death row resident slept fitfully for more than a month after his release. If they could send him to death row on a trumped-up charge once, he feared it could happen again. Even after he resumed his life, the constant flashbacks to the daily horrors and degradations he suffered in a tiny five-by-seven-foot cell on death row continued. This strapping, slow-talking man doesn't like to discuss his death row experience, yet the memories of those wasted years have scarred him for life.

Menard's death row is housed in a sandstone-and-brick building 150 yards up a hill from the main prison. "It was a demoralizing and dehumanizing human zoo," Burrows said. "Even animals in zoos are treated better than we were."

With their own facility and battalion of guards watching their every movement, Menard's death row prisoners were considered outcasts and throwaways. Compared to the death row building, the main prison was like summer camp. General population prisoners were confined to cells between 8:30 P.M. and 6:00 A.M. The rest of the time was spent either working one of three shifts, reading in the library, or working out in the yard.

Death row prisoners enjoyed none of these luxuries. They were confined twenty-two hours a day, six days a week (on Sundays, the entire day was spent in their cells). Meals were brought to them at 5:30 A.M., 11:30 A.M., and 4:30 P.M. They ate with plastic utensils.

Burrows never saw a sunset when he was in prison.

The two hours spent outside the cell, which included a half hour to shower and one and a half hours in the yard, changed daily, varying between 7:00 and 11:30 A.M. Once in the large yard surrounded by towering walls spiked with gleaming razor wire, Burrows played basketball, dominoes or cards, or just sat in the sun, soaking up fresh air and the sun's warmth.

Death row prisoners were allowed five visits a month. Handcuffed and leg-shackled, they met with loved ones and family in tiny locked rooms monitored by video cameras. "Humiliating doesn't begin to describe what it was like for my wife and kids to see me that way," said Burrows.

Yet those fleeting tastes of the life he left sustained him, providing hope and a reason to live. Unlike many death row prisoners, his family stuck by him throughout his ordeal. They truly believed he'd return home to take his rightful place at the family table. As difficult as it was, Burrows made himself believe it also.

One of ten children and a high-school dropout, Burrows grew up poor. His family moved frequently through central Illinois searching for work and opportunity. As they moved, Burrows got into trouble. At nine, he was arrested for theft. After that, he did two short stints in prison for burglary convictions. But he never hurt anyone.

Surviving death row for Burrows meant staying sane in a tiny, poorly ventilated room no bigger than a large closet. The air was always bad, but it was particularly stale on the top gallery housing Burrows. The closest windows were six feet below, spaced twenty-five feet apart. Regardless of the season, the cells were always uncomfortable. In the winter, they were cold and damp; in the summer, temperatures climbed to an oppressive one hundred degrees and more.

Nevertheless, Burrows mastered the art of killing

time. Whatever he did, he did for six to eight hours at a stretch. Making up for lost time, death row gave Burrows the opportunity to read the books most kids read in high school. And thanks to a teach-yourself-how-to-crochet book, Burrows created elaborate afghans and quilts. The rest of the time, he stared at the twelve-inch color TV set his wife had given him.

A tranquilizer for death row prisoners, TV often squelches outbreaks of violence, madness, and self-destruction. Suffering from insomnia and sleeping no more than four hours a day, Burrows found a way to keep from "bugging out." Others weren't so lucky. He recalls plenty of outbreaks of unbridled rage during which men snapped right before his eyes. Some took their frustration out on the guards by hurling pots of urine and feces in their faces. Others took it out on themselves, beating the state at its own game. They overdosed on sleeping pills or hanged themselves with homemade ropes woven secretly in the eerie predawn hours.

When Burrows looks back on his death row experience, he gets angry and bitter. It's hard to blame him. He sees himself as a victim, a helpless pawn of crooked politicians and an inefficient judicial system. "How else can I feel?" he asked, expecting no answer. "They sent me to death row on nothing. All the evidence was made up."

Sadly, Burrows's story is a variation on an all-too-common theme. Muneer Deeb, thirty-six, also got off death row, but he didn't fare as well as Burrows. He, too, was the victim of a trumped-up case. A Jordanian immigrant, Deeb came to the United States in 1979 to study engineering, marry, and build a life. He sought the American dream, but instead found a nightmare. In

1982, when running a convenience store in Waco, Texas, Deeb was charged with the brutal killings of three teenagers. In a complicated case, Deeb was railroaded and sentenced to death in 1985. He spent nine years on death row at Texas's infamous Huntsville Prison before he was finally acquitted on January 12, 1993.

Huntsville's death row prisoners are locked down twenty-one hours a day and allowed three hours of recreation, five days a week. Yet, Deeb says, if you got two solid hours, it was a lot. All it took was the slightest prisoner disturbance to lock down the entire death row population for weeks on end.

Where the food at Menard was tolerable, Deeb said the food at Huntsville was atrocious. Pork or a pork product was served at practically every meal. As a practicing Muslim forbidden to eat pork, Deeb survived on peanut butter, canned chili, beans, and macaroni from the prison commissary.

Bad food was the least of Deeb's worries. Death row prisoners weren't allowed to have TVs in their cells or contact visits. Communication only took place through a mesh screen.

Suicide was a regular occurrence at Huntsville. And the guards didn't much care. "I watched an inmate take a razor and cut his own throat," said Deeb, still horrified by the memory. "With blood spurting from his neck in all directions, you'd think the guards would rush him to the hospital on stretchers. Instead, they walked him there in no great hurry." If he died along the way, all well and good. Taxpayers would be saved one less death row inmate to feed and house.

Huntsville guards had no fondness for their wards. "They treated us like animals," said Deeb. "I remember one saying to me matter-of-factly, 'If it was up to me, I'd bring in my .357 and kill ya all right now.' On another occasion, the same guard said, 'One day I'm going to sneak in here and kill the bunch of you myself.'"

Where the guards only vent their desire to kill, the state of Texas picks up the slack by doing the deed legally. Texans don't take kindly to murderers. When Deeb arrived on death row, there were 240 prisoners. When he left, there were close to four hundred. Over his nine-year stay, he estimates close to forty executions took place, nineteen of them in 1988 alone. Today, not a month goes by without at least three scheduled executions. In June 1995, a banner month for Huntsville's execution team, thirteen executions were slotted, with a triple-header midmonth. However, only six of them were actually carried out. At Huntsville, it's the classic numbers game. With so many executions scheduled, you're bound to chalk up an impressive scoreboard of kills.

Knowing he was sitting in an execution factory, Deeb stayed sane by keeping busy every moment. During his last three years, he worked at the prison's garment factory, which has become a legend in the U.S. prison system. Texas prison officials herald it as a model program. Deeb called it slave labor.

Separate tiers at Huntsville house three classes of death row prisoners—the super-segregated (super-segs), segregated (segs), and work-capable. The super-segs are the incorrigibles. A threat to others and themselves, they can't be trusted to behave outside their cells. They're locked down twenty-three hours a day. When taken to the showers, guards escort them with six-foot Plexiglas shields to protect themselves and the prisoners from other super-segs who think nothing of flinging feces or semen at them as they pass their cells. Unlike standard barred cells, super-seg cells are reinforced with mesh wire.

Seg prisoners are the newer, probationary death row prisoners. Once deemed trustworthy, they're stamped work-capable and have a choice of working one of the garment factory's two four-hour shifts or be locked down twenty-one hours a day.

The factory is a large guarded cage where some forty prisoners sew guard and hospital uniforms. Each year, the factory yields a net income of more than $1.25 million. Aside from four hours of work time and a couple of extra hours in the yard a day, factory workers are rewarded for their hard work with a hamburger at Christmas. Like Deeb, most prisoners work at the factory to break up the day. Others deem it a futile effort since they're only going to be killed. Why make money for a state hell-bent on getting an execution record?

Deeb's most productive hours were spent studying law books and poring over his case's weighty transcript. The will to survive was enough motivation for him to spend the better part of each day working on his case. Struggling with inadequate English, no photocopying facilities, and attempts by prison authorities to sabotage his efforts, Deeb managed to commandeer law books from the prison library. In the process of going over every detail of his case, he discovered that his lawyers failed to investigate properly and discredit witnesses. "It was as good as having no lawyer at all," Deeb said.

A relentless Deeb finally won a hearing. In a five-hour interrogation of his prosecutors and police officials, he earned himself a new trial and finally freedom.

As much as he fantasized about the day he'd walk out of prison unshackled, freedom proved a bittersweet victory. Prior to his conviction, Deeb felt he could achieve anything with hard work. There were no barriers that couldn't be overcome. But nine years on death row made him paranoid and untrusting. America shattered his dreams. Like many men who channel all their hope and energy into establishing their freedom, once Deeb achieved it, it wasn't everything it was cracked up to be.

Like thousands of other convicts suddenly tossed back into society, Deeb had a hard time adjusting to freedom. Many death row prisoners, especially long-termers, think if they can survive prison, they can endure anything. To their horror, they find the outside world offers terrors for which they weren't prepared. They must call upon a whole new set of survival skills. Rather than reconquer the streets they left, they are swallowed up, overwhelmed and consumed by them. Those who can't hack it either wind up back in prison or, like Deeb, slink into the shadows, frightened and suspicious.

Instead of returning to Waco, Deeb moved to Dallas, changing jobs and residences frequently. For the time being, he works for a car service and lives in a tiny, sparsely furnished apartment. It's been two years since he was released from death row and he is still struggling to pick up the pieces of his shattered life. He's getting used to freedom, especially little things like going where he wants without handcuffs and eating whatever he wants anytime of the day. Occasionally, he awakens from a dead sleep and snaps his light on at 3:00 A.M., expecting breakfast to be wheeled around to his cell.

Deeb said he can't put the experience to rest until he gets some much-deserved revenge on the state of Texas. He has filed a $100 million lawsuit against the officials who prosecuted him and he's writing a book about his harrowing nine years on death row.

Yet, even if compensated for the mistake, Deeb is permanently scarred. Every time he sees someone in a uniform, he tenses, his heart races, and he walks the other way. Deeb has good reason to distrust the system. "I'm always suspicious," he said. "The system was supposed to protect me. But that wasn't my experience."

It certainly wasn't Andrew Golden's experience either. When he looks back on his twenty-six months on death row at Florida's State Penitentiary at Starke, the former college professor is still horrified by the shameful breakdown of the American justice system. It's been three years since his release, yet there is still disbelief in his voice and sadness in his eyes when he recalls the order of events leading to his imprisonment in 1991.

Golden, fifty, was sent to death row for murdering his wife, Ardelle, in September, 1989. According to the prosecutor, a deep-in-debt Golden orchestrated his wife's death to collect on her life insurance policies. Golden was the victim of a zealous prosecutor who had already sent seventeen men to death row. Worse still, he had the bad luck of hiring a lawyer who presented a halfhearted and poorly prepared defense. Golden didn't have a prayer.

After he had endured more than two years of some of the worst prison conditions in the United States, a different attorney proved Golden was innocent and got a reversal of his conviction from the Florida Supreme Court. Beyond any doubt, she proved Ardelle accidentally drowned after driving down an unmarked, unlit boat ramp into a lake. When the facts were dramatically brought to the surface, Florida's judicial system was justifiably raked over the coals by the media.

First, no crime had been committed, and more astounding still, Golden was an unlikely killer, a far cry from the career criminal. He was a pawn, a victim of a flawed system looking for scapegoats. Golden's case pointed up the unsettling fact that the same thing could happen to anyone. Meek and self-effacing, Golden is a model citizen, a family man right out of *Leave It to Beaver*. Holding master's degrees in social work and vocational education, he was a doting father who bragged about his two sons being honor students. He was proud of the fact that he raised his kids in the Lutheran faith and of his wife's role as church organist.

The saddest part is Golden was also a loving husband whose life revolved around his wife. Her death occurred just two weeks before the couple's twenty-fifth anniversary. To celebrate the landmark occasion, Golden had purchased a diamond ring for his wife, a gift he never got to give her.

His wife's death turned him into an emotional cripple for more than a year. He was so despondent he tried to take his life by overdosing on sleeping pills. Suffering from a crippling depression during the trial, Golden was so drugged up he only remembers bits and pieces of the harrowing event. It's no wonder he couldn't take an aggressive role in his defense.

Andrew Golden was just a regular guy who found himself plucked from the lap of middle-class comfort and dropped into hell. "One day I was home watching TV in my living room, two days later I was sitting in a cell on death row," Golden said. "It was quite a shock."

That's an understatement. No one could have prepared him for death row. And if he had been briefed, he would never have believed what he heard. When he went to prison, his oldest son, Darin, had just turned nineteen; his younger son, Chip, was thirteen.

Golden's first six months at Starke were the toughest. If not for antidepressants, he probably wouldn't have made it. On several occasions he thought about overdosing on tranquilizers or hanging himself. Thankfully, the antidepressants prevented that.

Of the 330 men on Florida's death row at the time, Golden was the most unlikely candidate for the electric chair. He was so humbled by the horrific conditions, he retreated into his own world, obeying the rules like a terrified and obedient schoolboy who expected to get up one morning and find the nightmare over. "I respected the guards and the other prisoners and kept to myself," said Golden, one of the smartest things he could have done. Sensing he was neither a threat nor a danger, both guards and inmates left this docile prisoner alone. But it didn't turn off the madness swirling around Golden twenty-four-hours a day. "No one sleeps very long on death row," he remembered. "The noise never stopped. Day and night, the prison walls resonated with an endless cacophony of moans, screams, cries, and endless cursing. Often, hundreds of men screamed at once. The sound was deafening. Even Arnold Schoenberg's cacophonous atonal symphonies sounded better than this. And there was no escaping it."

At times, the tension rose to nerve-racking levels. Violent outbreaks were regular occurrences. Golden estimates he witnessed at least twenty-five inmate stabbings. One day a guard was stabbed with a homemade shank and pushed off the second tier to his death. Beatings took place regularly. Golden remembered countless occasions during which guards stormed into prisoners' cells and beat them senseless. There was sexual harassment, too. "There was a gay guard who used to perform fellatio on prisoners, who in return would get special treatment," Golden said. At times, he wondered who was crazier, the prisoners or their captors. From his perspective, it really didn't matter. All he wanted was to get out.

Golden found himself in unlikely company. Most of the death row prisoners were career criminals; many were retarded or insane. The rest were helpless victims like himself who had gotten mangled by the system. "Like they say," said Golden, chuckling, "the only difference between a cop and a crook is the rate of pay."

The food at Starke was barely edible. During the first year, Golden dropped 38 pounds, going from 192 to 154. It didn't matter that most of the food was grown on the prison farm since death row prisoners were not served any fresh vegetables. Everything was cooked until it was tasteless. Most meals consisted of cooked greens, grits, corn bread, and something resembling chicken gumbo over flat noodles. Golden was never convinced he was actually eating chicken. Accompanying every meal was a glass of Kool-Aid. Throughout his stay on death row, Golden can't remember one hot meal. "Death row prisoners got the worst food," he said. "Maybe it's because they couldn't complain about it. They figured why bother giving us edible food when we're all going to be executed."

Golden wallowed in depression for six months. But even at his very worst, he knew there would be a day of reckoning when he'd walk out of Starke a free man. He was lucky it happened in just twenty-six months. For others, it takes two and three times that. For many more, it never happens. He discovered life was worth living again when he started taking an interest in the outside world. It happened when he began answering the dozens of letters he received from family, friends, and well-wishers. "Writing letters was a cathartic exercise," Golden remembered. "I was pulling thoughts and feelings from my mind and putting them on paper. It was a gratifying process."

He underwent other changes as well. Rather than feeling sorry for himself and remaining in his cell, Golden began taking his one hour of recreation in the yard. "For months all I saw was concrete," he said.

"Then I started noticing grass and feeling the warmth of the sun and cool breezes on my face. I felt like there was hope and that I was returning from the dead."

Finding the will to live didn't blunt the shock of reentering the world a free man. When that day finally came, like Deeb, he discovered freedom brought problems he never imagined. "I thought just by leaving prison I could pick up where I left off and return to my old life," Golden said. "But it wasn't that way." He couldn't sleep. He was constantly agitated and paranoid. He suffered from constant nightmares and flashbacks about his prison life. He was physically free, yet psychologically he was still locked in a dark and smelly little prison cell at Starke. On top of it all, he felt guilty for having gotten out as quickly as he had. In almost two and a half years on death row, Golden made some good friends. It upset him to realize most would never get out, while some would be executed.

Psychotherapy helped Golden readjust to freedom. It took more than a year, but slowly he put the pieces of his shattered life back together. It's been three years since he walked out of Starke, yet the memories of death row are stronger than ever, the effect permanent. And in some bizarre way, maybe it was a good thing. "Everything is different," he said, sitting in a lawn chair in the backyard of his house in Gainesville one muggy July day. "The big things in life don't mean a heck of a lot anymore. It's the little things—walking outside in the early morning, feeling the fresh air, being able to see grass and trees, and the thrill of getting in a car and driving."

Yet, no matter how much time passes, Golden's still trying to make sense of those wasted years of his life. Looking older than his years, he asked: "How can one human being treat another human being so terribly?" He knows he'll never find the answer.

*   *   *

It may not be much of a consolation, but Golden isn't alone. Fifty-two-year-old Walter McMillian, known to his friends as Johnny D, was also a victim of the legal system. McMillian, an African-American, was arrested for killing an eighteen-year-old white woman. Not only did he not commit the crime, but he was helping his sister run a fish fry to raise money for the local church at the time the woman was murdered.

McMillian was a self-made man who built his own pulpwood business in Monroeville, Alabama. He dropped out of school at age ten and has been working ever since. On June 7, 1987, his life came to a crashing halt when he was pulled off the road and surrounded by a battalion of police armed with twelve-gauge shotguns. From that point on, McMillian's life became a roller-coaster ride. A couple of weeks after being arrested he was transferred to death row at Holman Prison in Atmore, where he waited one year before he was tried. To this day, he can't explain why his basic rights were so blatantly violated.

The trial lasted two days. A half-dozen friends and family swore McMillian had been with them at the time of the killing. Yet an all-white jury sent him to death row, where he stayed for four and one half years. There he sat until he was proven innocent and released in March 1993, thanks to an attorney with the Southern Center for Human Rights in Atlanta and a *60 Minutes* TV segment, which provoked the outrage of America. McMillian became the first man in Alabama's history to be released from death row. In a statement to the United States Senate Judiciary Committee on April 1, 1993, he described his ordeal: "With the exception of forty-five minutes per day of exercise and a few rare hours per week in the day room, my days were spent in my cell—twenty-three hours a day. My cell, a mere five-by-eight-foot space, was my only world. Had it not been for the loving visits of my family and grandchildren, I may not have survived the experience. And even with their support, my experience on death row was traumatic. I was wrenched from my family, from my children, from my grandchildren, from my friends, from my work that I loved, and was placed in an isolation cell, the size of a shoe box, with no sunlight, no companionship, and no work for nearly six years."

During his confinement, he watched seven prisoners be taken away for electrocution. Says McMillian, "I experienced the executions with the greatest pain and with enormous fear about whether it would happen to me." From his cell, he could smell the stench of burning flesh wafting through the ventilation system. "The smell of someone you know burning to death is the most painful and nauseating experience on this earth," he said.

Hope kept McMillian going. In his concluding remarks to the judiciary committee, he said: "I survived those six long years, but I am a different man. I have suffered pain, agony, loss, and fear in degrees that I had never imagined possible. My life will never be the same now. That is something I have come to terms with. I have learned more knowledge about human existence in these last six years than I would ever have desired."

Lawrence "Bubba" Hayes can relate to everything McMillian said—and more. He, too, is a death row survivor. Like the others, the experience left him permanently scarred. Hayes, forty-two, finds it therapeutic to talk about his prison experience, yet there's a sadness in his eyes that will never go away.

Most of us can single out momentous years in our lives when everything suddenly came together and we had eye-opening experiences. For Hayes, that year was 1974, when New York's court of appeals overturned the death penalty law. That's when Hayes knew he wasn't going to be electrocuted.

On May 12, 1972, at the age of nineteen, Hayes, a former Black Panther who had joined the militant black activist group when he was seventeen, and his nephew, Cornelius Butler, were sentenced to death for killing an undercover cop in a Queens confectionery store. While the evidence proved he wasn't even present when the cop was shot, he was charged as "acting in concert" with the gunman, sending him to the death house at Green Haven Correctional Facility in Shoreham, New York. At the time, killing a cop was punishable by death.

The moment the judge told Hayes he would be electrocuted, time seemed to stop. He broke down and cried, groping for words to describe the terror that gripped him. All he could say was, "A grave injustice has been done." Twenty-four years have gone by since that chilling day, yet Hayes remembers every second of it as if it happened yesterday. Where he couldn't find the words to describe what he felt then, Hayes can do so eloquently now.

Before the death penalty was overturned, Hayes spent two and a half years on Green Haven's death row with six other men slated to be executed. After that, he was given a life sentence and transferred to the general population, where he served a twenty-five-years-to-life sentence until his parole in 1992.

Hayes's prison experience will haunt him for the rest of his life, but especially the years spent on death row. It was no consolation that no one was ever executed at Green Haven. All Hayes and the other death row prisoners knew was their days were numbered. "When the most powerful nation in the world says it's going to kill you, you believe it," Hayes said matter-of-factly. "It's absolutely shocking to have someone tell you they're going to kill you. It's one thing for someone to come up to you and kill you. But when they say they're going to do it—and they're serious about it—it's hard to imagine how that feels."

Hayes described his reaction on that ill-fated day. He immediately withdrew inside himself. "It's a survival mechanism condemned men experience, saving us from cracking," he explained. "It was so automatic I didn't even know it was happening. Although the events were real, I expected someone to come along at any moment and say, 'It's all a mistake, you can go home, we're sorry.' That's what I held on to."

It was no mistake. Hayes's two-decade nightmare was just beginning. As soon as they led him and his nephew away, cuffed and in leg irons, from the Queens House of Detention to Green Haven's death house, escorted by two dozen squad cars with sirens blaring, he knew no mistake had been made. The worst was still ahead. "I remember pulling up to this big old prison," he said. "It reminded me of a medieval fortress made of brick and concrete. Man, was it frightening. As we pulled up, the gates automatically opened."

Again, Hayes retreated. He felt like he was in a movie, but he also knew there was a good chance he'd never walk off the set alive. Guards and prisoners awaited at the entrance, anxious to clap eyes on the cop killers. They were curiosity pieces, hated by the guards and heroes to prisoners. All the fanfare and notoriety terrified him.

He and his nephew were speedily processed. After he was stripped and examined, his street clothes were taken away and he was given prison greens. He was no

longer Lawrence Hayes, but inmate number 72H001.
What's more, the H in his ID number stigmatized him
as a death house prisoner. Like Hester Prynne, in
Nathaniel Hawthorne's famous novel, forced to wear
the letter A on her chest so she could constantly be
reminded of committing adultery, Hayes wore his own
"scarlet letter."

For twenty years, he carried the stigma of the death
penalty with him. It was a noose around his neck, a
plank he walked daily. He was a target for prisoners
building reputations and racist redneck cops looking
for a captive who couldn't fight back.

Hayes was taken to the "Tank," a secluded section
of the prison reserved for death row prisoners. There,
he met the five other condemned prisoners who gave
him the rundown on prison routines. One tossed him a
carton of cigarettes, the others gave him a crash course
in survival. It was small consolation, yet the tension
eased slightly knowing he wasn't alone. It was the
immediate bond with other death row prisoners that
kept Hayes from snapping. "It's like suddenly you find
yourself drowning in the middle of the ocean and
someone throws you a life preserver," said Hayes.
"Those guys talked to me and showed me the ropes.
One guy told me to be cool and that I had a good
chance of getting a stay of execution."

Until he was transferred to the general population,
Hayes was locked down twenty-three hours a day. His
one free hour could be spent in the yard or showering.
Hayes opted for five hours in the yard and two showers
a week.

He survived prison on wits, a fierce will to live, and
a healthy degree of paranoia. Where most prisoners
survive on anger, targeting their rage at their keepers,
Hayes turned inward, beginning an introspective journey in search of answers. He credits a fellow death row

survivor for passing on priceless advice. "That wise man pulled me aside and said, 'There are five ways for a lifer to get out of prison. He gets a reversal, he gets a pardon, some kind of sentencing law changes, he escapes, or he goes out with a tag on his toe.' He said if you involve yourself in those first three things, you shouldn't have time for the fourth or fifth."

Hayes followed this senior convict's advice. He did things he never would have done on the outside. He painted, wrote, and became a voracious reader. "From the moment I realized I may never leave this place, I wanted to understand the insanity and why this was happening to me," Hayes continued. He studied semantics, linguistics, science, and literature, earning bachelor's and master's degrees. All the while he shuttled around the New York prison system, doing time in Clinton, Attica, Sing Sing, and Comstock, before ending up back in Green Haven.

Now free and working as a case manager for a publicly funded social agency helping indigent people in Brooklyn, Hayes has continued his quest for answers. Unlike most death row survivors, he says he's not angry. He views his death row and prison experience as an eye-opening experience that altered his take on life. He entered prison angry, but left as a contemplative man intent on understanding the human condition.

While he walked out of prison with a mission, Hayes admits the experience left its mark. As motivated as he was to make it in the free world, the adjustment was painful. Tougher still is going back to prison to see friends. Each time he returns, he sees men trapped in apathy and hopelessness, sinking in their own despair. They've resigned themselves to never leaving prison. Seeing his friends from the other side of the bars is tough to stomach. Now that he's out of prison, freedom is a mixed blessing, especially when he talks to his less fortunate prison buddies. Like others who have won their freedom through hard work, Hayes knows there's no such thing as rehabilitation or resocialization in prison. Rehabilitation comes down to a personal quest to overhaul yourself so you can convince the parole board you're no threat to society. That's a tall order for most men.

Nobody walks off death row unscathed. The lucky ones return to their families and pick up the shards of their former lives. Others trust no one and take to the road, constantly drifting from place to place. They figure they're safe because they never stay anywhere too long. It's like being invisible because they're hardly noticed.

Others are determined to understand the experience that permanently altered their lives. Like Hayes, they find salvation in learning.

Like all death row survivors, Hayes has good reason to be angry. He could wallow in self-pity and spend the rest of his days condemning a system that crucified him because he was poor, black, and the product of a dysfunctional family. In short, he was a victim of circumstance. Yet he insists that type of thinking is self-defeating. He compares the past to an open wound that will never heal. "I can't undo the past," he said matter-of-factly. "All I can do is start over. I'm thankful I have the chance."

Hayes made it and odds are that his forty-four-year-old nephew, Cornelius Butler, will, too. It's no small wonder considering Butler had to do four more years than Hayes before he got to see what prison walls looked like from the outside. And he never understood why. Both men did exemplary time, minding their business and staying out of trouble. Butler wasn't a scholar like his uncle, but nevertheless earned an associate's degree in hotel technology and became the head cook at Green Haven. Directing the daily preparation of meals for a couple of thousand men is no small accomplishment.

Yet those four additional years of penance were hard on Butler. He figured the government didn't think it was politically wise to release the two men at the same time. So it put a few years between them so the public would think justice was being served. That rationale didn't hold water for Butler.

Finally, in July 1995, Butler got the news he had been waiting for. He will never forget the day he was told of the parole board's decision and handed his release papers. He was to be let out on or before August 16. After hearing the news, he took the papers and walked to his cell, trembling in disbelief. "Not only couldn't I speak, I could hardly breathe," Butler said.

"I left the parole officer feeling paralyzed," he added. "I figured I'd wait to tell the general population. Yet they knew by the expression on my face. They've seen that look before and they knew what it meant."

For about ten minutes, Butler tried to be cool about the news. But as soon as he walked into his cell, the floodgates opened, his eyes welled up with tears, and he sobbed like a baby. "It was the first time I shed a tear since I was sixteen years old," he said. "And that was the day my father was buried."

Looking back on his last two weeks in prison, Butler said the separation procedure was surprisingly simple. A quick conversation was followed by the exchange of a legal document and he had his life back. He felt reborn. He would return to the wife who had never abandoned him all those years. He would see his twenty-six-year-old daughter, who was barely two years old when he was sentenced. He would taste freedom, a state he could formerly only fantasize about. "I was a kid when I was sent to prison," Butler said. "This is where I grew up and became a man. These guys were my family; many of the older men were a combination of father figures and mentors."

Butler's VE Day was Monday, August 6, 1995. At 9:00 A.M., he walked out of Green Haven's main gate in street clothes, carrying his possessions—two boxes containing books, photographs, and stacks of letters. As he walked to his wife, who was waiting by a car, men cheered from barred windows on every tier of prison. Butler heard the commotion but didn't look back. He couldn't, and the men understood. A prison superstition says if you look back, you'll *be* back, and Butler had no intention of tempting fate. The car pulled out of the parking lot, passing the observation towers and thick high walls topped with gleaming razor wire as the sound of cheering voices trailed off. Butler will never forget those parting moments. Finally, the page had turned on the longest chapter of his life.

Hardly three weeks after his release, Butler seemed to be making a healthy adjustment to freedom. Like Golden, he couldn't stop talking about the simple pleasures of walking without handcuffs, without guards in his face, or of feeling the sun on his face and seeing airplanes in the sky.

Nor could he stop talking about how much New York City and his Brooklyn neighborhood of Coney Island had changed. Apartment houses had been replaced with low-income projects and crime rates were soaring. But it was the change in Coney Island's amusement park that upset him the most. When he left it was a vacation mecca, home of two of the country's scariest roller coasters, not to mention its landmark Ferris wheel and parachute jump. Coney Island still draws crowds, yet it's only a shadow of what it was when he left two decades ago. Only one working roller coaster remains and the Ferris wheel and parachute jump are rusting and decayed. When Butler walks Coney Island's mile-and-a-half-long boardwalk, he sees throngs of people against the tarnished relics of his stolen youth.

Getting used to a changed neighborhood won't be half as difficult as living in a world that is not encased in bars. During his first month at home, his wife complained about the icy distance between them. "She said I acted cold and held back my emotions," Butler explained. "I wasn't aware of it because that's the way you act in prison. I was used to talking to convicts." The one thing you don't do in prison is telegraph your emotions. You keep them in check so you're in control and no one knows what you are thinking. "I'm fast discovering there's more to getting used to freedom than I imagined," he added. "It ain't gonna happen overnight. It'll take time."

Butler also knows he's not completely free. All it takes is a simple parole violation for him to be tossed back into prison. For the length of his five-year parole, he's expected to be in his apartment by 7:00 P.M. and he's not permitted to leave it before 7:00 A.M. Doing so requires permission from his parole officer. After twenty-four years of rules and regulations, Butler has no problems with these minor restrictions.

"After all I've been through, I don't intend to let anything stop me from making it out here," Butler said, staring out the window. "Some guys come out bitter and angry, always griping about the bad hand dealt to them. I'm not going to let my prison experience ruin the rest of my life or turn me into the monster everyone believed I was."

Butler's face relaxed into a grin. "I got the whole world out there and I'm gonna enjoy every minute of the time I have left."

*   *   *

Good or bad adjustment, many death row survivors take solace in writing about their prison experience. Whether they resume their lives or drop out of society, they're driven by a deep-rooted need to cleanse themselves of the awful experience by exploring and analyzing every particle of it. Sonia "Sonny" Jacobs, who is writing a book about her five years on Florida's death row, is one of these people.

In 1976, she was sent to death row with her ex-convict husband, Jesse Tafero, and his friend Walter Rhodes for killing two cops at a Florida highway rest stop. Tafero and Rhodes had gotten in a fight with the officers that escalated to a shoot-out. As soon as trouble started, Jacobs, who was sitting in the backseat, flung herself protectively over her two infants. She witnessed nothing. But being in the wrong place at the wrong time won her a death sentence along with her husband and his buddy. Rhodes got life imprisonment after he plea-bargained and insisted Tafero and Jacobs fired the shots.

In 1976, Jacobs had the distinction of being the only woman on death row. In 1981, her sentence was commuted to a life term and she was released into the general prison population. There she stayed until 1992, when, after complex legal maneuvering, she was released. Two years earlier, Tafero was executed in the electric chair in a textbook example of a botched execution. The prison's electrician made the mistake of replacing the rotted sea sponge in the device's headpiece with a synthetic sponge purchased at a supermarket. As soon as the switch was thrown, the sponge caught fire. Flames and smoke engulfed Tafero's head and spewed from his face mask. It took three jolts of electricity before Tafero was pronounced dead.

Margaret Vandiver also knew Tafero well, spending many hours with him before his execution. Right up until the last minute, he swore he was innocent. Like many other cases, there was a lot of confusion about the events and who did the shooting. What was certain was that Tafero didn't seem like a hardened killer. He was a talented artist who made museumlike copies of Van Gogh and Botticelli works. He was articulate and well-read. The elegant script in his letters looks like calligraphy.

Afraid that Tafero wouldn't have many people with him when he was executed, Vandiver offered to be a witness. "Jesse said 'absolutely not,' saying it was no place for his friends," she remembered. It was a good thing since Tafero's execution turned out to be a nightmare worthy of a low-budget horror film.

As terrifying as the event was, the execution of her husband proved to be the motivation Jacobs needed in order to prove her own innocence and walk out of prison a free person. Like Deeb and Burrows, her innocence gave her the strength to fight. The better part of her five years on death row was spent in isolation. The only person she saw was a guard who checked her cell every couple of hours. In the beginning, she paced for hours at a time, trying to work off bottled-up energy. Then she began to create routines for herself. She wrote letters, meditated, and painted. Her body remained caged, yet she managed to free her mind and stay sane.

After she was released, Jacobs began teaching meditation and kept in close touch with former prison friends. Like all death row survivors, as soon as she walked out of prison a free person, she joined an elite group of misfits who had been cruelly tried, convicted, and deprived of precious years of their lives.

*   *   *

Kirk Bloodsworth, thirty-five, doesn't like to talk about his nine years in the Baltimore County Detention Center, sixteen months of which were spent on death row. Since he was released in June 1993, he's been transcribing notes he tape-recorded about his prison experience. Unsure about what to do with them, his goal is simply to articulate the horrendous memories before he forgets them.

In the summer of 1984, Bloodsworth was accused of raping and brutally murdering a nine-year-old girl in a Baltimore suburb. An anonymous tip led police to Bloodsworth after a composite sketch of the suspect appeared in a local paper. There was no physical evidence identifying Bloodsworth as the killer, only an angry public demanding revenge. The jury found the twenty-four-year-old former marine guilty, sentencing him to die in the gas chamber. After a year and a half on death row, he won a second trial and reconviction to two life terms. He later won his freedom when a county-circuit-court judge ordered his case dismissed based on DNA testing that proved the semen found in the child's underwear could not be Bloodsworth's.

Once again, a revenge-hungry legal system punished the wrong person. It's tough enough for any condemned person to endure prison, but it's particularly hard if you're convicted of crimes against children. Even prisons have a code of ethics. Child molesters and sexual deviants are considered the lowest of the low, subject to ridicule, attack, and isolation. Serial killer Jeffrey Dahmer, convicted of sadistically molesting, killing, and eating six young men, was constantly attacked until he was brutally murdered by a fellow prisoner in 1994.

Bloodsworth often feared for his life. He was spat on, urine was hurled in his face, and there were constant fights. When the man in the next cell hanged himself,

Bloodsworth did all he could do to keep from snapping. Yet his innocence and the powerful belief that he'd once again fish and hunt in the Maryland woods he loved kept him going. When he was pardoned by the governor of Maryland, he won a $300,000 award for wrongful conviction, piddling remuneration for relinquishing nine torturous years of his life.

These are the stories of a few of the lucky ones who have managed to walk off death row and talk about the experience. Others could never make it on the outside. By the time they were released, they had become terrorized, broken men whose minds had turned to mush. Jerry Banks, a poor black man from Henry County, Georgia, was one of them. When Banks was finally proven innocent and released from Georgia's Diagnostic and Classification Center in Jackson, he wound up shooting his wife and himself. He, too, was a victim of shoddy legal representation. It was little consolation to poor Banks that his lawyer was disbarred at the time of his release. The damage had been done. When the police found Banks and his wife, a note was by his side that read, "Everything I have in this world has been taken away." For poor Banks, that included his dignity and self-respect.

Most of the people you're going to be reading about never will experience freedom, not even briefly. More than three thousand death row prisoners will never enjoy the luxury of controlling their own lives. Many will spend the rest of their days in a prison cell, waiting in terror for that dark, airless day when they meet their executioner.

Caryl Chessman will be remembered not so much for taking on the justice system and keeping the executioner at bay, but for his considerable writing talent. If the world had any doubts about what death row was really like, Chessman straightened them out. He wrote, "Life on the row is a blending of the real and the unreal; it's a clash of internal and external tension, the tension of everyday living magnified a hundred times. You're a prisoner in a strange land. You are and you aren't a part of the larger whole around you. You form friendships and your friends die. You dream and your dreams die. . . . On death row, life not only copies art, it creates a grotesque art form all its own that makes life its slave, death its master."

How About a Big Round of Applause for the Return of the Death Penalty

"They have sown the wind, and they shall reap the whirlwind."
—HOSEA: 8:7

"Capital punishment is our society's recognition of the sanctity of human life."
—SENATOR ORIN HATCH, 1988

"Let's do it."
—LAST WORDS OF GARY GILMORE BEFORE HE WAS EXECUTED BY A FIRING SQUAD IN 1977

JANUARY 17, 1977, WAS A BIG NEWS DAY. Intrigued by television reports and front-page newspaper headlines, Americans gobbled up the biggest news story of the year. On that blustery winter day at 8:07 A.M. in Utah, thirty-six-year-old Gary Gilmore was put to death by firing squad when four .30-caliber bullets ripped through his chest. Two minutes later, Gilmore's heart stopped beating, officially marking the end of a ten-year suspension of capital punishment in the United States. Gilmore's execution marked the modern era of capital punishment.

In 1972, the United States Supreme Court made a landmark ruling on capital punishment in a case known as *Furman* v. *Georgia*. In a five-to-four vote, the court declared that existing capital punishment laws were unconstitutional. The court's view can be summed up simply: the capital punishment laws in effect in certain states were being carried out unfairly. Some people—quite often those who were poor or black or both—were given the death penalty more often than other groups. Others who committed the same types of crime were often sentenced to life imprisonment. The Supreme Court said that this arbitrary or helter-skelter way of carrying out the laws amounted to "cruel and unusual punishment." Such punishment is forbidden by the Eighth Amendment to the U.S. Constitution. However, the court did not say that the death penalty itself was "cruel and unusual," just the manner in which the laws were being carried out. Soon after, states began rewriting their death penalty laws. For the most part, the new laws required the death penalty for specific crimes such as killing a police officer.

Four years later, in 1976, Florida became the first state to draft a law reinstating the death penalty. It was followed by Georgia and Texas, and all of these laws were upheld by the Supreme Court. Over the next two decades, thirty-five states reinstated the death penalty by updating their outmoded penal codes. Connecticut, for instance, reinstated the death penalty in 1995, overhauling harsh penal laws dating back to the 1630s. Similarly, records from the Massachusetts Bay Colony dating back to 1636 listed the following crimes as punishable by death: idolatry, witchcraft, blasphemy, murder (excluding self-defense), assault in sudden anger, sodomy, buggery, adultery, statutory rape (death sentence optional), man-stealing, perjury in a capital trial, and rebellion.

Today, with the exception of treason and wartime espionage, more than sixty crimes are punishable by execution in the United States, all of them variations on murder.

The death penalty once again is going to be around for a long time. Watt Espy, an eccentric gallows historian based in Headland, Alabama, is probably the only person who tracks executions in this country. Since the execution of George Kendall as a Spanish spy in 1608, more than 18,800 executions have occurred, according to Espy. He projects that in the future, the nation's executioners will experience no shortage of work. It won't be long before we will exceed the record of 199 executions in a single year, set in 1935. By the millennium, Espy is convinced we'll be dispatching almost three hundred criminals a year to their government-sanctioned deaths.

But it was the first few executions that captured front-page headlines, fertile ground for writers, producers, and fast-buck hucksters of every stripe. Gilmore set the stage. He created as well a lurid, national interest in the process and the controversial belief that legal vengeance prevents violent crime.

Convicted of killing two people, Gilmore wanted to die—and he insisted upon doing so by firing squad. Long before, he had confessed to going on a drug and booze rampage and killing Max Jensen and Bennie Bushness. Jensen, a twenty-four-year-old Brigham Young University law student, had been supporting his wife and child with a part-time service station job. Bushness, twenty-six, also a student, lived and worked with his pregnant wife in a little hotel next to the home of Gilmore's uncle's house in Provo, Utah.

A few hours before he was executed, Gilmore expressed sorrow for committing the cold-blooded, senseless murders. By then, it was too late.

Gilmore's execution went like clockwork. By 7:50 A.M., he walked down a short hallway in the one-story maximum-security building at Utah State Prison in Point of the Mountain, glanced for the last time at a clear blue sky, and entered a van that would take him to the prison's one-story concrete block storage building and former cannery. The temperature hovered in the low forties.

Escorted by guards and Prison Warden Samuel Smith, Gilmore walked quietly, almost heroically, to his death. One eyewitness account captured the drama and solemnity of Gilmore's execution:

He had stepped from the van into the cannery and immediately taken his place in the black leather-and-oak office chair set atop a six-inch platform and backed by plywood and sandbags. Prison officials had adjusted nylon bands, padded with heavy sheepskin, around his wrists, his waist and just above his red, white and blue tennis shoes.

About 25 feet in front of Gilmore was the gray sailcloth screen built to hide the executioners. Five 2x4–inch slits 2 1/2 feet apart, had been strengthened with leather. A smaller slit for the commander of the firing squad was to the far right as Gilmore faced it. A floodlight shone directly on Gilmore from the ceiling, 20 feet above.

The riflemen, all volunteers, then entered through a side door and took their places. Four had real bullets, one a blank. That is so no one knows who actually did the deed. But every one of them knows. You can tell from the recoil of the 30–30 deer rifles.

After some formalities, Gilmore looked up at Smith. "Let's do it," Gilmore said. Then a hood, the neck strap, the target pinned over the heart with a single straight pin, the religious formalities for the nominally Catholic prisoner.

Then the warden's slight hand motion, the commander's order, the sound of the rifles and it was all over.

An autopsy showed that all four slugs fired by the riflemen hit Gilmore's heart, and that Gilmore lived two minutes after being shot. "I couldn't tell you if he was sensing pain. All I knew is that he was breathing," Dr. Serge Moore, Utah medical examiner, said.

Outside the prison, it was like a three-ring circus. An army of print, TV, and radio journalists from all over the world covered Provo's most sensational news story to date. Every helicopter in the state had been chartered and it was practically impossible to get a rental car. The Hilton was filled to capacity, a rare event in this tiny city. And every superstar journalist was there to report on the event. Geraldo Rivera, looking cool in a black leather jacket and jeans, was shouting orders to his crew as if directing a military invasion. And former Baptist minister Bill Moyers shot a documentary of the historic event.

The carnival atmosphere surrounding Gilmore's execution was sickening. Like vultures hovering over a rotting carcass, spectators stampeded the prison for a glimpse of the action. Moments after Gilmore was pronounced dead, reporters and photographers swarmed the death chamber snapping photographs and scribbling notes, recording their first impressions of the scene. With flashbulbs snapping rhythmically and a cacophony of voices shouting at once, it was reminiscent of a raucous dance club sans music.

Describing Gilmore's execution as theatrical is an understatement indeed, but the irony is that he himself orchestrated it. What he couldn't achieve in life, he accomplished in death. The ultimate showman and con man, he finally got some recognition and, yes, respect, too, the very things he hungered for while alive. In Gilmore's mind, being shot to death was a just end. Those who live by the sword die by the sword. In accordance with his final request, his ashes were spread from a plane over the city of Provo. A few days prior to his execution, Gilmore told Larry Schiller, a literary agent who bought publication and movie rights to his story, "I want them to never be rid of me."

Gilmore got his way. The placid Middle American city of Provo will never shake the memory of Gary Mark Gilmore. Neither will the rest of America. More than a topic of conversation and a cause célèbre for the intellectual set, Gilmore was elevated to a larger-than-life commodity packaged and sold to waiting consumers. Besides prompting endless debates on the pros and cons of the death penalty, Gilmore's dramatic death triggered countless trashy tabloid news stories about his lawless, tragic life. A 1,056-page epic of a book, *The Executioner's Song* by Norman Mailer, came two years later, followed by a TV movie version starring Tommy Lee Jones as Gary Gilmore. More recently, Mikal Gilmore's sensitively written book, *Shot in the Heart,* described his brother's story.

In the course of serving justice, another phenomenon was taking shape. An "antihero" was born. Americans have an ongoing love affair with antiheroes. First we execute them, then we idolize them. Over the past two hundred years, there have been scores of them, from Billy the Kid to Bonnie and Clyde.

Gilmore greased and primed the execution machinery, but he also fueled our fascination with the American drifter, loser, and unrepentant bad guy. The product of a dysfunctional home, Gilmore was beaten and abused as a child. By the time he reached adulthood, he was looking for revenge. Instead of taking it out on his parents, he lashed out at anyone he deemed to be a threat. Playing by his own violent rules led to his untimely death. Yet underneath that tough restless facade, there was a reflective and sensitive person capable of close relationships.

Mikal Gilmore summed up his brother this way: "For millions, Gary provided a focus for revenge, while for others he fulfilled the American dream of hero and madman, saint and outlaw. Gary was a network of contradictions. He was a man who loved his mother with a childlike fervor and who protected children and dogs. But he was also a man who discarded opportunities and, in rage, could be violent and could kill. . . . If Gary was one of society's losers, then he was also one of its losses; a fine line separates the role of the breaker from the broke and Gary crossed that line many times."

After Gilmore's dramatic exit, the silent majority's appetite for revenge was aroused. They wanted blood and all the gory details to match. They got it with John Spenkelink, whose capital punishment case dominated the news for months. Like Gilmore, Americans couldn't read enough about Spenkelink. But unlike Gilmore, Spenkelink didn't want to die. He was Florida's chance to get its death machinery back in operation and for Governor Bob Graham to appear tough on crime.

Like most death row inmates, Spenkelink started out with two strikes against him. He was poor and had countless scrapes with the law, dating back to the age of thirteen. His family said Spenkelink's problems began when he was twelve years old and found his father's body slumped over the wheel of his car, a hose connected to the exhaust pipe running into its interior. But before Bernard Spenkelink's suicide, he had taught his son to smoke and bragged that the boy could hold his liquor. A lot of good it did. After his father's death, Spenkelink became a drifter and a career criminal. At the age of twenty-five, he was sentenced to death for murdering a hitchhiker he picked up while fleeing a California prison. Spenkelink made the fatal mistake of picking up Joseph Syzmankiewicz, forty-five, a parole violator. Their ill-fated odyssey ended on February 4, 1973, in Room Four of the Ponce de Leon Motel in Tallahassee, where Syzmankiewicz was shot twice in the back. Spenkelink then fled 2,300 miles back to California, but was caught and returned to Florida. Spenkelink later told a court that Syzmankiewicz had forced him to submit to a homosexual act at gunpoint. He was convicted anyway and, five days before Christmas 1973, sentenced to death.

Until the bitter end, Spenkelink insisted he had killed in self-defense and didn't deserve the death penalty. Many prominent attorneys agreed, saying he was a pawn of a criminal justice system looking for a scapegoat. Just prior to the execution, Spenkelink's attorney, Margie Pitts Hames, said officials "were determined to kill him." He didn't have a prayer.

The day after the execution, even arch-conservative pundit William F. Buckley wrote a scathing column decrying a breach of justice. He ended his column saying, "I am convinced they should not have executed John Spenkelink."

Just four minutes before his execution, the Supreme Court, by a vote of 6 to 2, rejected a last-minute request for a stay. Prior to his execution, it was rumored that Spenkelink's death row friend, James "Doug" MacCray, thirty, told the *St. Petersburg Times* that William Ziegler, an inmate locked up in the cell nearest the death house, heard Spenkelink shout: "Why you guys doin' this to me? This is murder."

Nevertheless, on May 25, 1979, at Florida's State Penitentiary in Starke, Spenkelink was strapped firmly into the electric chair and executed. A witness to the execution described what it's like to die by electric shock:

> The prisoner was given three surges of electricity. The first 2,500 volts were administered at 10:12 A.M. Mr. Spenkelink jerked in the chair and one hand clenched into a fist.
> Then came the second and the third, by two executioners in black hoods. A doctor stepped forward after the third surge, pulled up the prisoner's T-shirt and applied a stethoscope to Mr. Spenkelink's chest.
> He then checked for a pulse. Then he stepped back. He returned to the prisoner and examined him once more and backed away again. A third time, at 10:18, he checked the prisoner for a pulse, examined Mr. Spenkelink's eyes with a pocket pen-flashlight and nodded to the warden that the prisoner was dead.

Meanwhile abolitionists, many of whom had been camped outside the prison for almost a week, screamed and chanted, "Government murder! Government murder!" Nearby, death penalty proponents, who had also camped out for three to four days prior to the execution, cheered the warden and execution team. One group was even positioned in a mobile home with a silver coffin mounted on its roof bearing a placard that read GO SPARKY, the nickname for Florida's three-legged electric chair.

Thirty-year-old Spenkelink became the first person executed against his will since 1967. It ushered in a new dawn for capital punishment with operalike fanfare, sounding the death knell for many of the five hundred men and five women imprisoned on death rows in twenty-five states.

Waiting in the wings in Nevada State Prison in Carson City was Jesse Bishop, forty-seven, who, like Gary Gilmore, spurned all efforts to halt the execution machinery. Five months after Spenkelink was executed, Bishop walked unassisted to the gas chamber to die a grisly death.

Described as a colorful, cigar-smoking Nick Nolte look-alike, Bishop led a life full of drugs and violence. Authorities say he committed as many as 18 murders. Yet he had also a reputation as a lady's man with his own brand of humor. Bishop prided himself on being a macho man, and right until the end, he puffed on fat cigars and joked in a thick Southern drawl about his fate. After finishing his last meal of filet mignon and tomatoes, he said wryly, "Give my regards to the chef."

Liked by the guards, Bishop was feared and respected by other prisoners. He was a career convict who spent twenty of his forty-six years in prisons. The flip side of his ingratiating smile was an uncontrollable rage that could easily lead him to kill if provoked. A month before he was executed, he admitted to the Nevada State Pardon Board that if his sentence were commuted he'd go back to sticking up casinos and gas stations. He promised to pick up where he left off and return to a life packed with violence, new cars, pretty women, money, and drugs. Bishop insisted his craving for drugs began when he was being treated for wounds suffered as a paratrooper during the Korean War. Needing money to buy dope, he held up a Las Vegas casino. During the robbery in December 1977, he fatally shot newlywed David Ballard of Baltimore, who had tried to stop him. That was the only murder for which he was convicted.

Police think he was responsible for seventeen others, ten of them in California.

His last request was a bottle of Jack Daniel's and a private visit with his ex-wife. His comment: "They say they can't do it. They say, 'How will we explain it to the press?' If they can't explain the death penalty, I don't think they would need to explain a couple of hours of privacy. It's just a normal request from a man."

When he was finally taken to the execution chamber, he tested the metal chair and said, "It's not comfortable." Nevada's gas chamber was the oldest in the nation. It was first used in 1924 on a Chinese Tong War assassin, but a number of other states later also adopted the method, most notably California and Colorado.

Here's an eyewitness's short play-by-play of Bishop's death by gas on October 22, 1979, at 3:10 A.M.:

There were 14 witnesses, most of us reporters, in a small adjoining room.

The guards inside the death chamber raised the green shades covering the windows.

Inside we saw two metal chairs and Bishop was seated on the one on the left. His arms were strapped at the shoulders and wrists. He was wearing a neatly pressed white dress shirt, blue denim prison fatigues and white socks. He wore no shoes.

Bishop nodded at me. I nodded back.

I had covered his case and since his arrest had become friends with him. It appeared he didn't want to look at anyone else. He looked calm.

Most of the time he kept his face turned to the side.

Beneath his chair was a bucket filled with sulfuric acid. When cyanide pellets slid into the bucket through a tube, the poison would be created.

I heard a small clank. He nodded at me, again.

A half smile crossed his face and he pointed beneath the chair, where the pellet had just hit.

Suddenly he took a deep breath.

His eyes rolled upward.

His head dropped on his chest—then it snapped back. He took another deep breath and his eyes closed for the last time. His face reddened.

His head fell again on his chest.

Then his body went through a series of convulsions.

He jerked and trembled for what seemed two or three minutes. Finally, he was still.

The horrible scene lasted about five minutes.

There were no executions in 1980. Then on March 9, 1981, Steven Judy was voluntarily executed. About a year and a half later, on August 10, 1982, Frank Coppola was executed in Virginia, followed by Charlie Brooks, who voluntarily walked to his death four months later. Brooks has the distinction of being the first person executed by lethal injection in the United States.

Two years later, on March 31, 1984, Ronald O'Bryan also met his maker at the same Texas prison as Brooks. Ten years earlier, his sordid, horrific crime tugged at the heartstrings of America. O'Bryan was sent to death row for killing his eight-year-old son, Timmy, on a rainy Halloween night in Houston.

When O'Bryan rushed his vomiting and gasping son to the emergency room, no one suspected wrongdoing. The last person in the world they'd consider was his own father. As Timmy writhed in agony, O'Bryan played the role of the concerned father to the hilt. When a doctor solemnly told the parents Timmy was not going to make it, O'Bryan turned to the wall and beat his fist on it. "Oh, God, why did an eight-year-old boy have to die?" he wailed.

Timmy's death was a mystery. When they pumped his stomach, they found exactly what O'Bryan said they'd find—his last dinner of pork roast, vegetables, one sour tart, medicine, and some Halloween candy given to him by his dad.

But when an autopsy was performed, the picture suddenly turned murky. Doctors found an abundance of a red-gray frothy material in Timmy's lungs. His brain glowed an unusual shade of red. When the contents of the boy's stomach were tested, they confirmed the medical examiner's suspicions: cyanide. The plot thickened when Timmy's partially eaten candy was examined. The medical examiner noticed that the top end of the candy's plastic tube, which is normally melted shut, had been sliced open and stapled closed. And the top two inches of the Pixy Stix had contained enough potassium cyanide to kill several people.

When police urged parents to bring in all their children's candy for inspection, they found cyanide in the Pixy Stix of O'Bryan's daughter and two children of a close friend, all of whom were together on Halloween night. It didn't take long for authorities to fit the pieces together. When they discovered O'Bryan had purchased $20,000 life insurance polices on each of his children, had paid for them in cash, and specified his wife not be told, they knew they had their man. A few days later, O'Bryan was arrested for the murder of his son and charged with the attempted murder of three other children. The police figured that O'Bryan expected if several children had been killed, it would somehow focus less attention on him.

He was wrong. O'Bryan became a guest of the state of Texas for a decade before he mounted the death gurney.

*   *   *

After Gilmore, Spenkelink, Bishop, and a few others, the public was no longer interested in ordinary losers; they craved killers who sparked their imaginations. Americans can't read enough about serial killers, those predatory monsters who kill for the sheer thrill of it or because they're on an insane mission.

New York serial killer Joel Rifkin, intent on cleansing the world of human filth, got off lucky. He was sentenced to life imprisonment in 1993, just two years shy of New York's restoration of the death penalty. Chalk it up to good timing. If Rifkin had been caught in October 1995, a month after New York's death penalty was restored, he might have been the first to be executed by lethal injection in the state. Having killed seventeen prostitutes, Rifkin holds the dubious distinction of being New York's most prolific serial killer.

But if he were scheduled to be executed, Rifkin, warped egomaniac that he is, would be signing autographs right up until the moment they wheeled his gurney into the execution chamber. Prison gave Rifkin a celebrity status he never enjoyed on the outside. As one New York reporter put it, jail is "the only club he was allowed to join." Imagine if he was on death row. America would gobble up his delusions of becoming a millionaire and maybe he'd actually write some of the books he promised.

One of the all-time biggest carnival scenes preceded the execution of serial killer Ted Bundy in Florida. On January 23, 1989, the day before Bundy was to be executed, hundreds of cars and at least two thousand people gathered in a pasture near the state prison in Starke to celebrate. The scene was almost as horrifying as the one taking place within the prison walls, where a deranged but frightened man was trying to die with dignity.

In the makeshift parking lot, TV crews strategically

positioned themselves while pickups and trailers streamed in carrying families. Good ole boys carting hefty paunches and wearing sweaty T-shirts and cowboy boots brought six-packs while fraternity boys swigged Jack Daniel's and tequila from hip flasks. Many of them carried homemade signs: SPARKS ARE GOING TO FLY; CATCH THE CURRENT; TEDDY IS DEADLY; HAVE A SEAT, TED; and BUNDY, BURN IN HELL. Horns honked, firecrackers popped, and sparklers flared, providing shimmering light in the predawn hours.

Every time a superstar killer is executed, count on small-time entrepreneurs to hawk collectibles and memorabilia from the event. As a *Time* columnist put it, "Hey, there's gold in them thar psychos." If you had the stomach to capitalize on the event, Bundy's execution was an opportunity not to be missed. Someone was selling tiny electric-chair lapel pins for five dollars apiece, the perfect gift for a friend or loved one. It certainly was a money-making opportunity for local restaurant owners. They made fast cash peddling soda, hot dogs, coffee, and doughnuts. It's a wonder a pro–death penalty heavy-metal band didn't donate their services to the raucous event.

In 1992, serial killer trading cards triggered national outrage. Psychotic Charles Manson, who's practically an American institution, reportedly earned six hundred dollars in royalties from a line of caps, surfer pants, and T-shirts adorned with his image, carrying slogans like SUPPORT FAMILY VALUES, and CHARLIE DON'T SURF. Sales jumped after rock group Guns N' Roses lead singer Axl Rose began wearing the T-shirts in concert and actually covered a Manson song, on the group's 1993 live album, *The Spaghetti Incident*. And only California typographers could produce a typeface called Manson. For a reasonable ninety-five dollars, art directors can set type in Manson Regular, Manson Alternate, or Manson Bold.

John Wayne Gacy had his own interview line, a 900 number offering a recording of the monotone-voiced killer of thirty-three trying to pin the crime on others. (Gacy actually buried the bodies under his house.) A twelve-minute call cost $23.88.

On the night of Gacy's execution in 1994, a veritable festival atmosphere was taking place outside Illinois's maximum-security prison near Joliet. The crowd roared, "Let the clown die!" Gacy had worked as a clown at children's birthday parties.

Following his execution, Gacy's paintings became collectors' items, bringing hefty price tags in art galleries. A hard-rock group called Bloody Mess used Gacy's art on its album cover.

Stay tuned for more. The execution machinery grinds on, and if you want to keep up, just follow the national pages of your daily newspaper. Among the routine executions of ordinary killers are superstars waiting in the wings. A mega-event sure to titillate world press is Texas's pending execution of Henry Lee Lucas, a self-confessed serial killer.

It was like the traveling circus coming to town when Lucas went to trial on September 13, 1983, for the 1982 stabbing death of eighty-year-old Kate Pearl Rich in Montague, Texas. Initially, Lucas was charged with twenty-two killings in the state. He says he killed over a hundred women, raping his victims and committing numerous acts of necrophilia.

Until Lucas put the tiny hamlet of four hundred people on the map, no one ever heard of Montague. Suddenly this speck of a town was invaded by newspeople from all over the world. Twenty-four hours a day, helicopters hovered, making a constant whopping sound that nearly drove the town's tobacco-spitting old men to distraction.

For more than three weeks, Lucas was hot news.

Americans couldn't read enough about the forty-seven-year-old drifter and ex-con with a long history of mental instability. Since his arrest, Lucas had led lawmen and the media around the state, pointing out spots where he said he dumped the bodies of the women he murdered.

Lucas's story only got better as the investigation proceeded. Changing his original story, Lucas admitted to an incredible six hundred killings throughout the United States as well as in five foreign countries. Investigators in thirty-five states came to help the Texas Rangers close the investigation. After more than a hundred interviews with people who knew Lucas and sixty hours of taped interviews with Lucas himself, plus exhaustive examination of court records, they concluded that he was most likely responsible for three of the killings credited to him.

Following the trial was like watching a real-life Western with a cast of characters plucked right from a Hollywood back lot. Lucas, the one-eyed drifter and perennial loser, was center stage. Behind him was Montague County sheriff W. F. Conway, who has worn a badge for twenty-six of his sixty-one years. Sporting a straw cowboy hat and pointy boots, the paunchy slow-talking Conway epitomized the righteous Texas sheriff popular in Western movies. A former newsman turned prosecutor and a defense attorney who used to be a prosecutor rounded out the cast.

But all good things come to an end. When Lucas was sentenced to death, the public quickly forgot about him and Montague again fell into obscurity. Today, Lucas, pasty, paunchy, and looking much older than his sixty-one years, sits in a hot dirty prison cell in the Huntsville Correctional Facility waiting to die. When that day comes, the media will once again invade Texas to close the book on the reputed serial killer. Expect the likes of Mike Wallace, Peter Jennings, Dan Rather, and Diane Sawyer. Expect some pithy but sensitive observations from Bill Moyers, while Geraldo Rivera, sensational news' perennial piranha, milks the occasion for all it's worth. And you can only imagine what they'll be selling during Lucas's execution. Count on a sprawling country-style picnic, replete with barbecued ribs and down-home fried chicken, biscuits, and gravy. You may even get a guided tour of one of the hobo camps he hid in for years at a time.

New York is the most recent state to return to capital pumishment. Mario Cuomo fought hard against the death penalty during his entire tenure as govenor. With Cuomo's defeat in 1994, new govenor George Pataki made capital punishment a number one priority. New York's experience in this new quest and the issues the state encountered are instructive.

New York was once a trendsetter in the execution department. The first execution by electrocution in the world took place at New York's Auburn Prison in August 1890. Prior to that, the favorite execution method had been hanging, usually administered by county sheriffs. From 1890 through 1963, 695 people were executed by the state. Of this total, 26 were executed at Clinton, 55 at Auburn and 614 at Sing Sing. For opponents of the death penalty, New York's reinstatement marked a step backward. The majority, however, welcomed it with open arms, hoping capital punishment would serve as a deterrent and crimestopper.

The drive to rural Shoreham, home of Green Haven Correctional Institution, is eighty miles from bustling Manhattan. After Attica, Green Haven is the second largest prison in the state and the currrent resting place of New York's electric chair. Most of New York's thirteen prisons were built around the turn of the century in rural areas so they could be self-supporting. Hence, Auburn Prison boasted workshops; Sing Sing, marble quarries; Dannemora, iron mines; and Green Haven, dairy farmland. Green Haven has attracted curiosity seekers from all over the world, anxious to see its infamous electric chair, and chat with Warden Christopher P. Artuz.

No sooner was Green Haven unofficially proclaimed the "designated" location where New York would resume executions than it began to draw a steady stream of print and broadcast journalists. They came to experience the calm before the storm, to say they visited the site before New York staged its first execution in more than three decades. Green Haven was only a temporary site. New York correctional bigwigs had elaborate plans for its permanent death house that they weren't prepared to release until every detail was worked out.

Until exact place and procedures were determined, the spotlight was on Green Haven. It housed one of the world's most famous electric chairs, the original "Old Sparky" from Sing Sing Penitentiary in Ossining. Sing Sing had once been the sole site for executions in the state.

The last execution in New York was in 1965. Althjough the chair was moved to Green Haven in 1970, no executions took place there before *Furman* v. *Georgia* ended executions nationwide. By the time Governor Pataki restored the death penalty in 1995, making New York the thirty-eighth state to reinstate a capital punishment provision, there hadn't been an execution in the state in thirty-two years. By changing the law, prosecutors can now seek death by lethal injection for serial murderers, contract killers, people who kill witnesses or police officers, and people who kill as part of a terrorist act, among other crimes.

Seeing Green Haven for the first time is like stumbling on Dracula's castle on a rainy night. Suddenly you encounter this towering fortress in the middle of a serene rural countryside. The prison's massive gray cement walls violate the rich, fertile farmland and rolling green hills and valleys surrounding it. With its stark high-banked walls and watchtowers, Green Haven is an ugly, yet breathtaking, architectural monstrosity.

If you didn't know for certain that the prison was located in Stormville, which boasts one general store/gas station combination, you'd have a hell of a time finding it. Perhaps prison officials figure it's better to keep a low profile and not make a big deal about this sprawling maximum-security jail housing 2,220 prisoners and 1,300 security and administrative staff. If New York's first execution had taken place at Green Haven, a media circus would have arrived to televise the event around the world. Convoys of uplink satellite trucks with flagpolelike antennas would have been strategically positioned around the prison. There would have been food trucks, rows of portable toilets, and battalions of photographers, journalists, and curiosity seekers trying to get as close to the prison as possible.

Instead of taking the main road, it's easy to mistakenly turn onto a deserted unpaved, winding back road leading to the prison. You pass the prison's cemetery with its large twelve-foot wooden cross at the rear. There rests Green Haven's unclaimed prisoners, marked by cheap headstones inscribed with prison numbers only, no names. Who said death was liberating? No flowers are seen on this unkempt, overgrown cemetery plot. No visitors either. If you want to see Old Sparky, you have to be processed, stamped, and searched, then an escort takes you to a deserted section of the prison. It is a short stairway from the old K Unit, once the prison's death row, which has been converted to a fifty-cell SHU (Special Housing Unit) block for the prison's most dangerous inmates. This is where Lawrence Hayes and his nephew Cornelius Butler spent more than two decades. Visitors aren't allowed to walk through this cell block for fear of stirring up the prisoners.

One of the guides who will take you through the facility is Lieutenant Daniel Connolly, a career corrections officer in his early thirties, so far the youngest lieutenant in New York's entire correction system. Clearly, he is on the fast track. Maybe Connolly will someday make associate warden, maybe even warden.

He'll show you the tiny holding cell furnished with a cot, sink, and toilet, whose inside walls are covered with rust. The guides are quick to tell you that this state of disrepair is being corrected, as if they didn't want anyone thinking the prison staff had let the old death house fall to ruin.

Outside the holding cell, a video camera is positioned to monitor the prisoner twenty-four hours a day. Around a corner, there is a small conference cell where prisoners can meet privately with attorneys or a chaplain. Off to the right, just beyond the entrance, a door leads to a tiny fenced-in courtyard holding a lone basketball hoop perhaps so the prisoners can pass some time honing their jumpshots while waiting to die.

They save the worst for last, the old execution chamber itself. If the electric chair wasn't securely planted dead center in the front of the room, the place could easily pass for a chapel. Facing the chair are seven or eight dark mahogany pews that can seat more than fifty witnesses. No screen or window separates spectators from the gory event. Even the exhaust vent above the chair can't suck all the smells of burning flesh from the room. If the smells themselves are repugnant—and they most always are—imagine the sounds and sights. Witnesses would hear the shattering crack of electricity and then watch the jerking, squirming prisoner strain the leather restraints to the breaking point. Not a sight for the faint of heart. To the right of the chair is a large two-way mirror, behind which is the execution booth housing executioner and controls. This is where the killing machinery is stored—the power source and lever for releasing massive doses of electricity, a skull cap with electrodes, the black hood that is draped over the prisoner's face so spectators are shielded from his terror and pain, cables, and additional leather restraints for securing the prisoner in the chair. Paraphernalia that would make the Marquis de Sade proud.

The execution booth is off-limits to visitors. No one says why. But the party line is that Warden Artuz "has his reasons." "He is a very powerful man," said Connolly. "He runs the jail." No one questions him. So no one sees all the instruments of death. It's no wonder a mysterious aura surrounds the death props.

Artuz's reason for keeping the room locked is that he doesn't want to feed the overly curious and morbid. Actually, the last word on the secretive execution booth actually comes from his boss, the commissioner of corrections. Perfect public servant Artuz is doing his job—and taking all the heat himself. If you show all the lethal toys, especially the lever, it becomes chillingly clear that one person does the job by throwing the switch that fatally zaps the guy strapped in the chair.

A former Green Haven staffer who has been inside the little execution booth several times couldn't understand the big deal about the tiny room. "There's just a lot of electric panels, switches, and cable, that's all."

According to an ex-con who spent twenty years in prison, corrections officials are very protective over what they consider to be their most valued piece of equipment, the coveted centerpiece of the correctional system. "Hell, this is what it's all about," he said. "Punishing people. The electric chair or any other execution device is a symbol of the system. It means justice."

Despite the passage of time, "Old Sparky" doesn't seem any the worse for wear. The high-backed sturdy oak chair had been made to last. Only the leather straps and seat are faded and worn. After 614 executions, it's a wonder they've held up this well.

Walking through the old death house, one imagines what this room would be like if it were turned into a temporary execution chamber. It would be simple enough to do. Remove the electric chair and replace it with a hospital gurney. Then divide the large room to include a separate observation room with chairs, not pews, for witnesses to watch the execution from a distance. Tear down the control room, remove its contents, and turn it into a storeroom housing chemicals, IV lines, stethoscopes, and other hospital-like equipment needed for the lethal injection procedure.

Weeks before the execution, this section of the prison would be bustling with activity. Doors would clang open and shut as guards filed in and out. Family members would take turns seeing the prisoner for the last time as attorneys worked around the clock trying to secure last-minute stays. Like a frightened animal sitting in a zoo cage, the death-bound prisoner would be on display twenty-four hours a day. Once placed on death watch, there wouldn't be a moment of privacy. Every blink would be recorded and so would every word, grunt, or sob. For good reason. Perish the thought that a man about to die should short-circuit fate and take his own life.

While the guides can provide historical information about the prison, the only person who can explain how

Green Haven works is its top cop, Warden Artuz. Artuz is a short, bull-necked man sporting a marine-style crew cut and neatly trimmed mustache who has spent twenty-four of his forty-nine years in corrections. He enjoys being called "boss" by his men.

What effect is greenlighting an execution going to have on this outwardly steely bureaucrat? Oddly, he seemed nonplussed by the awesome events surrounding him. Does he relish the potential glory of a well-orchestrated execution? Once the execution countdown begins, with a nod of a head, a wave of a hand, or a mere look, the warden holds the awesome power of life and death over another human being.

Artuz made it clear he was not about to be intimidated by questions he had no intention of answering. This tough little man who deals with murderers, rapists, and drug dealers on a daily basis has neither time nor patience for small talk.

Between questions, he pulled Marlboros from his pack and lit them with a disposable plastic lighter. If cigarette smoke is a problem, don't stop in to see Artuz. Green Haven is *his* show

Artuz looks like he was yanked right out of central casting. He reveals nothing but the party line. If he has any secret thoughts or fears about Green Haven's role in New York's execution drama, he isn't about to share them. But he makes it very clear that prisons are run on a paramilitary model. Everyone's expected to do his or her job and do it well. His job is to carry out the commissioner's orders—no questions asked! You leave confident he will unflinchingly do just that. Artuz also seems unconcerned about any moral ambiguities surrounding the death penalty. Like a faithful servant, he intends to follow orders. Artuz would be a good man to lead troops into battle. The best place to be is right behind him.

Ex-convicts who spent many years at Green Haven can tell you Artuz is as tough as he seems. "You don't ever forget a man like Artuz," says Lawrence Hayes. On the other side of the fence, however, employees within New York's correctional system aren't as forthright with information. Most refused to comment about the man, on or off the record.

Artuz took over as Green Haven's warden in 1989. Prior to that he held Connolly's job. Visitors at that time probably had the same feeling about Artuz that they share about Connolly. One day he'd be warden. As for his future role as New York's executioner, Hayes says if anyone can do the job, it's Artuz. "He's ideal for it," he added.

Eddie Ellis, another ex-convict, agrees. Ellis spent twenty-three years of a twenty-five-year-to-life prison sentence in New York prisons. Fourteen of those years were spent in Green Haven. In the mid–1960s, Ellis was a key decision maker in the Black Panther's elite central committee. As the party's director of community relations, he shaped policy for the militant black organization that had a major impact on the civil rights movement in the black community. In 1969, Ellis was arrested and convicted of killing a Harlem resident. To this day, he maintains his innocence, insisting he was framed by the FBI, which was hell-bent on destroying the Panthers and other radical black organizations.

Ellis remembers Artuz well. He calls him a "factory-approved bureaucrat, a 100-percent-no-deviation, by-the-book kind of guy. He was fair, but he didn't tolerate rule breaking of any kind. If he had an order, he carried it out. Guys like that are scary."

"Nobody liked him much and nobody wanted to go before him," Hayes added. "Artuz is a complex man who loves his job and believes in the system. At Green Haven, he *is* the system." Chances are no visitors will ever understand that system—or see the inside of that room—until the behemoth called Green Haven is closed down. That's when its secrets will be revealed.

As the grounds and buildings fade behind you when you leave Green Haven, you're inclined to wonder about what Artuz thinks as he drives up to the prison every morning. At times, he has to feel like a feudal lord surveying his kingdom. He runs the show, sets the pace, and everyone else keeps in step. Technically, Artuz is just another civil servant, a powerful cog in a big wheel. But at Green Haven, he's the cog and the wheel. If you're on the wrong side of the bars, it's best to be on Artuz's good side.

What effect is an execution going to have on this tight-lipped bureaucrat? Maybe he'd glance at the execution technician hovering over the prisoner on the gurney, IV lines plugged into veins in both arms, and nod his head to give the "go ahead" signal. It's hard to believe that naked second in time wouldn't have a profound effect on Artuz for the rest of his life. Following the execution, he'd give a press conference, guided by the state's official version. But what happens to Artuz once he leaves the prison at the end of the troubling day? Surprise wife and kids with some takeout from KFC?

Or might a macho warden be more likely to head to the nearest bar and get quietly sloshed while chain-smoking his Marlboros. He might drink himself into oblivion to blur the events of the day. Or maybe he'll drink because he got off on the grisly event, an awesome power trip. There are as many possibilities as there are wardens. The big question is will he ever get over the event? But let's not be too hard on the man. If Artuz doesn't green-flag New York's executions, someone else will have to do so. Ditto that for every death row jurisdiction.

One thing is certain, the shock waves from this kind of work don't hit you immediately. They come later, growing more intense following each execution. Inevitably, memories of such events begin eating away at executioners like slow-acting acid. One day, they suddenly find the moral gyroscope that kept them centered and balanced has stopped working. Their world is suddenly askew. It has happened to many wardens who presided over executions. And it usually happens later in life. It happened to Lewis E. Lawes, the famed Sing Sing prison warden, who wrote five books about his prison reign. It happened to Clinton P. Duffy, the warden of California's San Quentin Prison, who carried out ninety executions. More recently, it happened to Don Cabana, former warden at Mississippi's State Penitentiary at Parchman and author of the recently published *Death at Midnight: The Confession of an Executioner.* Their belief systems shattered, many executioners do a complete about-face and become abolitionists—and staunch ones at that.

On September 1, 1995, New York State's death penalty law took effect and the Department of Corrections released its official plans. Nothing was "designated" or "temporary" anymore. Everything was ready to roll. New York's corrections heavies put a lot of time and money into getting their execution act together. Releasing reams of paper explaining procedures and costs, New York's acting commissioner of correctional services, Philip Coombe, Jr., said Green Haven would be the execution site for one year while other sites were being renovated. Male death row prisoners were to be housed at Clinton Correctional Facility in Dannemora, the state's largest maximum-security prison. Females were to be housed at Bedford

Hills Correctional. The permanent death house or execution chamber would be located at Sullivan Correctional Facility, a small maximum-security prison housing 585 prisoners in Fallsburg. The execution chamber at Sullivan is to be located in a large storage area on the ground floor. Three cells are ready, with accompanying showers, visiting areas, and closed-circuit television monitors. As more prisoners await execution dates, the unit can be expanded to include forty-eight cells. The reason for these elaborate plans is that Green Haven's old death row is too small.

Dannemora's residents are thrilled about the new death row arrangements. Just as there are company and college towns, Dannemora is a prison town and proud of it. Forget about the politics of execution, to this tiny village on the northern edge of the breathtaking Adirondack Mountains, it spells steady employment. One local corrections officer who has worked at the Clinton County Correction Facility for twenty-nine years said, "For us the death penalty is just another job." Many more Dannemora residents said they have no problem calling their hometown death row. A local hairstylist whose clients include prison staffers commented on Clinton's 2,800 inmates, "If they could all be put on death row and be fried tomorrow, the guards would have a party."

3

Don't Hold Your Breath—
THE SECRET TO GETTING A MERCIFUL
EXECUTION, FIRST TIME, EVERY TIME

> *"I don't want that on my conscience.*
> *Only God can decide to take a life."*
> —A JUROR REFUSING TO SERVE ON A
> SOUTH CAROLINA CAPITAL MURDER TRIAL

THE FOLLOWING IS AN EYEWITNESS ACCOUNT
of the 1962 execution of Leanderess Riley from the chaplain of San Quentin Prison:

At 9:50 P.M., Associate Warden Rigg and the doctors came in. I told Leanderess to say a prayer to himself if he did not care to have me pray and to relax into God's care. He did not seem to hear me. When the doctors approached his cell, he made a throaty, guttural growling sound. Frantically, at random, he picked up some of the old legal papers on his table and began passing them through the bars to the associate warden, as if they were appeals or writs. A guard unlocked his cell. He gripped the bars with both hands and began a long, shrieking cry. It was a bone-chilling, wordless cry. The guards grabbed him, wrested him violently away from the bars. The old shirt and trousers were stripped off. His flailing arms and legs were forced into the new shirt and fresh blue denims. The guards needed all their strength to hold him while the doctor taped the end of the stethoscope in place.

The deep-throated cry, alternately moaning and shrieking, continued. Leanderess had to be carried to the gas chamber, fighting, writhing all the way. As the witnesses watched in horror, the guards stuffed him into the chair. One guard threw his weight against the struggling little Negro [sic] while the other jerked the straps tight. They backed out, slammed the door on him.

Leanderess didn't stop screaming or struggling. Associate Warden Rigg was about to signal for the dropping of the gas pellets when we all saw Leanderess' small hands break free from the straps. He pulled at the other buckles [and] was about to free himself.

The associate warden withheld his signal. San Quentin had never executed a man raging wildly around the gas chamber. He ordered the guards to go in again and restrap the frenzied man. One of the guards said later he had to cinch the straps down so tightly the second time that he was ashamed of himself.

Again the door was closed. Again Leanderess managed to free his small, thin right wrist from the straps. Riggs gave the order to drop the pellets. Working furiously, Leanderess freed his left hand. The chest strap came off next. Still shrieking and moaning, he was working on the waist strap when the gas hit him. He put both hands over his face to hold it away. Then his hands fell, his head arched back. His eyes remained open.

His heartbeat continued to register for two minutes, but his shrieking stopped and his head
slowly dropped. (From pamphlet published by the
American Civil Liberites Union.)

About 250 miles away from New York state's
brouhaha over resuming capital punishment, in the
Boston suburb of Malden, Fred Leuchter must have
been upset. During the several months of planning,
Leuchter didn't receive a single call about the nifty
high-tech lethal injection machine he designed. He
must have wondered how anyone could think of buying
execution machinery without talking to him first.

In the execution game, Leuchter is considered an
innovative architect of cutting-edge killing machinery.
The *Boston Globe* dubbed him "Dr. Death." If he
wasn't so modest, he'd probably tell you he's to execution machinery what Edison is to electricity or Frank
Lloyd Wright to modern architecture. "I'm the only
expert in the world dealing with execution equipment,"
Leuchter stated simply.

He's not just an expert on the lethal injection procedure, but on death by electrocution, gas, and hanging as
well. This multifaceted specialist can also design and
build state-of-the-art gas chambers and gallows. There
isn't a warden on either coast who doesn't know his
name. Leuchter's electric chairs and components can be
found in prisons in Indiana, South Carolina, and
Tennessee. His $35,000 (excluding installation) comput-
erized lethal injection machines are used in Delaware,
Illinois, Missouri, New Jersey, Colorado, Oregon, and
Wyoming. "I believe in capital punishment, not capital
torture," Leuchter says with conviction.

So, understandably, Leuchter had to be hurt when
New York's corrections heavies didn't call him. The
fifty-four-year-old inventor has the strangest job in the

world. Yet someone has to do it, and Leuchter puts his heart and soul into it. In fact, to hear him talk about his work, it's clear he loves the execution game. Ask him about the history of capital punishment, specifically, the evolution of execution technology, and he's like a broken water faucet. Thin, nondescript, and bespectacled, Leuchter is a grown-up version of the prototypical nerd. He's the ninety-nine-pound weakling who got even with the bullies who kicked sand in his face. One journalist described him as a carbon copy of *Mad* magazine's legendary mascot, Alfred E. Neuman.

One wonders how anyone would choose the execution industry as his life's work. In Leuchter's case, the choice can be traced back to his childhood. While his peers were batting baseballs into center field, prison inmates were teaching him how to pick locks and break into safes. Leuchter's father supervised transportation for the Massachusetts prison system. As far as young Leuchter was concerned, there was nothing strange about hanging out with hardened criminals. As for his mechanical aptitude, even as a child Leuchter demonstrated a knack for inventing. Prior to getting into the execution game, he designed navigation equipment for the navy and holds patents for the first electronic sextant as well as several optical coding and surveying devices.

In 1980, while working as a private engineering consultant, he got a call from a New England prison warden asking if he could repair an electric chair. Knowing nothing about execution equipment, but welcoming a challenge, Leuchter said he'd like to research the subject before agreeing to tackle the assignment. So began his intense journey into the science of execution technology.

If Leuchter thought designing navigational equipment was fun, the science of killing had it beat. Researching execution machinery became an all-consuming passion. Leuchter pored over medical journals and spoke with

prison administrators and engineers all over the United
States. He even studied electric chair blueprints.

Weeks later, Leuchter got back to the New England
warden and told him he was confident he could repair
the chair and tackle other execution problems as well.

As in any business, good work brings its own
rewards. After Leuchter gave the New England warden
more for his money than he expected, word spread
quickly. Fred Leuchter was the man to call when you
had an execution glitch. There was no shortage of
work. According to Leuchter, he stumbled into a field
where he was the sole practitioner. He had cornered the
market. By his third or fourth job, he folded his engineering consulting firm, American Engineering, Inc.,
and formed Fred A. Leuchter Associates, Inc., specializing in execution equipment. By the mid–1980s,
Leuchter not only made the four types of equipment
used in the United States for hanging, electrocution,
gas, and lethal injection, he also trained and certified
personnel as hands-on execution technicians.

In the past, making execution equipment was a hap-
hazard affair prison officials didn't think a lot about
until faced with an execution. Practically all execution
equipment was designed and built at prison shops.
Most electric chairs were built by prisoners with the
wiring and circuitry done by prison electricians. But
that's a sore subject with Leuchter, who sees himself as
the Mother Teresa of the execution industry, a humane
savior committed to preventing needless suffering.

Leuchter said prison wardens desperately needed his
services. Muddled executions were happening on a regular basis. Executees were being senselessly tortured
because of archaic equipment and inexperienced technicians. His mission was to educate prison wardens, bring
them up to date, and end the primitive means of snuffing human life. Leuchter will provide you straight out

with plenty of bloodcurdling examples. He loves citing the classic case of Jesse Tafero, executed in Florida on May 4, 1990. "You're familiar with Jesse Tafero's case?" he asked, as if mentioning an historical turning point as important as the signing of the Declaration of Independence. The problem, as Leuchter saw it, was not just a rotted sponge in the headpiece, but a defective electrode in the helmet. "The voltage dropped—and I have no way of knowing how much—but I would guess from the damage done to Tafero's body that it dropped somewhere in the vicinity of seventy volts and then worked its way up."

The minimum number of volts needed to execute someone painlessly, according to Leuchter, is between 2,000 and 2,500 volts, depending upon the equipment. According to Leuchter's operation and instruction manual for his modular electrocution system, exactly 2,540 volts should be applied in two one-minute jolts, spaced ten seconds apart. The manual reads, "On occasion, the subject's heart will spasm, instead of seizing, during the first application of current, and the application of the second jolt will generally eliminate this problem."

Simply, if the execution is done improperly, the executee suffers extreme pain. Leuchter emphasized the importance of that first jolt of electricity. "The first jolt should render the body unconscious," he said. "But when you start with seventy volts, as they did in the Tafero execution, it ain't gonna happen."

Leuchter is also fond of citing the case of the man who came back to life thirty minutes after his execution because the electricity had not been applied in the right voltage. "They had to bring all the witnesses back, strap the person back in the chair, and do it all over again," he added.

Leuchter, however, has left nothing to chance. Not

only did he design a state-of-the-art chair and control
console, he also created a detailed operational procedure. The instructions are similar to those telling lay-
men how to put together an assembly-line desk, Jungle
Jim, or barbecue grill. Here is a slightly abbreviated
version of Leuchter's multi-step electrocution process.

Modular Electrocution System, Operation and Instruction Manual

*(A setup procedure outlines the arming of the chair,
a check of the control cable, control console,
power source, switches, etc.)*

1. Determine that the main disconnect is off and the
   input circuit breaker to the power supply is off. Do
   not proceed unless electric chair energized light is off.
2. Prepare subject for electrocution: Shave approximately a three-inch diameter spot on the top of the
   executee's head. Cut off pants to knees, slit pants to
   knees or supply subject with short pants.
3. Mix a saturated saline (saltwater) solution (add salt
   until it will no longer mix to lukewarm water).
4. Wet sponge in helmet (saturate).
5. Wet ankle sponges if a determination is made that
   they are to be utilized. Use of sponges is recommended in most cases.
6. Loosen all adjustments in restraint system and move
   backrest all the way back.
7. Sedate subject either orally or by injection if permissible. A 5cc injection of Verset (Midazolam HCL) 1
   mg/ml has been used in the past for sedating executees. Another alternative would be 1.5 ounces of
   eighty-proof whiskey. This should be done one half
   hour prior to the execution.
8. Curtain on witness window should be opened.

9. Subject must walk into execution chamber and speak (demonstrating he's alive).

10. Curtain on witness window should be closed.

11. Executee should be strapped into chair in the following manner:

   A. Connect and tighten waist harness.

   B. Tighten shoulder adjustments.

   C. Connect and tighten arm restraints, centering connectors.

   D. Insert subject's legs into electrodes on leg stock and connect and adjust the restraints, keeping the connectors in the center. The saturated saline sponges are recommended and may be placed behind the subject's leg between the leg and the electrode.

   E. Install saline-saturated helmet on the executee's head and tighten chin strap as tight as possible. The face curtain is optional and may be installed at this time.

   F. Insert helmet conductor into electrode on helmet and tighten hand screw. Tighten further with wrench.

   G. Loosen backrest adjuster, pull backrest as far forward as possible (tightening the subject) and tighten backrest adjuster, locking the backrest in place.

   Note: Subject is now ready for execution.

12. Open the witness window curtain.

13. The doctor should now examine the subject and certify that he is alive.

14. Turn on main disconnect.

15. Turn on input circuit breaker to the power supply.

16. On order from the warden, the key will be inserted and the "power on" switch will be turned on. The "system on" light will be verified. The key will be removed.

17. On order from the warden, the key will be inserted and the "computer on" switch will be turned on only if a two-operator procedure is to be utilized. The "computer on" (double) light will be verified. The key will be removed.

18. When the warden determines that the execution will proceed, he will order that the key be inserted and the "electric chair fail-safe" switch be turned from the center position to the operating position to the left.

WARNING: THE SYSTEM IS NOW ARMED. DO NOT TOUCH THE ACTIVATION BUTTONS (SINGLE OR DOUBLE).

19. On order from the warden, the electrocution will commence. One or two executioners will push either the single or double buttons simultaneously (if two). Verify the "electric chair energized" light.
Note: The system will now deliver two jolts of current, each for one minute with a ten-second off time separating the jolts. If a failure occurs on double operation, simply activate the single button and the timing sequence will proceed. If a further failure occurs, operate the system manually by turning the "electric chair fail-safe" switch to test position (right) and time with a watch: sixty seconds on; ten seconds off; sixty seconds on. Upon completion, turn "electric chair fail-safe" switch to off (center) position.

20. Upon completion of the timing sequence the subject should be dead. Verify that the "electric chair energized" light is off. Do not proceed unless this light is off.

21. Use key to shut off "computer on" switch and "power on" switch.

22. Shut off input circuit breaker to the power supply and the main disconnect in this order.
23. The doctor should now verify the heart death of the executee.
Note: If death has not occurred, proceed with steps 16 through 23 again.
24. The execution is now over.
25. Close witness window curtain and witnesses exit.
26. The executee should be removed from the chair.
27. Clean chair seat with disinfectant and mild soap.
28. Verify all switches and power are off.

Leuchter accompanies his literature with maintenance and test procedures to make sure the electrocution system delivers consistent results.

Of the three commonly used execution methods, Leuchter's favorite is electrocution. "If I were going to be executed, I'd rather be electrocuted, provided it was done properly," he explained. His reason is that this method is fast and painless. "With electrocution, you're strapped into the chamber, and within two or three minutes, you're dead."

While he admitted lethal injection is also painless, there is a psychological component to the procedure that's rarely talked about. "The problem with lethal injection is the executee lies on the gurney for thirty-five to sixty minutes with an IV line of saline going into his arm to prevent any coagulation at the tip of the catheter in the vein," Leuchter said.

The most dangerous, not to mention most expensive, execution method is the gas chamber, which Leuchter charges $300,000 to fabricate. He'll also build a gallows for a more reasonable $85,000, an electrocution system for $35,000, and a lethal injection machine for an affordable $30,000.

Even though Leuchter can build a first-rate gas

chamber, it's the method he recommends the least. The prisoner is placed in a supposedly airtight chamber where cyanide tablets are dropped in sulfuric acid to release lethal fumes. If the prisoner quickly breathes in the toxic fumes and then drops off into a deep sleep, it would be halfway humane. But that seldom happens. More often than not, the prisoner holds his breath until the last minute. When he finally inhales the deadly fumes, he gasps violently and uncontrollably, practically choking to death. Minutes later, he nods off, eyes bulging, writhing in his seat, and foaming at the mouth.

"I don't advise anyone to spend that kind of money on a gas chamber," Leuchter said. "About six years ago, I had a contract with Missouri to completely revamp their entire gas chamber. My recommendation was that they switch to lethal injection. You're talking about thirty thousand dollars for just the parts alone. Even after the new parts are installed, you still have something that's dangerous. The prison staff still has to handle the cyanide and make provisions for the elimination of the waste."

The business of disposing of the gas chamber's waste products bothered Leuchter a lot. "You'd be surprised what's done with the waste products," he complained. "Although the gas that is left is not dangerous in the long term, it's a hazard for the first twenty-four-to-forty-eight hours following the execution." Leuchter refuses to name the states, but says some "have dumped their wastes in harbors or buried them underground."

When it comes to the proverbial bottom line, Leuchter again endorses electrocution. It costs only thirty-one cents to electrocute someone, compared with over $600 for lethal chemicals and $250 for pellets and sulfuric acid for the gas chamber.

While there isn't much of a demand these days for

gallows, Leuchter can design a state-of-the-art product. Even though America has been lynching people since the *Mayflower* landed, Leuchter said hanging is tricky and can be easily botched.

Washington, Montana, New Hampshire, and Delaware are the only states with hanging statutes, but Leuchter strongly felt they'll soon be eliminated. Delaware, for example, had no idea how to hang anyone and once contacted Leuchter for advice. He wrote out the procedure, which was upheld by the Supreme Court.

Leuchter explained that hanging must be done precisely or the prisoner suffers excruciating pain. A mistake can cause strangulation, even decapitation. Leuchter designed a gallows based on a formula perfected by British military executioners. The hand-crafted gallows drops prisoners with a force of 1,600 pounds. Dropping this quickly severs the prisoner's spinal cord and painlessly snaps his neck.

To hear Leuchter go on about execution methodology and his obsessive goal of achieving a merciful execution, you'd think he had witnessed several executions. But he has no compunction about saying he hasn't. "It's not necessary that I watch someone be executed in order to understand what has to be done," he said. "I rely on the reports of doctors who are better qualified to make a judgment as to what is happening than I am."

What better example than the first lethal injection machine he developed for New Jersey. "Doctors determined lethal injection couldn't be done properly by hand," Leuchter continued. "They figured some kind of machine could do the job properly. The state's department of corrections approached me about building the machine."

Just as he had thrown himself into researching elec-

trocution methods, Leuchter took off to the nearest
medical library to research lethal dosages. The lethal
injection was invented by Karl Brandt, personal surgeon and friend of Adolf Hitler. Hitler's goal was to rid
the German race of imperfect specimens and freaks.
Brandt was entrusted with that mission and authorized
to expand the authority of physicians to determine who
was considered incurable and granted with mercy
killing. He developed the lethal injection in 1939 and
tested it on ten thousand retarded children.

Leuchter, true perfectionist that he is, had surpassed
Brandt. Beyond finding the best chemicals for the job,
he designed a computerized lethal injection machine
that introduces the drugs at appropriate intervals.
Here's how it works. First, the prisoner is given an
antihistamine in order to keep choking, coughing, and
spasms to a minimum. To calm the prisoner, Leuchter
suggests a preinjection of sodium pentothal five minutes prior to entering the death chamber. About forty-
five minutes prior to the execution, an IV line is
inserted in one arm, delivering saline solution, for easy
passage of the drugs into the veins.

Then the actual execution begins. First, Leuchter's
machine releases 15cc of 2 percent sodium pentothal
over a ten-second period, causing unconsciousness.
After a one-minute pause, the machine injects 15cc of
pancuronium bromide, followed by another one-minute
wait. The clincher is the injection of 15cc of potassium
chloride. If all goes according to plan, the prisoner
expires within two minutes.

By the mid–1980s, Leuchter had established himself
as an execution specialist with no competitors. If he had
only kept his mouth shut and gone on providing wardens with electric chairs and lethal injection machines,
his career would have been secure. Instead, he foolishly
agreed to be an expert witness at the trial of reputed

neo-Nazi German/Canadian publisher Ernst Zundel. In 1988, Zundel was being prosecuted for violating a Canadian law that forbids citizens to knowingly disseminate false information about the Holocaust. Zundel had reprinted and distributed a booklet, "Did 6 Million Really Die?", which presents evidence countering the claim that six million Jews were gassed to death in the "so-called Holocaust." As an expert on gas chambers, Leuchter was hired to visit concentration camp sites and gather evidence that would once and for all explain whether the Germans actually gassed millions of Jews. With Zundel footing the bill, Leuchter visited Poland's most notorious concentration camps—Auschwitz, Birkenau, and Majdanek—and took soil samples back to Massachusetts for analysis.

Alpha Analytical Inc, a Westborough, Massachusettes–based testing laboratory, analyzed the samples and found little or no trace of toxic gases. This startling bit of data became the centerpiece of the infamous 192-page "Leuchter Report." It said, "None of the facilities examined could have supported, or in fact did support, multiple executions utilizing . . . lethal gas . . . they were never used as gas chambers."

Leuchter and Alpha executive James Roth flew to Toronto to testify on Zundel's behalf. In great detail, Leuchter explained that "the alleged gas chambers at Auschwitz would have been too damp to perform an execution function. They lacked the heating systems required to bring Zyklon B"—trade name of cyanide used by Nazis—"to its proper killing temperature of 78.3 degrees Fahrenheit." It's hard to understand why Leuchter would jeopardize his career, reputation, and credibility over such absurdities. Was it chutzpah, madness, prejudice, stupidity, or all of the above?

Ironically, it took about two years for the media to jump on the story. When they did, Leuchter was drawn and quartered by major dailies, especially Leuchter's hometown *Boston Globe*, as well as Jewish and liberal organizations such as the American Civil Liberties Union and Amnesty International.

All the while, Leuchter continued to defend his position. He told one reporter, "Using those facilities would be tantamount to trying to operate a gas chamber in your living room." When asked about the "Leuchter Report," he flippy said, "It was just another job" for an expert on execution systems.

For a couple of years, Leuchter was hot copy for the legitimate press as well as sensational tabloids and TV news shows. Even ABC's popular *Prime Time Live* did an eerie segment on him, called "Dr. Death," on May 10, 1990. During it, he proudly demonstrated the gallows he built for Delaware by putting a noose around a bag of sand the same weight as a man and pulling the trapdoor.

Meanwhile, Leuchter was investigated, discredited, and publicly humiliated. He was forced to admit he wasn't an engineer and didn't have a state license to practice engineering, just a bachelor's degree in history from Boston University. Massachusetts attempted to prevent him from functioning as an execution systems specialist. Florida, Alabama, Virginia, and Illinois all but ceased doing business with him. Illinois reportedly cut off a contract with him for building a lethal injection machine and supervising in the execution of Charles Walker. (Because of citizen outrage, Illinois executed Walker without Leuchter on September 12, 1990.)

Leuchter's life became a daily nightmare. By 1991, he had enough of the limelight. He lay low and monitored his calls to avoid journalists, outraged citizens, and curiosity seekers.

When he does choose to take a call, he is quick to put

a price tag on the conversation: a two-hundred-dollars-an-hour consulting fee with a five-hour minimum. Leuchter made a big point of saying he wasn't going to talk about the Holocaust and how he was hurt by the public's insensitivity. Nevertheless, he said, "I don't want to get into any details on this [the Holocaust] because it's all ancient history. And I hope it's over! Suffice it to say, I'm not a Holocaust revisionist or a neo-Nazi. I have been condemned by everyone. I got caught in the middle. Everyone is after my head. No one likes me. I'm simply an expert on execution procedures. I was contacted by the Canadian court system because of referrals from several prison wardens in the United States to act as an expert witness for the court. I was sent to Europe, investigated alleged execution facilities, and simply reported that the facilities I inspected were not execution facilities. I said nothing about the Holocaust."

Leuchter sees himself as a victim. If the public had understood the magnitude of his mission, it would have been more forgiving. He explained that he's not in his line of work for money or publicity, but to make sure capital punishment is administered humanely. As far as he is concerned, his actions were above reproach.

It didn't take much prodding to get him to talk about his favorite subject: execution technology. He rambled about the importance of his role and how his goal is to replace outmoded execution methods with modern and humane technology. Beyond improving execution devices, Leuchter contended that the execution environment, especially during lethal injection procedures, should be upgraded. Putting himself in the executee's shoes, he imagined that it was no fun staring at a cold painted or concrete wall.

The solution, he says, is beautifying the execution chamber. Good intentions aside, Leuchter has never considered that the execution chamber's decor is not a high priority to the petrified prisoner. He insists it's an important issue that ought to be addressed. He felt the execution chamber ought to have wood-paneled walls and television or music to help the executee pass the time on the gurney waiting to die. As for the gurney itself, it should be replaced with a comfortable, reclining chair, the kind used in dental offices or blood banks.

Why stop there? Shouldn't the executee of the nineties be able to kick back in his electric Stratolounger and put on a little Henry Mancini or maybe pop in his favorite video, possibly *Murder in the First* or the *Bird Man of Alcatraz,* while the lethal chemicals take hold.

All in all, Leuchter feels execution technology is sorely neglected. What's needed, he proclaimed, is a textbook on execution technology. "There are a lot of prisoners being tortured to death in poorly administered executions," he said. "It doesn't have to happen."

Clearly, Leuchter is his own best spokesperson. No matter how much he's raked over the coals, he manages to sound like a misunderstood martyr. Nevertheless, plenty of impressively credentialed professionals think otherwise. Over the past couple of years, his lethal injection machine has been a subject of controversy because of glitches in the process that caused pain and suffering, not only for the prisoner on the gurney but for everyone participating in the grisly event. With all his alleged research, many medical professionals are outraged because he's not a physician and is thus unqualified to prescribe lethal dosages.

Dr. Edward A. Brunner, a board-certified anesthesiologist and chairman of the department of anesthesia at Northwestern University Medical School, is among a handful of experts who criticized Leuchter's lethal injection machine. Following the painful execution of

Emmitt Foster on May 3, 1995, Brunner was asked to provide expert advice in a prisoner complaint seeking a restraining order to prevent further use of Leuchter's machine at Missouri's Potosi Correctional Center.

Foster took thirty minutes to die after the chemical cocktail entered his bloodstream. The forty-three-year-old prisoner was executed for the murder of a softball-team mate during a robbery twelve years earlier in St. Louis County. In Missouri's previous executions by injection, death came anywhere from seven to twenty minutes after administration of the first of two lethal doses. Potosi officials said an overly tight leather strap binding Foster's arm slowed the process to a snail's pace. Even though it took far longer than it should have, they insisted Foster didn't suffer. Reporters covering the execution had a different story. A Missouri radio network reporter said Foster was "gasping, slightly convulsing" when prison officials closed the blinds to the execution chamber. An Associated Press reporter said Foster was having "some abdominal convulsing."

After analyzing Potosi's lethal injection procedures, Brunner concluded that it "poses substantial and unwarranted risks of subjecting the prisoner to extreme pain and suffering during his execution." Doing the job properly would take qualified personnel to select the chemicals, prepare the injection, insert the IV catheter, and supervise the event from beginning to end.

Dr. Paul LeVesque, a professor of anesthesiology at Tufts Medical School in Boston, agreed with Brunner. LeVesque said the chemicals will do the job, but it's the quantities of chemicals used that can cause unnecessary suffering. "You can't have one recipe for all prisoners," he said. "Fifteen ccs of sodium pentothal will put out an average man of 165 to 170 pounds, but it wouldn't knock out a guy weighing over 200 pounds. It will also have little effect on prisoners who were habit-ual drug users. Some patients have an enhanced reaction to pain after sodium pentothal is given."

LeVesque also said giving potassium chloride intravenously can cause intense pain. "During operations, we give it through a central line right into the heart so it doesn't hurt," he said. He concluded by saying that three quarters of prisoners using Leuchter's technique will suffer. "This is not a humane way to kill a person," he said. "It's worse than the electric chair." A British documentary filmmaker describes the lethal injection process as "medical theater." "Don't be misled," he said. "It only looks like medicine."

Emmitt Foster's long, painful death is just one of many similar instances. Medical experts say it isn't just Leuchter's computerized lethal injection machine that's flawed, it's the procedure itself, regardless of how the chemicals are administered. Rickey Ray Rector's execution on January 24, 1992, in Varner, Arkansas, dramatically points up the glaring incompetence of technician executioners. Because Rector weighed 298 pounds, it took the medical staff more than fifty minutes to find a usable vein in his arm. Witnesses were not permitted to view the bloody comedy of errors, but they said they heard Rector's loud moans throughout the process. During the ordeal, Rector, who suffered serious brain damage from a lobotomy, tried to help the medical personnel locate a vein. The administrator of the state's Department of Corrections Medical Programs reportedly said, "The moans came as a team of two medical people, increased to five, worked on both sides of Rector's body to find a suitable vein." The administrator said that this may have contributed to his occasional outbursts.

Plenty of other similar mishaps have been reported in the back pages of newspapers. On March 13, 1985, Stephen Peter Morin lay on a gurney for forty-five minutes at the Huntsville, Texas, execution site while bungling technicians repeatedly pricked his arms and legs with a needle in search of a vein suitable for the lethal injection. On August 20, 1986, Randy Wools had to help his Texas executioners find a good vein for the execution. On June 24, 1987, a similar drama was repeated in Huntsville when Elliot Johnson waited on the death gurney. Johnson lay awake and fully conscious for thirty-five minutes while Huntsville's medical team searched for a place to insert the needle.

It was a ghoulish scene at Huntsville on December 13, 1988, when Raymond Landry climbed on the gurney. Landry was put to death at 12:45 A.M. after a fourteen-minute delay when one of two needles sprang a leak, sending lethal liquid shooting across the room toward media observers. The delay was caused by what officials call a "blowout," when the syringe comes out of the vein. The warden then had to order the execution team to reinsert the catheter.

On May 24, 1989, Stephen McCoy had such a violent physical reaction to the drugs (heaving chest, gasping, choking, etc.) at Huntsville's execution factory that one of the witnesses fainted and fell onto another witness.

Even the well-publicized execution of John Wayne Gacy on May 10, 1994, in Illinois, was botched. After the execution had begun, one of the three lethal drugs used to execute Gacy clogged the tube. Blinds were drawn to block the scene and obstruct witnesses' views. The clogged tube was replaced with a new one, the blinds were reopened, and the execution resumed. Anesthesiologists blamed the problem on the inexperience of prison officials who conducted the execution. One doctor said the proper procedure taught in "IV 101" would have prevented this error.

* * *

While execution experts still insist lethal injection is the cleanest and most humane way to snuff a life, old-line corrections bureaucrats are reluctant to abandon electrocution or the gas chamber. One prison official, who insisted on anonymity, said, "It's hard to teach an old dog new tricks." Most times these tried-and-true methods get the job done. But when they backfire, the execution chamber suddenly turns into a medieval torture chamber.

The following eight executions by electrocution and in the gas chamber are practically textbook cases of botched executions.

On April 22, 1983, in Alabama, sparks and flames erupted from the electrode attached to John Evans's leg after the first jolt of electricity. The electrode then burst from the strap holding it in place and caught on fire. Smoke and sparks came out from under the hood. Two physicians entered the chamber and found a heartbeat. The electrode was reattached to Evans's leg, followed by more smoke and burning flesh. Again the doctors found a heartbeat. Ignoring the pleas of Evans's lawyer, Russ Canan, a third jolt was applied. The execution took fourteen minutes and left Evans's body charred and smoldering.

After a first jolt of electricity failed to kill Otis Stephens in Georgia on December 12, 1984, he struggled for eight minutes before a second charge finished the job. The first jolt took two minutes. Officials waited six minutes to allow Stephens's body to cool before physicians could examine him and order another jolt. Witnesses said Stephens took twenty-three breaths.

On October 16, 1985, in Indiana, William E. Vandiver was still breathing after taking a first jolt of 2,300 volts. The current had to be applied three more times before he died. Department of Corrections officials admitted the execution "did not go according to plan."

Leuchter's favorite botched execution is the goriest screwup of all, the electrocution of Jesse Joseph Tafero on May 4, 1990. Six-inch flames erupted from the headpiece and three jolts of power were required to stop Tafero's breathing.

On October 17, 1990, Virginia's Department of Corrections increased the voltage on the electric chair to compensate for Wilbert L. Evans's large size. When the electricity hit him, Evans lunged forward, smashing his face against the hood. Blood from his nose and eyes flowed from the hood, staining his shirt.

At 11:00 P.M. on August 22, 1991, Virginia corrections officers strapped Derick Lynn Peterson into the chair and administered the normal dose of a 1,725-volt surge for ten seconds, followed by a 240-volt surge for 10 seconds. His head jerked and his fists clenched. Prison Doctor David Barnes felt Peterson's neck and checked him with a stethoscope at 11:05 and again at 11:09. "He has not expired," Barnes said after each check. At 11:10, the electrocution cycle was administered again and Barnes pronounced Peterson dead at 11:13 P.M.

The reported foul-ups in the gas chamber are equally upsetting.

During the execution of Jimmy Lee Gray in Mississippi on September 2, 1983, officials had to clear the room eight minutes after the gas was released when Gray's desperate gasps for air repulsed witnesses. His attorney, Dennis Balske, criticized state officials for clearing the room while the inmate was still alive. Gray died banging his head against a steel pole in the gas chamber while reporters counted his moans.

On April 6, 1992 at 12:18 A.M., one pound of sodium cyanide pellets dropped beneath Donald

Eugene Harding's chair into a vat containing six quarts of distilled water and six pints of sulfuric acid. Cameron Harper, a reporter for KTVK-TV, said, "I watched Harding go into violent spasms for fifty-seven seconds. Then he began to convulse less frequently. His back muscles rippled. The spasms grew less violent. I timed them as ending six minutes and thirty-seven seconds after they began. His head went down in a little jerking motion. Obviously, the gentleman was suffering. This was a violent death, make no mistake about it. It was an ugly event. We put animals to death more humanely. This was not a clean and simple death." Another witness, Carla McClain, a reporter for the *Tucson Citizen*, said, "Harding's death was extremely violent. He was in great pain. I heard him gasp and moan. I saw his body turn from red to purple."

Corrections officials admit there is no perfect way to kill a person. No matter how much planning goes into the process, glitches can occur. Even when the process goes smoothly, it is nerve-racking. To prevent screwups, prison officials create strict detailed procedures or protocols. A. J. Bannister, a death row prisoner at Missouri's Potosi Correctional Center, neatly summarized the execution protocol's purpose: "It makes sure everything goes according to schedule and it also diffuses responsibility so the entire weight of the execution doesn't fall on one person."

Aside from keeping the execution wheels humming smoothly, detailing every step of the execution dehumanizes a painful process. Despite abolitionist cries, most prison wardens struggle to squelch empathetic feelings so they can get the job done. The protocol is a way of sanitizing the killing process.

Whatever the reasons for the execution protocol, it

amounts to a macabre shopping list of events and procedures for speedily ending a prisoner's life. New York's methodical execution protocol was officially released on September 1, 1995, the day the state's new death penalty law took effect. A thirty-page numbered list, covering every aspect of a condemned prisoner's life and death, it includes the clothing he or she is permitted to wear on death row (one pair of pants, one shirt, one set of underwear, one pair of slippers, one pair of socks), personal items (one pair of prescription eyeglasses), one medically approved denture, one prescription hearing aid, toiletries (one bar of soap, one toothbrush, one tube of toothpaste, one plastic comb, one roll of toilet tissue), and writing materials (writing paper, envelopes, pencil or pen).

Seventy-two hours after being moved to the death house, or the "Unit for Condemned Persons," at New York's Sullivan Correctional Facility, prisoners are permitted the following personal items: one religious book, one plain wedding band, one kufi or yarmulke or fez, one set of rosary beads, up to ten photographs, stamps, cigarettes (one carton per week), or twenty cigars per week, one prayer rug, and one prayer shawl.

Every moment of the chilling sequence of events is synchronized, right down to the twenty-nine words the security adviser says once the prisoner is executed: "Ladies and gentlemen, the physician in attendance has pronounced the inmate dead at [time]. The execution is complete and the officers will now escort you out of the institution."

Whether it's a lengthy booklet or a short list of procedures, the protocol is designed for the agonizing last two weeks prior to the execution date when every step is planned. By then, the prisoner has used up his or her appeals. There's no hope and the end is imminent. Typically, the execution order is signed by a

Superior Court judge in the county where the inmate was convicted.

Until the execution order is delivered, execution is often an abstract idea to most condemned prisoners. Many think the day will never come. They're betting on indefinite stays. When the event becomes real, all the tension, anxiety, and numbing fear that's been building for several years is suddenly focused.

Typically, the prisoner is notified two weeks before the scheduled execution date. The warden reads the order and asks about final arrangements, witnesses, visitation, and disposal of the body. Prisoners ask questions they never thought they'd ask. Most agonize over soiling themselves and whether they'll have to wear diapers. A. J. Bannister wondered how he'd get on the gurney. Would he be lifted or would he climb on it unassisted? Not a day goes by when Bannister doesn't run the execution drill over in his head. He knows what chemicals are used, in what order they're administered, and the effect they will have. Knowing all that, he can pretty much guess how long the process takes until he's dead.

Rumors circulate about what happens during the execution process. Every botched execution is blown out of proportion, looming as a potential nightmare. Prisoners facing execution wonder whether their eyes will pop out or if their skin will be burned clean off their bones.

Every prison has its own protocols, yet they're all variations on the same theme. Only minute details differ. At Texas's Huntsville execution factory, the well-rehearsed protocol runs with clockwork efficiency. When Texas revised its penal code in 1974, it became the first state to adopt lethal injection as an execution method. When it finally tested it, Texas became a trendsetter. The Lone Star State boasts the most executions in the twentieth century, with Georgia right behind it. Not only did Texas master the free-flow lethal injection system, it perfected the protocol keeping the execution wheels running smoothly.

At Huntsville, the execution moves into high gear when the prisoner is placed in a death watch cell thirty-six hours prior to the execution. The cell is in front of the cell block so the prisoner can be observed. The afternoon prior to the execution, the inmate is transported fifteen miles to the execution chamber at the Walls Unit, which ironically lies smack in the middle of bustling little Huntsville. One would hardly suspect that this unpretentious little building with neatly pruned shrubbery is one of America's most famous execution sites.

The last hours of the prisoner's life are spent in a holding cell next to the execution chamber. Except for an attorney or spiritual adviser, the prisoner is not permitted to see friends or family.

A few hours before the execution, the prisoner is given a last meal and waits out the final hours with his attorney and spiritual adviser.

It's pretty much the same at other prisons. Outside the prisoner's cell, there's often a television and an accessible telephone. Typically, the prisoner's last hours are spent saying good-byes to friends and relatives and watching television. If the case has captured local or national coverage, he can even catch live updates on any last-minute appeals.

In states where prisoners are electrocuted, the procedure is slightly more elaborate. Two hours prior to execution at Georgia's Jackson Diagnostic Center, the prisoner's head and right leg are shaved where the electrodes are to be placed. The inmate is given a fresh uniform, which has been modified for the execution. Except for the slit to the knee in the right leg part, it's a

standard uniform of white pants and shirt with blue
stripes.

All states with a death penalty require the prisoner
be in reasonably good health before execution. A
month before forty-seven-year-old George Del Vecchio
was executed in Illinois on November 22, 1995, he
underwent an angioplasty to clear a blocked artery
after suffering a heart attack. (In a botched burglary in
1977, Del Vecchio almost decapitated a boy with a
knife and raped the boy's mother.)

The last half hour of the prisoner's life moves like a
dirge. The witnesses are escorted into an observation
room with a window facing the execution chamber.
Surrounded by the warden and guards, the prisoner is
strapped into the electric chair or brought into a gas
chamber and secured in a chair. With the lethal injection, the procedure is slightly different. Typically, the
witnesses are brought in when the prisoner is already
on the gurney and the saline solution is flowing into his
system, opening the veins so the lethal fluids can be
quickly absorbed.

Regardless of prison or execution method, the last
ritual before the warden gives the technician the go-
ahead is the prisoner's final statement. Most prisoners
say something. John Spenkelink took the opportunity
to ask Governor Bob Graham to seriously think about
what he was doing. Even prosecutors who favor capital
punishment admitted Spenkelink should not have been
executed. Said Spenkelink: "I would like Governor
Graham to come see me. It seems to me that if he is to
judge me, he should know me. He cannot know me
through papers or the words of my lawyers. That's just
common sense. If he had investigated my case, he
wouldn't be doing this. If he's so sure of himself, he

wouldn't be afraid to come. I know who I am. I want him to know who he is killing—the real person, not some idea he has in his head about me."

Some decline the opportunity to make a final statement and a few use this last theatrical moment to lash out at the system or proclaim their innocence. Nicholas Ingram, executed on April 7, 1995, in Georgia's Jackson Diagnostic Center, used his final statement to aim a huge wad of spit at Warden A. G. Thomas. Ingram, thirty-one, shot to death J. C. Sawyer and tried to kill Sawyer's wife after robbing them.

In Florence, Arizona, Jimmie Wayne Jeffers's last words were a stream of obscenities directed at Corrections Director Sam Lewis. On October 20, 1976, Jeffers killed his former girlfriend with an overdose of heroin, then left her in a shower stall for three days.

When white supremacist Richard Wayne Snell, executed on April 20, 1995, in Varner, Arkansas, was asked if he had any last words, he took the opportunity to threaten Governor Jim Guy Tucker, who had declined to block the execution. Said Snell, "Governor Tucker, look over your shoulder; justice is coming. I wouldn't trade places with you or any of your cronies. Hell has victories; I am at peace." Snell was convicted of the 1984 murder of a Texarkana pawnbroker, William Stumpp, during a robbery, and of the 1985 killing of an Arkansas state trooper who had stopped Snell's car for a traffic violation.

Dozens of prisoners have proclaimed their innocence right up until the very end. In 1995, there were at least three such cases: Emmitt Foster, on May 3, in Missouri; Bernard Bolander, on July 18, in Florida; and Carl Johnson, on September 19, in Texas. "I do have remorse for the legal system," Foster said, "because I did not commit this particular murder."

Bolander insisted he was framed and verbally slammed the legal system. "As I walk through this final point in my life," he said, "I want to tell all of you who may be writing about this there are many people living here who had lawyers who were incompetent, lazy, ignorant, or simply too busy to do a good job."

Johnson's final words: "I want the world to know I am innocent. I have found peace. Let's ride. I'm ready."

Many more express regrets for what they did and try to make peace with themselves and the world. Thomas Lee Ward, fifty-nine, executed at Angola, Louisiana, for killing his stepfather-in-law soon after being released from jail for molesting his daughter, said, "I feel remorse for the things that I did."

Just before Thomas Mann was put to death in Huntsville, Texas, for killing two people in Dallas in 1980, he said, "I would like to tell my family I love them. My attorneys did their best. All my brothers on death row, those who died and those who are still there, hang in there."

Thirty-year-old Karl Hammond's last words before he was put to death by lethal injection in Huntsville on June 21, 1995, for the 1986 rape and murder of an FBI secretary, were: "I just want to say I know it's so hard for people to lose someone they love so much. I think it's best for me to just say nothing at all."

A few welcomed the end. Philip Lee Ingle, thirty-four, said he had stopped all appeals "so that the victims can maybe find some peace and put an end to what has happened." Ingle was executed in Raleigh, North Carolina, on September 22, 1995, for the brutal 1991 murders of two elderly couples. One couple was beaten with an ax handle, the other was bludgeoned with a tire iron. As he was rolled into the death chamber, Ingle shouted, "I'm going to heaven."

After spending fifteen years on Virginia's death row,

forty-nine-year-old Willie Lloyd Turner said he had so many stays, he knew the death warrant by heart. By the time his appeals finally ran out, he wanted out. Turner was convicted of shooting a jewelry store owner to death in 1978 in Franklin, Virginia. Said Turner, "Even a cat has only nine lives. Enough is enough. This is psychological torture."

Ironically, many cold-blooded killers take these last moments to lecture on morality. Thomas Lee Ward concluded his last statement with, "I hope that young people today will learn that violence is not an answer. I hope that the legal system learns that lesson, too. The death penalty is not a solution."

Just before Robert Lee Willie, convicted of raping and murdering an eighteen-year-old woman, was executed in Louisiana on December 28, 1984, he said: "Killing people is wrong. It makes no difference whether it's citizens, countries, or governments. Killing is wrong." Two weeks later in South Carolina, Joseph Carl Shaw was executed for murdering two teenagers. His last words were an appeal to the governor: "Killing is wrong when I did it. Killing is wrong when you do it. I hope you have the courage and moral strength to stop the killing."

And some take this last theatrical moment to preach. After being strapped into the gurney in Huntsville on December 8, 1995, Hai Hai Vuong, forty, said, "I hope whoever hears my voice tonight will turn to the Lord. I give my spirit back to him. Praise the Lord! Hallelujah!" Vuong was executed nine years after killing two people and wounding five others in a pool hall-shooting spree.

Even when the prisoner is making his final statement, there is a fleeting chance his life will be spared. Every execution chamber has a telephone, with an open line to the attorney general, who has the power to grant a last-minute reprieve.

*   *   *

Once the final statement is completed, the chances of being saved by the bell are slim. The warden takes over, quickly closing the door on the prisoner's life. With a nod of the head or a hand signal, the last sound the prisoner hears prior to electrocution is a soft click when the electricity comes on, slamming the body unconscious with more than two thousand volts for four seconds. If gassed, the inmate hears he cyanide pellets drop into the sulfuric acid, releasing deadly fumes that envelope the chamber and, if he is lucky, quickly end his life. If it's lethal injection, no sound is heard as deadly chemicals rapidly invade the body, quickly shutting down all vital organs.

None of the above events is speedy or painless for any of the players—including the victim's family. Even under optimal conditions, it's seldom a clean kill.

There Are No Millionaires
on Death Row
THE POLITICS OF DEATH

*"I don't know of a wealthy person ever
executed in the United States."*
—CLINTON P. DUFFY, THE LATE LONGTIME WARDEN OF
CALIFORNIA'S SAN QUENTIN PRISON,
WHO CARRIED OUT NINETY EXECUTIONS

"Society prepares the crime; the criminal commits it."
—FORTUNE COOKIE, NEW VIET HUONG RESTAURANT,
NEW YORK CITY

*"To die is poignantly bitter, but the idea of having
to die without having lived is unbearable."*
—ERICH FROMM, *MAN FOR HIMSELF*

IT'S EASY TO LAND ON DEATH ROW. IF YOU
are poor, black or Hispanic, uneducated, and/or have a
prior prison record, you have most of the qualifications.
The chances increase enormously if you are a loner,
drifter, are eccentric, or retarded. And if you had the mis-
fortune of committing the crime in a desolate law-and-
order-abiding Southern town that doesn't take well to
itinerant strangers, you don't have a prayer.

Most of death row's inhabitants are losers, wanderers, and small-time crooks not smart enough to figure out how to avoid the law. You're not going to find superstar crooks, Mafia warlords, hit men or white-collar fraud mongers on death row. Nor will you find celebrities.

Lewis A. Lawes, the famed warden of New York's Sing Sing Prison, summed up the death row population in his prophetic *Twenty Thousand Years in Sing Sing:* "In my twelve years of my wardenship I have escorted 150 men and one woman to the death chamber and the electric chair. In ages they ranged from seventeen to sixty-three. They came from all kinds of homes and environments. In one respect they were all alike. All were poor, and most of them friendless."

Football legend O.J. Simpson, for example, would never have wound up on death row. His spectacular sixteen-month trial, which ended on October 3, 1995, offers a scathing picture of America's criminal justice system. The darling of well-heeled jet-setters, Simpson enjoyed an international following. His trial pointed up the power of wealth and privilege. Most of all, it drove home the fact that the death penalty debate is just as much a political issue as it is a moral and ethical one.

After less than four hours of deliberation, the jury of ten women and two men rendered a not-guilty verdict. Prior to the reading of the verdict, the entire world was waiting with baited breath. The media wasn't exaggerating when they called the Simpson case the "trial of the century." It cost the state of California $4 million to prosecute Simpson, plus an additional $3 million to sequester the jury for 474 days. Simpson's legal fees for a battalion of lawyers were $10 million. The trial spawned a niche industry. About thirty Simpson-related books were published, plus there was a TV miniseries, a few documentaries, and at least two full-length feature films. Anything the football great had touched suddenly became a big-ticket collectible. Years from now, entrepreneurs will still be making money hawking O.J. memorabilia.

But change the above scenario and you could wind up with a more troubling outcome. What would have happened if O.J. Simpson hadn't a celebrity athlete, but a poor-schlump regular guy holding down a minimum-wage job. What if he hadn't been a millionaire boasting a Bentley and a Ferrari, but just another black man accused of two brutal murders? The result would have been another, far less spectacular trial. American justice would have moved at warp speed. Prosecutors most likely would have asked for—and gotten—the death penalty. If a capital crime were committed in Escambia County, Alabama, Simpson would have experienced assembly-line justice. The average length of a capital murder trial in Alabama is three days.

But, like they say, money talks. Influence and status equal power. And power, more than issues of right and wrong, defines how justice is doled out and whether someone lives or dies.

The Simpson trial proved that two kinds of justice exist: justice for the wealthy and privileged and justice for everyone else. If you're lucky enough to be in the former camp, the system can be manipulated so you don't wind up on death row. But if you fall into the latter group, you become a pawn of a political machine fueled by ambitious prosecutors looking for notches on their résumés. What could be more impressive than sending a bad guy to death row?

As frustration and anger over violent crime grows, most people feel that death is the only proper punishment. Politicians have discovered that the secret to holding on to their thrones is to support the death penalty with evangelical force. Present a strong get-tough-on-crime package to voters and you're practically a shoo-in. Come across as soft on crime and you'll never enjoy the perks of political office. For well over a decade, the death penalty had been a key political issue in Florida. After conquering the governor's job for two straight terms, Bob Graham quickly learned that nothing captures votes faster than promising to campaign for the death penalty. They called him "Governor Jell-O" until he started signing death warrants at reelection time. But Graham was a mere foot soldier compared with Bill Clinton when he was hot on the 1992 presidential campaign trail. After he was defeated for the 1980 Arkansas gubernatorial race, he wholeheartedly supported the death penalty when again seeking office. And in the heat of a presidential campaign, Clinton returned to Arkansas to preside over the execution of Ricky Ray Rector, a pathetic killer who had tried to commit suicide, but survived, blowing away half his brain instead.

Executions have escalated because many believe politicians have convinced voters that the death penalty is a solution to violence. A Georgia reporter covering death row put his finger on it: "The United States is in a killing mood." More executions took place in the first six months of 1995 than in all of 1994.

During the 1980s, the U.S. averaged about twelve executions per year. But in the 1990s, the country has averaged thirty executions per year. During the current decade, twenty-six states have conducted at least one execution so far, with the South (particularly the "Death Belt" states of Georgia, Texas, Florida, and Mississippi) leading the pack. Executions are as much a part of the South's judicial machinery as writing out parking tickets. Most states stage executions at midnight; in Georgia, it's done at 7:00 P.M. so it can be reported during morning newscasts while commuters drive to work. Georgia set a national record in the

1940s (131 executions) and the 1950s (85 executions). But in 1995, Texas surpassed Georgia. The Lone Star State boasts roughly half the nation's executions in the 1990s.

Many historians believe the death penalty became popular in the South when Congress was dickering with an antilynching law in the 1920s. Prior to that, about 4,700 people had been lynched. Right up until the early 1930s (there was a lynching as recently as 1981) lynching remained popular. Ninety percent of the lynchings took place in the South with 75 percent of the victims being black. If you think these numbers are exaggerated, ask eighty-one-year-old James Cameron. Sixty-five years ago on a steamy August night, the sixteen-year-old Cameron watched a screaming mob of fifteen thousand people, led by the KKK, lynch two of his best friends, Tommy Shipp, eighteen, and Abe Smith, nineteen, from a tree in Marion, Indiana. Shipp was clubbed, stoned, and garroted at the bars of a jailhouse window and someone jammed a crowbar through Smith's chest while another person cut off his pants and distributed the pieces as souvenirs. Both men were long dead before they were strung up on the courthouse tree.

But luck was somehow on Cameron's side. He had been beaten bloody and dragged to the tree where his friends were already hanging. He had stinging rope burns around his neck from the noose. He was supposed to be the last to be hanged without a trial for the robbery and killing of a white man. By the time they got to Cameron, the mob had had enough blood for one night and spared his life. To this day, he thinks divine intervention saved him. He was convicted as an accessory before the fact to voluntary manslaughter and spent four years in prison. In 1993, he was officially pardoned by the governor of Indiana.

The belated acknowledgment of the event didn't do much to squelch Cameron's rage over the brutal miscarriage of justice. He has never forgotten the August night that permanently altered his perception of the world. After a visit to the Holocaust Museum in Israel, he decided never to let Americans forget. The former building engineer and self-taught historian opened America's Black Holocaust Museum in Milwaukee in 1988 as a permanent record of the terror and injustice inflicted upon black Americans. The museum is full of gruesome images of lynchings, including a chilling poster-size photograph of the hangings of Cameron's friends. If you pull Cameron aside, he'll tell you about the last minutes of his best friends' lives and what it was like every grueling second. He'll even show you a Klan souvenir he's kept from the event, a piece of the rope that was used to hang either Shipp or Smith.

Yet, despite these horror stories, prosecutors win the death penalty only in a fraction of cases. Victor Streib, a law professor at Cleveland State University, observed that the 22,000 homicides, 18,000 arrests, and about 300 death sentences each year lead to approximately 60 executions. Regardless of the state, a number of key factors make it more likely a particular murderer will get the death penalty over another criminal. Most candidates are poor and were given inexperienced or disinterested state-appointed attorneys. Typically, lawyers in the Death Belt earn about 50 dollars an hour to defend people facing the death penalty. Attorneys earn more than three times that amount to draw up wills and oversee real-estate closings.

Another deciding factor is the race of the killer and victim. Almost half of all the people murdered each year in the United States are black. Yet since the execution of Gary Gilmore by firing squad in 1977, the majority of executed murderers—85 percent—had been convicted of killing a white person. Only 11 percent had killed a black person. Civil-rights advocates insist that the judicial system puts more value on the lives of whites than those of blacks.

Also, the particular scene of a crime can strongly influence the decision to seek the death penalty. Many states and counties contain populations and district attorneys that support the death penalty. Local politics, more than the crime itself, often plays a major part. If a prosecutor feels the case is a stepping-stone to a higher office, maybe a judgeship, he seeks the death penalty. A gruesome murder case may even sweep an obscure prosecutor into Congress. Georgia in particular is notorious for pockets of circuit courts in which murderers are more likely to face the prospect of capital punishment. The irony is that the same crime, if committed in a neighboring county, would not be considered a capital case.

Former District Attorney Joe Briley gained notoriety for thirty-five capital prosecutions in Georgia's Ocumlgee Circuit between 1973 and 1994. Even in metropolitan Atlanta, capital punishment is meted out inequitably. Kill someone in DeKalb or Cobb counties and an effort to seek the death penalty is a certainty. But commit the same crime in Fulton County and it doesn't even qualify as a capital case. The infamous six-county Chattahoochee Judicial District alone is responsible for twenty-eight capital trials and twenty death sentences, more than any other district in the state.

Finally, the decision to ask for the death penalty is predicated on jury emotions regarding the identity of the victim. If the victim is a child, a person with a disability, or a sick older person, juries are more inclined to vote for the death penalty. Legal experts who have studied jury decisions found that people identify more with the victim if he or she is a stranger to the killer. It's the random murders that upset people most. Female inmates are less likely to get the death penalty because their victims are usually lovers or family members.

Defense attorneys specializing in capital cases are appalled that justice is applied so unevenly, even randomly. They say it's not supposed to be based on who was killed and where it happened. Yet, on practically every level, the death penalty is doled out differently from state to state. For example, the only crimes punishable by death in New Hampshire are contract murder, murder of a law enforcement officer or a kidnapping victim, or committing murder after being sentenced to life imprisonment. In many Southern states, however, the death penalty can be imposed for any first-degree murder. Leaving no stone unturned, Georgia law stipulates that a murder defendant may be given the death sentence if the jury finds that the case meets one of ten criteria, called aggravating circumstances. These occur when: a murder is committed by a person previously convicted of a capital felony (murder, rape, armed robbery, or kidnapping); an offense is committed during the commission of another felony, such as a murder during an armed robbery; during a murder, the defendant creates a great risk of harm to others in a public place using a weapon or device (such as a bomb) that normally would be hazardous to more than one person; a murder for hire; a judicial officer is murdered; another person is employed to commit a murder; a murder is outrageously or wantonly vile, horrible, or inhuman in that it involves torture, depravity of mind, or aggravated battery to the victim; a peace officer, corrections employee, or fire fighter who was performing his or her duties is murdered; an escapee from a prison or jail commits murder; a murder is committed to avoid or interfere with a lawful arrest or imprisonment.

Georgia's attorney general, Mike Bowers, said there is nothing peculiar about the differences in capital punishment from state to state, nor about Georgia's failure to try capital cases uniformly from county to county. "You'll always have differences in the way government is transacted," he said. "That's the way it is in a democracy."

Even the minimum age required to seek capital punishment for a prisoner differs among the states, although a 1989 U.S. Supreme Court ruling banned executions for murders committed before age sixteen. For example, the minimum age is eighteen in California, Colorado, Connecticut, Illinois, Maryland, Nebraska, New Jersey, New Mexico, Ohio, Oregon, and Tennessee; seventeen in Georgia, New Hampshire, North Carolina, and Texas; sixteen in Alabama, Delaware, Indiana, Kentucky, Mississippi, Missouri, Nevada, Oklahoma, and Wyoming; fifteen in Louisiana and Virginia; and fourteen in Arkansas.

To see capital punishment in action check out Atlanta, the seat of Georgia's judicial system. The man standing at the apex of the state's prison system is its chief enforcer, the governor-appointed commissioner of corrections, fifty-nine-year-old Alan Ault. He oversees a $700 million budget, 15,000 staff members, 34,000 prisoners, 131,000 probationers, and 112 facilities.

Ault is no down-home redneck. Yet he quietly defends Southern eye-for-an-eye style of justice. Smartly dressed in a starched white shirt, muted tie, and a conservative gray business suit, Ault is a soft-spoken man who could pass for a high-ranking executive in a Fortune 500 company. With a master's degree in rehabilitation counseling and a doctorate in counseling psychology, Ault symbolizes the South's new breed of corrections professional. Starting out as warden at Georgia's Diagnostic and Classification Center in

Jackson, he was quickly promoted to commissioner, in which capacity he served under five governors, including Jimmy Carter.

Ault has earned points as a hands-on commissioner, a position he has held under five wardens, especially A. G. "Jerry" Thomas, warden at the Diagnostic and Classification Center, home of Georgia's death row and legendary electric chair. Unlike other corrections commissioners, he has made a point of witnessing all six executions held under his administration. Speaking just above a whisper, he almost apologized for a system that flaunts the death penalty as its ultimate weapon. Ault detailed how difficult executions are and the toll they take on everyone involved.

Appearances can be deceiving, but Ault seems like a sensitive man struggling with the hardest part of his job, the legal taking of a human life. He complained that politicians as well as most citizens expect corrections officials to be macho about the death penalty. "They don't know what's involved," he said. "They don't have to carry out the sentence."

Yet not a week goes by when Ault's office doesn't get calls or letters from people from all walks of life volunteering to be witnesses to executions. There is no shortage of volunteer executioners either. Ault has yet to figure out whether these requests stem from good citizenship or morbid curiosity.

The battle-worn corrections chief feels the taking of a life has devastating repercussions. He once told a reporter, "This is the absolute worst aspect of the job. No matter how vile the crime might have been, I am not predisposed to killing people. I was trained to kill in the army, but that was in the most impersonal way: I would fire at the enemy in the distance. But this is very close, very personal." Because it is so intensely personal, Ault said he and his staff work hard at handling it in the most professional way possible.

That means dehumanizing the process through countless trial runs and mentally and emotionally separating themselves from the convicts they're going to kill. It's understandable why Ault referred to the condemned as "individuals" rather than people and why the execution process and its accompanying protocols are so rigidly choreographed. Perish the thought the quivering prisoner should sense fear, reluctance or hesitancy on the part of his executioners.

In another breath, though, Ault said he supports the death penalty, insisting it's a deterrent. "If a small percentage of criminals think through the consequences of their actions, the death penalty is worth it," he said. "As long as the six o'clock news keeps on scaring the hell out of people, it will be necessary."

Ault has plenty of company. Retired prosecutor Briley said he believes in retribution. He once told a reporter, "The state provides a legally acceptable means of exacting retribution. Retribution is part of the healing process. . . . I've never put a man on death row who I didn't believe deserved to be there."

Briley and Ault echo the sentiments of the state's second-most-influential elected official, Attorney General Bowers. Where Ault gropes for words to describe the difficulty of carrying out a death sentence, Bowers has no qualms about overseeing them. "Whatever Ault does I do," he said. "I'm not saying that it is a time of levity or is anything other than a solemn occasion. But after the fact, I cannot say it gives me a great deal of trouble either."

Bowers never questions his decision to punish society's predators to the full extent of the law. He cited the case of Darrell Gene Devier, executed on May 17, 1995, for the 1979 rape and murder of a twelve-year-old girl. Prior to witnessing the execution, he reread every word of the court transcript. Devier brutally murdered the young girl by hurling a fifty-pound rock on her head while she lay on her back pleading for mercy. "To be quite frank with you, I didn't have much sympathy for the guy," Bowers said. "I remembered full well what he did in the most graphic details." Execution "is the law of the state and it has to be done. I'm no Rambo, but when you read about what these guys have done and try to understand the trauma and the tragedy of the lives of the families of the victims, they don't evoke a lot of sympathy."

If Bowers had his way, he'd accelerate the appeals process so killers like Devier don't while away fifteen years on death row before justice is served. He noted that Devier had been on death row longer than his victim had been alive. "The system is so screwed up because it constantly replays a crime ten and fifteen times per crime," he said. "The sad part is the victim's families have to replay these tragedies every time. It's my job to tell them about a last-minute delay when they're waiting at the prison to witness the execution of some scumbag. No one ever says a word about that. It's a disaster."

Bowers is a career bureaucrat who takes his job very seriously. After getting his bachelor's degree from West Point and a law degree from University of Georgia, he went to work for the office of Georgia's attorney general and moved through the ranks. Starting as a clerk, he was quickly promoted to the real-estate division, then to division chief, where he handled civil rights cases, before he was boosted to assistant attorney general and finally, attorney general, a job he's held for fourteen years. Bowers is proud of the fact that he's worked for the same employer for twenty-two years.

It's easy to understand why voters like and respect

Bowers. He comes across as a regular guy concerned about making his state a safe place to live. Tack on a tough-on-crime pro–death penalty stance and Bowers is a shoo-in for the next gubernatorial race.

Georgia's prosecutors share Bowers sentiments. Some lust for glory and power, but many more believe the baddest of the bad—serial killers, child molesters, and those who commit sadistic murders—deserve to die. It's the natural order of things. A few officials, however, are torn by the enormity of their mission. Georgia's Houston County district attorney, Ed Lukemire, said the decision to seek the death penalty is not made lightly. He once said, "We are prosecutors, not persecutors. There is a lot of thought that goes into the decisions we make. In many cases, those decisions are painful."

Nevertheless, Lukemire stands by the death penalty. A mere virgin in the execution business, he's not yet witnessed an execution and admitted he can't begin to speculate on the effect it will have on him. He does believe in the legitimacy of capital punishment and said, "It is necessary in a fallen world. The depravity of man is one of the things, apart from God, that is ingrained in me."

Neither Lukemire nor Bowers feels he has to justify the death penalty. Lukemire traced it to religious upbringings and the Southern view of law and order, right and wrong. "You have a different mind-set down here," he said. Bowers insisted the South has always been ahead of the rest of the country. "I guess we're just more progressive than y'all," he said. As for other states firing up their execution machinery, Bowers responded, "The rest of the country is just trying to get right again."

But he also made a point of saying Southerners don't appreciate being judged by the rest of the country, particularly by smart-ass Northerners. "Georgians, in particular, take a very dim view of people who sit on Mount Olympus and say, 'We know better than the unwashed masses.' They don't like that. Oh boy, that doesn't go over well down here."

While Southern prosecutors and district attorneys quote scripture while revving up the execution machinery, defense attorneys burn the midnight oil trying to keep their death penalty clients alive. Often it's a losing battle. Every time a defense attorney goes one-on-one with a superstar prosecutor and his army of supporters, it's a courtroom version of the David and Goliath story. Yet the most skilled practitioners love the challenge and can't conceive of doing anything else. One defense lawyer said, "If you're a lawyer, and you want to be a lawyer, this is it. It doesn't get any heavier." For some attorneys, it's practically a religious crusade. The hardest part is that it's thankless, lonely work. Where prosecutors are seen as heroes, gloating in public support, death penalty lawyers are ridiculed by the public and scorned by their colleagues. After all, they represent society's dregs, scavengers, and irredeemable predators.

Among the high priests of capital law attorneys is native Georgian Millard Farmer, a fifty-eight-year-old lawyer who has defended hundreds of death row prisoners and participated in some aspect of the proceedings in more than a thousand capital cases. He's been verbally sparring with officials like Bowers and Lukemire for more than thirty years. During this time, Farmer witnessed the execution of six of his clients, experiences that left indelible images in his memory. He has defended some prisoners for twenty-plus years; others he's defended for just the last few weeks, often hours, of their lives. When all of John Spenkelink's appeals had dried up, Farmer was called in as a court of last resort. Even he couldn't stall the execution machinery and pull a petrified Spenkelink from the jaws of death. Florida officials were hell-bent on making Spenkelink the second person to be executed in the United States since the restoration of the death penalty. To judges and prosecutors, Farmer is an abrasive rule breaker. One tough judge, who would just as soon see Farmer drawn and quartered, cited him for contempt twenty times in a single trial.

A tall, lanky man with a high forehead and a curly shock of gray hair, Farmer speaks with a thick gravelly Southern accent that sounds like laryngitis. Unlike many of the feisty Northern abolitionist lawyers who moved south to fight the death penalty, Farmer is a Southerner through and through. A progeny of an old-line upper-class family, he grew up in a sprawling mansion in Newnan, a town his family practically owned. When he returned from college to run the family's fertilizer and coal business and oversee their thousands of acres of peach orchards, he was embarrassed by all this wealth, much of which he felt was a result of exploiting black people. As part of the landed gentry, Farmer felt personally responsible for this situation. He shocked the people of Newnan by doing something about it. He never intended to specialize in death penalty cases after passing the bar exam in the mid–1960s. "Like most young lawyers, I thought I'd be a lawyer lawyer, build a general practice and make a lot of money," he said.

It didn't take him long to find his mission. In 1967, just a few years out of law school, Farmer was given his first court-appointed unpaid death penalty case by a judge. It's common practice for judges to parcel out destitute capital cases to novice attorneys. While their fledgling attorneys get experience, being verbally bullwhipped and brought to their knees by seasoned prosecutors, defendants often wind up on death row.

Farmer got more than experience, he found his life's calling. From that moment on, he immersed himself in capital cases and became a crusading death penalty opponent. In 1976, he formed Team Defense, an organization that specialized in capital cases. When its funding dried up in the early 1990s, Team Defense accepted other cases, the fees from which were used to help its death row clientele. Not a week goes by when Farmer doesn't get called for a death penalty case. Even after all these years, each case presents new challenges and problems. Remarkably, he remembers every one.

Defending death row prisoners was tough in the mid–1970s, but Farmer said it's even harder now due to the escalation in the number of executions. Equally upsetting to Farmer are distortions of the death penalty issue and the conditions under which death row prisoners live. He was appalled by Tim Robbins's film, *Dead Man Walking,* which is based on Sister Helen Prejean's book about death row prisoners at Louisiana's Angola prison, the largest federal penitentiary in the United States, and her relationship with condemned prisoner Pat Sonnier. Farmer was one of the lawyers who tried in vain to save Sonnier's life. Since Farmer has a reputation as a pugnacious contrarian and was featured prominently in Sister Helen's book, Robbins asked him if he would like to play himself and serve as a consultant on the film.

No great fan of Hollywood or its overpaid superstars, Farmer declined the opportunity to make his film debut but, at Sister Helen's insistence, agreed to read the script and render a candid opinion. The naive Robbins didn't know what he was in for.

This feisty attorney wasn't thrilled with Robbins's

script. Characters and situations were grossly exaggerated. Farmer found the script more sensationalistic than accurate. He wasn't shy about letting Robbins know it either. "I told Tim that the entire script had to be rewritten from beginning to end so dignity would be restored to all the characters, just as Sister Helen wrote it," he said.

Whether Robbins wanted to hear it or not, Farmer systematically tore the script to pieces. He tried to persuade Robbins to remove anti-Semitic and other racist remarks from the mouth of the death row prisoner. Farmer felt the portrayal of the prisoner was unfair and unrepresentative of the many death row inmates he'd represented. He argued that the poor guy was in his grave and couldn't speak for himself and that other people facing a similar fate shouldn't be pictured as insensitive animals.

Farmer's urgent pleas to overhaul the script fell on deaf ears. All Robbins knew was that his film had to create a strong impression in a short period of time. As for removing the foul and offensive language that Farmer insisted detracted from the real story, Robbins wouldn't hear of it. "The film script for *Dead Man Walking* suffers from a very fundamental problem," Farmer said. "It didn't have a theme or a message."

As he saw it, the remedy was simple. All Robbins had to do was to try to capture Sister Helen's powerful message. More than describing Angola's death row and its prisoners, Farmer explained that Sister Helen's underlying theme was that "all participants in the death penalty process insist they are doing their duty. Everyone says the same thing, 'I'm only doing my job.'"

Farmer said Sister Helen's simple yet provocative book focused on what is wrong with the criminal justice system. "The problem with the system is everyone is so righteous," he said in a slow drawl. "That includes the arresting officer, prosecutor, jurors, judge, prison guards, and executioner."

As a man who has spent his entire career trying to get people to question and challenge this "duty," Farmer has come to accept the fact that Southern judges refuse to listen to him. "Southerners see violence as a better way to deal with problems," he said quietly. "And I don't know why."

Farmer will go to his deathbed a staunch abolitionist. After bucking the system for so many years, he's slowing down a bit. Unofficially, though, he's passed the baton to a younger crop of lawyers with more energy and enthusiasm.

Stephen B. Bright runs the Southern Center for Human Rights from a tiny town house near the courts in downtown Atlanta. Praised as a brilliant trial strategist who's pulled many execution-bound men from the jaws of death, he has also, like Farmer, suffered through a heart-rending share of losses. Over the course of his twenty-one-year career, he has witnessed the execution of five clients.

Tall, lean, and fair-skinned, with clean-cut all-American good looks, Bright could easily have landed a classy job in a big-name corporate law firm. But he had other goals. His colleagues drive expensive foreign cars, wear designer clothes, dine in haute cuisine restaurants, and spend their handsome salaries on homes, boats, and vacations. Bright is lucky if he has five business suits to his name. He couldn't tell a Giorgio Armani from a Kmart, nor does he care. His clothes are worn and frayed. His blue oxford-cloth shirt and khaki pants look like they could use a good ironing. The soles of his Topsiders have seen better days. He drives a ten-year-old Dodge Colt that's clocked well over 150,000 miles. For exercise, he rides a beat-up secondhand bicycle. He lives in a low-rent apartment in a less-than-fashionable part of Atlanta. "It is not necessary to have a Rolex watch or a Mercedes or expensive clothes," he said. "You can go to the factory outlet and get a suit for just sixty-five dollars. It will hold up for a long time."

Even if he could afford the conventional trappings of his profession, he'd pass them up. Bright just doesn't have the time to take advantage of them. In the courtroom, where lives are won or lost, he's an impassioned and articulate fighter for the downtrodden. This is where Bright has earned his stripes and built his reputation as an agile and articulate strategist, hated and feared by prosecutors who have neither his intellectual nor verbal skills.

The Southern Center for Human Rights exists on a meager $600,000 annually, which comes from foundations, churches, and individuals. It supports fourteen workers, nine attorneys, and a support staff of five. Everyone in the office, including Bright, earns the same salary of $23,000 a year. Miraculously, they manage to carry fifty capital cases and cover the costs of litigation, travel expenses, and experts' fees.

When Bright teaches at prestigious law schools like Harvard and Yale or lectures to attorney organizations, he refuses his salary and doantes a good portion of his lecture and speaking fees into his organization. "When I speak to law students about how they want to spend their lives, I tell them our whole budget here is less than one partner makes in an Atlanta law firm," he said. "There are law firms in town that pay salaries of $750,000 a year. Plenty of law firms in New York pay salaries of $1 million a year. Our problem is just trying to get by year to year."

Bright sounds too good to be true. He's part martyr, do-gooder, contrarian, and outrageous character all rolled into one. His destitute clients could care less about his motivations. They just thank their lucky stars he's found time to represent them. As soon as he accepts a case, a defendant's chances of cheating the executioner jump enormously.

Whether it's schoolboy idealism or a sense of fair play instilled in him by his folks, Bright is outraged by injustice, vehemently believing everyone is entitled to their constitutional rights. When lecturing to students at St. Louis University Law School, he once posed these questions: "Why are so many members of the legal profession wasting their time on silly things that only make them a lot of money when there are people wrongfully convicted, wrongfully sentenced to death, wrongfully evicted from their homes, discriminated against because of their race, gender or sexual preference, or mistreated because they are HIV positive? How can lawyers stand by when there is so much injustice?" Bright is convinced the legal profession has lost its way. "If you talk about lawyers as a helping profession today, people laugh at you."

Beyond the noble mantle of martyrdom, Bright is doing what he loves. "Some people might say that by now I should be doing better," he said. "But it comes down to this: It is better to be doing something and getting nothing for it than to be doing nothing and getting something for it."

Bright grew up in Danville, Kentucky, in a family of fourth-generation farmers. In his early college years, he had no burning ambition to be an attorney. He planned to be a journalist, but got sidetracked, stumbling into law. He got his bachelor's degree and took a year off before enrolling in the University of Kentucky's law school. Once he decided on law, he wanted to specialize in poverty cases. It wouldn't be long before he combined it with his fascination for criminal law.

Fresh out of law school, Bright trekked off to Appalachia to work as a legal service attorney before taking a job as a public defender in Washington, D.C. It was during the late 1970s when an attorney from the

American Civil Liberties Union asked him to represent Donny Wayne Thomas, an inmate on Georgia's death row. Bright read Thomas's case and was horrified by the slipshod, shoddy defense his attorney had offered. "It was a travesty, as almost all of these cases are, although I didn't realize it at the time," Bright continued. "The transcript was hardly a half inch thick, which tells you everything. The lawyer basically showed up. I couldn't believe someone could be sentenced to death in such a perfunctory process."

The ultimate shocker was meeting Thomas, who turned out to be a frightened eighteen-year-old paranoid schizophrenic. The tragic part was that the record mentioned nothing about his mental condition. The case was a real eye-opener for Bright.

Over the next couple of years, he participated in a number of death penalty cases before moving to Atlanta in 1982 to work with the Southern Center for Human Rights. The center's goal is to enforce the Eighth Amendment, the prohibition of cruel and unusual punishment.

Before he could catch his breath, he was practically drowning in capital cases. Each one presented formidable obstacles and numbing amounts of work for Bright and his overworked staff. He quickly discovered why his colleagues avoided capital cases like the plague. "There is no harder way to make a living than by specializing in capital cases," he said. "Not only is it a brutal practice, it is also unappreciated. It's emotionally draining, and what's more, it holds no prestige or political advantage."

Tack on endless hours and insulting pay and you'd realize why only feisty idealistic attorneys like Bright would be turned on by the job description. It wasn't only the daunting workload that fired him but the incredible odds against succeeding. Firsthand, he learned that equal justice is a myth in the Death Belt states. On several occasions, Bright has bluntly stated that practically all of the people executed in Georgia and Alabama were victims of shoddy legal representation. "Unless you're in metropolitan areas like Atlanta or Birmingham, the only person at the trial who is not white is the person on trial," he said. "In many of the courts I go to, 65 to 70 percent of the crime victims and 85 to 90 percent of the people accused of the crime are black. Yet all the people making the decisions are white. It really amazes me that no one is bothered by this."

If he discovered that someone was poorly represented, Bright tried to reopen the case and get a new trial. "You have to go back and start all over again," he said. "There is no other way to go. It is virtually impossible to say what the outcome would have been if the person had been able to find adequate legal representation."

What other attorneys consider a losing proposition, Bright considers a necessity, every American citizen's birthright. Behind that noble thought lies grueling by hard work. A retrial means total immersion in the case, poring over hundreds of pages of transcripts and reinterviewing everyone—cops, friends, witnesses, leads, and anyone else connected to the case. Most defense attorneys avoid all this exhausting drudgery because the pay is so bad. In Alabama, defense attorneys are paid as little as twenty dollars an hour for out-of-court time and given a two-thousand-dollars ceiling on pretrial preparation. In Georgia, the rate goes as high as fifty dollars an hour.

Several years ago, Bright represented a man in Jackson, Mississippi, and spent eight hundred hours on the case. For his efforts, the city of Jackson paid him one thousand dollars, less than two dollars an hour. Because of insulting fees, most defense attorneys wind up putting in only fifty to sixty hours preparing for a death penalty case. "That's preposterous," Bright shouts. "You can't do it in that amount of time."

Typically, Bright spends about a thousand hours preparing for a death penalty case, with an associate attorney putting in about half that amount of time. "If you're only being paid two thousand dollars, it's just not worth it for most attorneys to put in that kind of time," he said. "The thing I hear from these lawyers is "I'll never do another death penalty case.' They do one and it ruins them financially and it probably didn't help their reputation much in the community either." Bright complained about prosecutors walking away from capital cases as heroes, guardians of the American justice system and protectors of the common man. "The prosecutor gets political capital, name recognition, and a staff of salaried people to help him," he said.

Fire questions at Bright and he'll mercilessly rip the criminal justice system to threads. The sad fact of life he repeatedly drove home is if you're destitute, it's the luck of the draw. The cards are stacked against you from the outset. If a capital defendant is fortunate enough to have a committed and experienced lawyer like Bright who'll tirelessly pour every ounce of energy into the case, he stands a good chance of escaping the death sentence. Unfortunately, only a handful of lawyers like Bright can be found across the country.

Since experienced fast-track lawyers can't be bothered with them, many capital cases are given to young and green attorneys right out of law school. Or they're doled out to lawyers who have lost their edge. After all these years, Bright still finds it hard to believe that capital cases, which are the most difficult of all, could be handed over to young lawyers who've never seen the inside of a courtroom.

He explained how the politically driven criminal justice

system worked in the South. "The court is supposed to appoint a lawyer to an indigent defendant within seventy-two hours. Often the person is interrogated by the police for a long time before the accused is even assigned an attorney."

Problems for the condemned begin when the judge appoints an attorney. "Lawyers are not appointed by anyone who cares about the client," Bright explained. "Usually, in death penalty jurisdictions, the judge is a former prosecutor who was himself gung ho death penalty. This is how he got the publicity to get on the bench."

Bright said, "One of the most frequently traveled routes to the state trial bench is through prosecutors' offices. A capital case provides a prosecutor with a particularly rich opportunity for media exposure and name recognition that can later be helpful in a judicial campaign. Calling a press conference to announce that the police have captured a suspect and the prosecutor will seek the death penalty provides an opportunity for a prosecutor to obtain news coverage and ride the popular sentiments almost any politician would welcome. The prosecutor can then sustain prominent media coverage by announcing developments in the case as they occur. A capital trial provides one of the greatest opportunities for sustained coverage on the nightly newscasts and in the newspapers. A noncapital trial or resolution with a guilty plea does not produce such coverage."

Bright is convinced that judges intentionally appoint incompetent attorneys. "Judges are efficiency experts when it comes to getting cases rapidly through the system," he added. "The pity is the guys who are good become personal injury, estate, or corporate attorneys," he explained. "They stay clear of indigent defense cases. The guys picking up the scraps and taking cases for thirty-five dollars an hour tend to be alcoholics and broken-down lawyers who really can't do anything else. The judges give them capital cases because they're so bad."

Many of these burned-out lawyers place low bids for indigent defense cases and wind up becoming contract defenders and handling all the capital cases within a region. Bright pointed out they're not to be confused with public defenders. "A contract defender gets $25,000 a year, for example, to represent every indigent capital case, but he can do whatever he wants in his private practice."

He cited one contract defender from Georgia. "He's been the contract defender for three years and he's never tried a case. He probably never will. He pleads everyone guilty, and if the accused doesn't plead guilty, he lets the inmate languish in jail for a while and then ultimately pleads for time served. That's the way it is in many other counties as well."

On countless occasions, Bright has said inadequate legal representation is rampant in those jurisdictions that account for most of the death sentences. He quoted Supreme Court Justice Thurgood Marshall, who said, "Capital defendants frequently suffer the consequences of having trial counsel who are ill-equipped to handle capital cases," and cited the cases of John Eldon Smith, John Young, and James Messer. "Smith's sentence was upheld and he was killed despite a constitutional violation that was overlooked due to his lawyer's ignorance of the law. Meanwhile his codefendant won a new trial due to the same constitutional violation and later received a life sentence," Bright said.

Sentenced in the same county as Smith, Young was represented at his capital trial by an attorney who was dependent on amphetamines and other drugs that affected his ability to concentrate. Additionally, "the lawyer was physically exhausted, suffering severe emotional strain, and distracted from his law practice because of marital problems, child custody arrangements, difficulties in a relationship with a lover, and the pressures of a family business," Bright said. It's no wonder the lawyer hardly prepared for Young's trial, where he turned in an inept performance. Young received a death sentence. The story doesn't end there. A few weeks later, Young met his attorney in the prison yard of the county jail. The incompetent attorney had been sent there after pleading guilty to drug charges. John Young was executed on March 20, 1985.

James Messer, as Bright explained it, was represented by an attorney who offered no opening statement, presented no defense case, barely cross-examined witnesses, and made no objections. "He emphasized the horror of the crime in some brief closing remarks that could not be fairly described as a closing argument," said Bright. The attorney also failed to bring forth any evidence of his client's mental impairment. "He also failed to introduce Messer's steady employment record, military record, church attendance, and cooperation with the police," Bright continued. "In closing, the lawyer repeatedly hinted that death was the most appropriate punishment for his client. Messer was executed July 28, 1988."

Raking up well-documented cases of attorney incompetence doesn't even raise Attorney General Bowers's eyebrow. "If the lawyers are so damned bad, how come they [prisoners] stay alive twelve years when there is no dispute about their guilt?" he returned. "Explain that to me! Somebody is doing something right. I don't care what he [Bright] is talking about. We don't execute anybody until after ten or twelve years."

As for the screwups and mistakes made by young or incompetent attorneys who ought to be working behind deli counters rather than arguing death penalty cases, Bowers had an explanation for that, too. "The constitution doesn't promise you F. Lee Bailey as an attorney. It says you will have a fair defense. And when you tie back into the fact that all these cases have guilty pleas or an admission somewhere along the line, what difference does it make?"

While Bowers and prosecutors argue for shorter appeals, death penalty opponents insist innocent people could be wrongly executed because of it. Mike Mears, director of Atlanta's Multi-County Public Defender's Office, once said he didn't think nine years was an unreasonable amount of time for a thorough review of a capital case.

Bowers disagreed vehemently, refusing to buy any arguments pointing to innocence of the accused. "It's bullshit," he snapped. "It's just a lame excuse not to carry out the law."

As for mistakes, Bowers replied, "My God, we're human. From my experience—and I think I've had a fair amount of experience in dealing with these cases—guilt or innocence isn't even a question. The vast majority admit their guilt. So what are we worried about? All the review is about delay. If you're defending a death penalty case, delay means winning because you're keeping the guy alive. If we're going to have it [the death penalty], we have to bite the bullet, belly up, and recognize that there is an inherent risk, just like when we put someone away with life without parole. There is always a risk. If we are going to take counsel of our fears, we will never do anything."

Defense attorneys vehemently argue against playing those kind of odds. Juries were convinced Muneer Deeb in Texas, Andrew Golden in Florida, and Kirk Bloodsworth in Maryland deserved to die until they were proven innocent several years after their convictions. There are many more cases where justice was perverted by articulate prosecutors and ambitious

judges. It took eleven years for Gary Nelson's attorney
to establish his innocence and get him released from
Georgia's death row. A shortened appeals process
would have meant his sure death. Earl Patrick Charles
was under a death sentence for three and a half years
for a 1975 double murder before he was proven innocent in 1978. And Jerry Banks spent six years on
Georgia's death row before he was exonerated of a
double murder in 1980. His attorneys spent four thousand hours on the case discrediting the testimony of a
detective who testified against Banks.

If it were not for Bryan Stevenson, Bright's counterpart
in Alabama, Walter McMillian would have been executed long ago. In 1987, McMillian was arrested for
murder in Monroeville County, Alabama, in what the
judge called a "vicious and brutal killing of a young lady
in the first full flower of adulthood." In an unprece-
dented move, McMillian was sent right to death row
where he waited a year and a half before he was even
tried. After a one-and-a-half-day trial, he was given the
death sentence on the perjured testimony of three witnesses, one of whom had a long criminal record in connection with another killing in nearby Escambia
County. Both judge and jury failed to consider the
absence of physical evidence to convict McMillian and
the more than one dozen witnesses who swore he was
participating in a fish fry at the time of the murder.

It took Stevenson four years and well over five thousand hours of exhausting investigation to gather all the
evidence and reinterview all the witnesses, not to mention shuttling between the appeals and appellate
courts, before the state of Alabama freed McMillian.

Thirty-six-year-old Stevenson is doing exactly what
Bright does but with a bigger caseload and less money.

As director of the Equal Justice Initiative in Montgomery, Stevenson barely makes ends meet on a $350,000 budget to support himself, five attorneys, and a support staff of six. On an annual salary of $27,000 a year, he puts in more than seventy-hour weeks, working virtually every waking hour.

Like Bright, Stevenson can also recount endless cases of lawyer abuse and misconduct by judges and prosecutors who would just as soon build execution chambers next to courthouses so defendants can be speedily convicted and killed. The McMillian case, especially, drove home blatant inequities in the system for Stevenson. He identified with McMillian, just as he did with so many of his other clients who were poor and uneducated.

Stevenson's story is even more dramatic than Bright's. Bright, at least, had the advantage of being white and middle class. The son of a factory worker, Stevenson grew up in a poor black family and remembers attending segregated schools as a child. He lived in Milton, Delaware in the heart of rural Sussex County, which is more Southern than Northern in its attitudes.

Stevenson crossed paths with Bright in the early 1980s when he spent a few months in Atlanta working with the Southern Center for Human Rights doing fieldwork for a Harvard course in race and poverty litigation law. The experience hooked him. After receiving his law degree, he moved to Atlanta to work with Bright for five years. Then he moved to Alabama in the late eighties to head the Alabama Capital Representation Resource Center in Montgomery.

Since then, Stevenson has worked on hundreds of death penalty cases. Despite his youth, that first death penalty case brought home all the critical issues with a compelling force he'll never forget. "The first client I met was a young guy exactly my age," Stevenson said. "I was startled at how familiar the other side of the table was. Many of his experiences growing up were also my experiences. I realized then that it was too easy for someone like me to be cast in this kind of situation. This man suffered deprivation in ways I could relate to."

Yet Stevenson was lucky. He was on the other side of the law. What's more, he was dealt a better hand than many of the killers he represented. Stevenson was appalled someone could be convicted and sent to death row without having a lawyer. "Here I was graduating from Harvard and told about the surplus of lawyers trying to get jobs in big law firms, and there were all these people on death row literally dying because they could not get any kind of legal assistance. I found that very troubling. When I put it all together, I knew I had made the right career choice."

It was the McMillian case that put Stevenson, along with infamous Monroeville County, on the map. As he wound down his investigations, Stevenson contacted *60 Minutes,* which sent anchorman Ed Bradley to cover the story. As soon as the show aired, the entire world identified with McMillian and the real-life characters in Monroeville, deep in the heart of Jim Crow country.

The facts were out: McMillian, father of ten and a hardworking pulpwood worker who cut down trees for ten hours a day, was framed because he was black and poor. He also committed the unpardonable sin of having an affair with a white woman. Soon, to the horror of townspeople, Monroeville was overrun with reporters from every major news agency. The story was so compelling, author Pete Earley immortalized McMillian and all the God-fearing folks in Monroeville in *Circumstantial Evidence: Death, Life, and Justice in a Southern Town.*

The TV coverage combined with indisputable evidence of McMillian's innocence catapulted Stevenson to national attention. At the same time, Monroeville County was suddenly seen as a perverted throwback to the Old South. Ironically, it's the home of author Harper Lee, whose haunting novel, *To Kill a Mockingbird,* tells a gripping story of race and justice in a tiny Southern town.

As Bright and Stevenson will testify, getting an innocent person off death row is a Herculean feat. Equally difficult is saving the lives and securing the freedom of prisoners who've admitted their guilt. Sitting on death row, many hard-core felons have undergone radical transformations. Prosecutors argue that they are the exception to the rule. Yet death penalty attorneys like Bright and Stevenson insist there are plenty of them out there. Bright's former client William Neal Moore is one of them. In 1984, Moore had said his last good-byes and had resigned himself to dying in Georgia's electric chair. Seven hours before he was to be strapped into the sturdy oak chair, Bright secured a stay. Six years later, in 1990, his sentence was commuted, and in 1991, he was paroled. Moore stands among four dozen Georgia killers who walked off death row.

Moore's story is not uncommon. In 1974, Moore, a twenty-two-year old soldier at Fort Gordon, killed Fredger Stapleton. At that time he had a passion for fast living and easy money. Moore admitted his guilt and was ready to suffer the consequences. But in prison, he underwent an epiphany when a prison minister converted him. Searching for inner peace, Moore began helping others. He started death row Bible classes. He wrote about capital punishment and sent

letters to the relatives of his victim asking forgiveness.
Lucky for Moore, they believed he was sincere and
asked the parole board to save his life. Upon his
release, Moore married a pastor in Michigan, became
ordained, and devoted his life to keeping others off
death row. Said Bright, "It proves we are not very good
at deciding who should live and who should die. We
never have been."

Farmer, Bright, and Stevenson are fighting insur-
mountable odds. "We're kind of like the dance band on
the *Titanic*," Bright said, battling a public hell-bent on
priming the execution wheels.

Yet despite the odds, fighters like Bright grow more
committed by the challenge. The question is how long can
they sustain the exhausting pace, the numbing tension,
and staggering workloads. Farmer has already eased up on
the reins. Whether its age or because he's slightly burned
out is anybody's guess. Inevitably, the younger crop of
defense attorneys will slow down as well. Will there be a
new batch of idealistic defense attorneys to take their
place and work for starvation wages? It's a safe bet they
won't multiply as fast as ambitious attorneys concerned
with big dollars and status and prosecutors who are determined to score power points with judges. If the pace of
executions accelerates, jailers and executioners will be elevated to high-demand jobs with rosy futures.

Let He Who is Without Sin Cast the First Stone
PORTRAIT OF AN EXECUTIONER

"I'm just doing my job."

"He that diggeth a pit shall fall into it."
—ECCLESIASTES, 10:8

"Eye for eye, tooth for tooth, hand for hand, foot for foot."
—EXODUS, 21:24

"There is part of the warden that dies with his prisoner."
—DON CABANA, FORMER WARDEN AT THE MISSISSIPPI STATE PENITENTIARY AT PARCHMAN

"A slim, gray-haired gentleman approaches the chair with a nervous, jerky tread. He bends low to examine the electrode on the right leg; makes his final adjustments of the hood and steps rapidly away to the instrument panel, ten feet to the rear of the chair.

"Now there is a sputtering drone. The body of what a moment ago was a living human being leaps forward as if to break its bonds. A thin, gray wisp of smoke curls slowly up from under the hood—there is a faint odor of burning flesh.

"The hands turn red, then white and the cords of the neck stand out like steel bands. The drone increases in volume, the body is still straining at the straps. The hands grip the arms in an ever-tightening grasp. The raucous droning continues. There is a general subsidence and the body relaxes. . . ."
—LEWIS A. LAWES,
TWENTY-THOUSAND YEARS IN SING SING

JULY 8, 1987, IS A DATE PERMANENTLY ETCHED on Don Cabana's conscience. It still triggers nightmares when he recalls the nerve-racking seconds leading up to the midnight hour when he had to give the order to gas Connie Ray Evans at Mississippi's State Penitentiary at Parchman. He still wrestles with the question of why he had to green-light the kill. When they carried a dead Evans out of the chamber like a sack of potatoes, Cabana became a different person. He had committed a cardinal sin no prison warden can afford to make: becoming too close to a convict he had to kill. When Cabana brought down the curtain on Evans's life, he also killed a part of himself.

A decade earlier, Cabana would have never imagined he'd get into a mess like this. All of the debate surrounding the pros and cons of the death penalty never concerned him until he actually had to give the order to execute someone. Even when the ten-year-old moratorium on the death penalty ended in 1977, he never thought it would touch his life. When it did, he suddenly discovered he had a new job function as prison warden. While, technically speaking, he wasn't the guy who pulled the lever, dropping cyanide pellets into a vat of sulfuric acid to release deadly fumes, it was he who had to give the order telling someone else to do the deed. Putting semantics aside, Cabana had become the executioner.

While the politicians and poster-carrying do-gooders argue about the rights and wrongs of capital punishment, he and his staff had to kill the bad guys. By the time he got his orders, everyone else had finished his or her part. The judges and prosecutors had green-lighted the execution and defense attorneys had done everything possible to save the convict's life. But Cabana's work was just beginning. If he was lucky, all went smoothly and it was a clean kill, but that seldom happened. Nobody warned him his emotions would get in the way, causing him to question everything he'd been taught. He wasn't alone. His staff had to grapple with their own demons.

After finishing a job, Cabana was greeted with both applause and outrage from the public. If it was a particularly sticky execution, he also received a pat on the back from superiors. Until Cabana's world went haywire, he loved his job. For thirty years, the corrections business was his life, consuming every waking second. Yet, after working his way up through the ranks to the top job, Cabana decided to throw in the towel.

Even now, Cabana doesn't want anyone to get the wrong idea. He's no bleeding-heart liberal. He gets pissed off when someone accuses him of being soft on crime. Having dealt with some of America's most savage criminals, he's the first to admit there are plenty of nasty guys behind bars who you shouldn't turn your back on for a second. But when it came time to play God, Cabana found himself wrestling with himself, his morals, and a bureaucracy that made him what he is today.

*   *   *

Cabana is far from the stereotypical sadistic prison warden portrayed in crime novels and prison films. He's a short, balding man who wears wire-framed glasses. He is very round in the middle and small on top and bottom. He has the energy of a teenager and looks far younger than his fifty years. During his life, he has seen more of the world than most men do in three lifetimes. Cabana walks quickly, drives too fast, and speaks rapidly with a thick Southern drawl that would win free drinks in any watering hole located in a Death Belt state.

He doesn't seem tough or mean-spirited, but don't be deceived by appearances. Ask the hundreds of men who've worked closely with him and they'll tell you differently. As one guard put it, "This guy can be a mean-spirited son-of-a-bitch when he wants to be." Another said, "He could turn blood to ice water and be one cold-blooded bastard."

They could cite plenty of examples. He was criticized for making prisoners at Parchman pick cotton in the hot sun. Cabana figured he'd make incarceration as unpleasant as possible so they wouldn't come back. Countless times, he broke up riots or quelled escalating hostage situations by means of unorthodox tactics. Back in the early eighties, there was a particularly nasty incident at Parchman during which a scrawny white ringleader took a half-dozen guards hostage, all of them black. The demented creep was hell-bent on slitting one of the guard's throats if his demands weren't met. To make his point, he popped a tiny vein in the guard's neck with a homemade shank, drawing a tiny stream of blood that trickled down the man's white shirt. Rather than calling in state police and SWAT teams, Cabana ripped off his suit jacket, loosened his tie, grabbed a sawed-off shotgun from his gun rack, and charged into the cell block with a handful of guards scrambling behind him. He zeroed in on the

ringleader and broke his ranks. To the horror of the
hostage guard, Cabana looked the ringleader straight in
the eye and said in a polite drawl, "If you wanna fuck
with that pig's neck, go right ahead." Just as he said
that, with a sweeping Schwarzenegger-style right-hand
motion, he pumped a shell into the shotgun's chamber
and leveled the fat round barrel at the convict's head.
"If you don't let the guard go, I'm going to take you
and the rest of these motherfuckers with you," he said
matter-of-factly. "Then I'm gonna call your mama and
tell her I killed your worthless fucking ass. So what you
wanna do, boy? Yer call."

To this day, his men are convinced Cabana would
have blown away the convict at point-blank range if he
had dared to draw another drop of blood from the
guard. Thankfully, the cowardly ringleader backed
down while the petrified guard nearly had a coronary.

Although Cabana learned early on that there are no
rules when it comes to stopping problems in their
tracks—"Do whatever's necessary" was his best advice—
he could also be compassionate and understanding.
During countless occasions, he'd put his arm around
inmates' shoulders and console them when they got
bad news from home or a Dear John letter from their
girlfriends. Cabana discovered that being a prison warden is not like other jobs. "You gotta be more than a
little schizophrenic and better be a pretty goddamned
good actor, too," he said.

That same goes for the tough-guy stuff. He certainly
didn't broadcast it, but after dangerous confrontations,
Cabana struggled to regain his composure. Good actor
that he was, only men who had worked with him for
years knew about his skill at bottling up his emotions.
When deep into his Rambo act, it was almost impossible
to tell that his stomach was in knots and his head felt
like it would split open. Only in the privacy of his office

did he allow himself the luxury of breaking into a cold sweat or uncontrollably shaking until the fear dissipated.

"A lot of people think we're machines, sadistic bastards because we run prisons," Cabana complained. "Well, that's the Hollywood version. The fact is nobody sees the other side of the coin. They don't see we're human and that this has got to be the loneliest job in the world. The folks in the central office making policy are away from the real fucking world. But we're deep in the shit, in the trenches. We're the ones who are running the penitentiaries and getting caught up in the issues."

This little man who instilled fear and respect in his inmates and awe and respect in his men could be as tough and calculating as a convict and as understanding and forgiving as a priest. Cabana had the perfect credentials for the job. In many respects, he wasn't far removed from the convicts. He's the first to admit it was only a stroke of good luck that he himself didn't wind up behind bars.

Cabana grew up on the other side of the tracks in one of Boston's tough blue-collar neighborhoods. His mother was a prostitute and heroin addict, his father was a drunk. He had nine brothers and sisters, all of whom were abandoned, many of whom were sexually and physically abused by their father. Cabana was lucky. When he was six months old he was taken in by a foster family who adopted him when he was nine years old.

When his mother was tossed in jail for heroin possession and his father left for good, Cabana's brothers and sisters wound up in foster homes all over Boston. As difficult as things were for the kids, it would have been far worse if their parents had raised them. To this day, Cabana thanks his lucky stars he was adopted by a poor but loving working-class couple.

When he was an adult, Cabana had an opportunity to meet the mother who had abandoned him and his siblings. He declined the offer, but regretted it afterward. "I wanted to ask her point-blank why someone would have ten kids and abandon every one of them," he said. Still, he felt his biological mother left him with a priceless gift. "She taught me there are only two paths to take in life," he said. "You can travel the low road or the high road. She took the low road and look where it got her."

Knowing the sordid details of his past, it wasn't hard for Cabana to choose the right path. When you consider his roots, it doesn't seem strange that he chose a career in corrections. Without knowing anything about him, convicts sensed a bond, a meeting of the minds. They knew he was neither intimidated nor afraid of them. They also knew he didn't feel sorry for them. The warden was streetwise and not to be fucked with. When Cabana made a promise, he kept it, and the inmates respected him for this. When you're sitting in prison for a couple of decades, or worse yet, on death row, that's as close to a comforting feeling as you're likely to get.

Initially, Cabana thought he'd become an attorney specializing in criminal law. After getting his bachelor's degree in criminal justice from Northeastern University and doing a one-year stint in Vietnam as a paramedic, he returned to Boston to get a job and sock money away for law school. It was 1969 and the state prison system was hiring prison guards. Cabana jumped at the opportunity. He thought it would be a valuable experience.

His three years at the Massachusetts Correctional Institution at Bridgewater set the stage for a thirty-year career in the corrections business. The century-old prison was a relic of a bygone era. Short on modern conveniences, it had neither hot water nor indoor plumbing. Instead of the standard sink and commode, each cell here had a chamber pot.

Charles Gaughan, Bridgewater's warden, made a vivid impression on Cabana. A wiry little man who sported a pencil-thin mustache and spoke in a high-pitched nasal voice, Gaughan impressed Cabana when he actually took the time to interview him for a menial guard's job. Cabana was pleasantly surprised when Gaughan took him under his wing and told him the hard facts about building a career in corrections.

After a few months at Bridgewater, Cabana abandoned any thoughts about going to law school. This was what he wanted to do, and it was Gaughan's straight-on advice that put him on the right track. He told Cabana that the best way to work his way up the ladder to an administrative job was by moving through the security ranks. This is where the wardens come from. Ironically, Gaughan was the exception to that rule. With a master's degree in social work from Harvard, he initially took a job as a social worker in Bridgewater. He rapidly scaled the career ladder, eventually winning critical security jobs. Because he was both aggressive and smart, he was chosen for the warden's job. He held the job for thirty years, making him somewhat of an anomaly in the corrections business.

Gaughan emphasized the importance of spending time in the trenches. He advised Cabana to start at the bottom, work as a guard, and get to know the inmates on a hands-on basis. Learn their lingo and culture so you can talk to them and gain their respect. Excel at that and you've got a good shot at working your way into a warden's job.

But that's not all Gaughan taught Cabana. He told

the young man to put aside any romantic illusions about a career in corrections. If he was looking for danger and adventure, or if he wanted to be adored by the public, corrections was a bad choice. And he had better like "stinking filthy politics," too, because the corrections bureaucracy is riddled with it. In a nutshell, Gaughan said that a job in prisons was thankless, low-paying work.

"But when Gaughan finished reeling off a long list of negatives, he said you can also find your own private measure of satisfaction that you won't find doing anything else," Cabana reported.

Once Cabana made his decisions he discovered that prisons were a unique subculture where the keepers were as fascinating as the inmates. During his three years at Bridgewater, he learned how corrections bureaucracies worked and hung out with the prison's resident superstars who had booked accommodations for life.

The most famous of these was Albert DeSalvo, better known as the Boston Strangler, the Jack the Ripper of the 1960s. DeSalvo had a thing for nine- and ten-year-old boys, whom he assaulted, molested, strangled, and then buried in shallow graves in parks. "You'd think DeSalvo would seem like a real bad guy," said Cabana, surprised. "He didn't. The creepy thing was he seemed so normal, just like you and me." And he died an ordinary convict's death as well. DeSalvo was stabbed to death for cheating another convict.

In fact, most of the cons Cabana got to know were variations on DeSalvo. "They didn't have horns or scary eyes that glow in the dark," said Cabana. "They were pretty ordinary looking, which made them all the more intriguing."

Early in the game, Cabana also concluded corrections wasn't for everyone. Beyond guts, you have to truly love the power a warden commands. This was driven home several years later when he was working as a deputy warden at the 2,200-bed maximum-security Missouri State Penitentiary. "I remember walking out into the yard with the warden to see that everything was okay," he said. "Some guys were working out with weights or playing basketball, others were just hanging out smoking cigarettes. The warden turned to me and said, 'Isn't that the prettiest damn sight in the world?' He was kind of surveying his kingdom and talking about the thrill of running a maximum-security prison."

The warden was telling Cabana how only the best, brightest and toughest get to work in maximum-security pens. "This old warden was staring into the yard of this 150-year-old prison and feeling like he was on top of the world," Cabana said. "These guys were not nice people. Every one of them was a badass killer who wouldn't think twice about killing again."

But all you get for having balls and courage are merit points instead of incentive pay. In the 1970s, wardens at maximum-security prisons were paid between seventeen and twenty thousand a year and given housing. Today, they're paid about sixty thousand a year, which is precious little considering the responsibility and dangers of the job.

None of these jobs' shortcomings bothered Cabana much. He relished being part of the correction industry's equivalent of the Special Forces, the steel-nerved tough guys who ran the maximum-security pens. He had all the qualifications for the corrections fast track. He was smart, aggressive, and fearless. More important, he was well liked by the brass, who were quick to reward him with good jobs.

In 1972, he left Bridgewater and began job hopping, starting in a Mississippi detention center and a minimum-security prison, then moving to Missouri to take a job as warden of a women's prison, followed by jobs as deputy wardens in two maximum-security men's prisons, then back to Mississippi in the early 1980s to take the warden's post at Parchman.

By the late 1980s Cabana's career was in high gear. However, the political climate had changed. When *Furman* v. *Georgia* was reversed in 1976 and Florida became the first state to reinstate the death penalty, the mood shifted. The dawn of the modern era of capital punishment was ushered in carnival-style with the execution of Gary Gilmore in 1977. But it was the execution of John Spenkelink two years later that brought the whole death penalty issue home to Cabana and to every warden working at a death row facility. He didn't talk about it much, but the whole idea of an execution made him uncomfortable, and he hoped he wouldn't have to deal with it.

For a short while, it looked like he might get his wish. Many corrections heavies treated the Gilmore execution as an aberration. By asking to die, Gilmore had made it easy. As Cabana saw it, Gilmore couldn't take his own life, so he had Utah do it for him. But it was a different story with John Spenkelink. While Gilmore tossed all his appeals out the window, Spenkelink fought every step of the way. According to many wardens at the time, Spenkelink should have been way down on the list of potential execution candidates. "He was the exact opposite of the Ted Bundy type," Cabana observed. "He was a very quiet, decent kind of guy."

Nevertheless, Florida executed him, and Cabana knew that sooner or later, he'd be asked to step up to the plate and execute someone, too. He wasn't looking forward to it, but he controlled his growing anxiety by thinking that complete detachment would get him through it. He kept on telling himself, "Hell, it's part of my job. What choice do I have in the matter?"

Cabana had dreamed about being the top cop at the six-thousand-bed maximum-security prison at Parchman, one of the biggest and toughest prisons in the country. Within a month of landing the job, the confident little man with the slight swagger established himself as the prison boss. He set the rules and expected everyone to follow them. Cabana enjoyed the power and respect he commanded, and for three years, he did a hell of a job.

Then one ordinary spring morning in 1987, Edwin Pittman, the attorney general of Mississippi, called to tell him, "We're going to have an execution in just a few weeks." The death warrant for Edward Earl Johnson had been signed. On May 5, 1987, he was scheduled to be killed, making him the seventy-second person to be executed since the reinstatement of the death penalty. Johnson had been convicted of the 1979 killing of a town marshal and the attempted rape of a sixty-year-old woman.

Cabana hung up the phone, lit a cigarette, slumped back in the big old swivel chair behind his desk, and stared out the window. At first, he couldn't believe it. Then he looked at the facts. How could he be so naive? He had been running one of the biggest prisons in the Death Belt; it was a wonder he had gotten away without executing anyone for this long. There were five executions in 1983, twenty-one in 1984, and fifteen in both 1985 and 1986. Nobody knew 1987 was going to boast twenty-five executions, the most since the death penalty was reinstated. Within six years, there would be thirty-eight.

If Edison had only known the form his discovery would take. Georgia's original "Old Sparky" was built and installed at Milledgeville, Georgia, and was known as the Old Prison Farm. The first electrocution occurred on September 13, 1924.

(*Courtesy Georgia Department of Corrections*)

The machinery of death, an executioner's eye view. The final act of a grisly process. Lever in hand, the executioner awaits the go-ahead from the warden.

(*Courtesy Georgia Department of Corrections*)

Death row prisoner Thomas Grasso defied liberal New York Governor Mario Cuomo's extradition request. Oklahoma gave the green light on March 19, 1995. Grasso strangled an eighty-seven-year-old woman in Tulsa with her Christmas tree lights on Christmas Eve 1980 while stealing a cheap television set and $12.

(Courtesy State of New York Correctional Services)

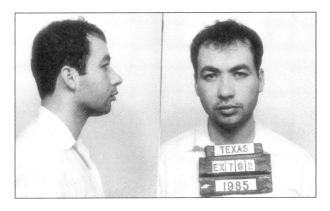

Death row is not an irreversible situation. Texas inmate Muneer Deeb beat the system after nine years on death row.

(Courtesy Florida Department of Corrections)

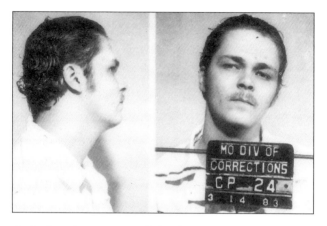

A. J. Bannister—one of death row's most articulate spokesmen.
(Courtesy Missouri Department of Corrections)

Can you believe it? Bannister and spouse, Lindsay, tied the knot at Bannister's exotic Potosi, Missouri, hideaway (actually the prison waiting room, Potosi Correctional Center, the state's newest maximum-security prison.)
(Courtesy Lindsay Bannister)

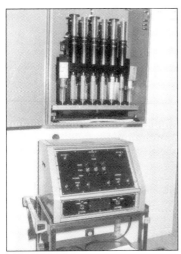

The latest development in execution technology is lethal injection. The computerized machine shown here is one of only a handful designed by Frederick Leuchter, America's most controversial designer of execution machinery.

(Courtesy Missouri Department of Corrections)

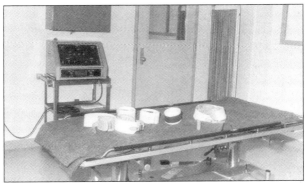

The gurney used in most lethal injection procedures is the same kind used in hospitals. The trend in executions is toward a more sterilized medical approach. The condemned prisoner is firmly strapped onto the gurney so intravenous lines can be inserted into the veins of his arms, allowing the free flow of lethal drugs. If there are no glitches, the prisoner is unconscious within 30 seconds and dead in less than six minutes.

(Courtesy Missouri Department of Corrections)

Willing, competent counsel for the condemned is in short supply. Atlanta-based abolitionist attorney, Stephen B. Bright has made a mission out of defending America's most despised clientele.

(*Courtesy of Stephen Bright*)

Walter McMillian is the only black man ever to legally beat the reaper in Alabama, thanks to the efforts of legal wizards like Bryan Stevenson (*right*).

(*Courtesy of Bryan Stevenson*)

Second only to a state's governor in the execution hierarchy is the attorney general. As Georgia's attorney general, Michael Bowers has overseen the execution of six men.

(Courtesy of the Georgia Attorney General's Office)

Next to Bowers in Georgia's chain of command is Corrections Commissioner Alan Ault.

(Courtesy Georgia Department of Corrections)

The little executioner who wouldn't—Don Cabana now stands adamantly against the death penalty.

(*Courtesy of Don Cabana*)

The Last Mile. The last place on earth. The final few hours before execution are typically spent in holding cells like these, adjacent to the execution chamber. Holding cells are often several miles from death row itself.

(*Courtesy Georgia Department of Corrections*)

95 MAR 20 AM 9:18
IN THE SUPERIOR COURT OF COBB COUNTY,

~~STATE OF GEORGIA~~

THE STATE OF GEORGIA   INDICTMENT NO. 83-1135

V.

NICHOLAS LEE INGRAM   MURDER (Count 1)

O R D E R

The Court having sentenced the defendant, NICHOLAS LEE INGRAM, on the 21st day of November, 1983, to be executed by the Department of Corrections at such penal institution as may be designated by said Department, in accordance with the laws of Georgia, and ;

The date for the execution of the said NICHOLAS LEE INGRAM having passed by reason of supersedeas incident to appellate review;

IT IS CONSIDERED, ORDERED AND ADJUDGED by this Court that within a time period commencing at noon on the 6th day of April, 1995, and ending seven days later at noon on the 13th day of April, 1995, the defendant, NICHOLAS LEE INGRAM, shall be executed by the Department of Corrections as such penal institution and on such a date and time within the aforementioned time period as may be designated by said Department all in accordance with the laws of Georgia.

A genuine death warrant, first step in the execution protocol. In this case it's official authorization to execute Nicholas Lee Ingram. Electrocuted on April 7, 1995 at Georgia's Jackson Diagnostic Center, Ingram's final statement was to aim a huge wad of spit at Warden A. G. Thomas. Ingram, 31, shot to death J. C. Sawyer and tried to kill Mrs. Sawyer after robbing them.

(Courtesy Georgia Department of Corrections)

Lawrence "Pliers" Bittaker. Why didn't they call him "Icepick"?
(*Courtesy California Department of Corrections*)

Freeway Killer William Bonin had an affinity for "little boys."
(*Courtesy California Department of Corrections*)

Judi Buenoano, Pensacola's infamous Black Widow, did her dirty work with arsenic.
(*Courtesy Florida Department of Corrections*)

"Stuttering Dave" Carpenter, California's Trailside Killer.
(*Courtesy California Department of Corrections*)

Douglas Clark is lucky he didn't shoot his penis off. The Sunset Strip Slayer liked to blow women's brains out during fellatio.
(*Courtesy California Department of Corrections*)

While in prison on an assault charge, Daniel Corwin made the confession that got him the death penalty under a new Texas statute.
(*Courtesy Texas Department of Corrections*)

Nurse Robert Diaz seems to have gotten the Hippocratic oath turned around.

(*Courtesy California Department of Corrections*)

Richard Wade Farley cracked as a result of rejection by a coworker. He turned his former workplace into a killing field.

(*Courtesy California Department of Corrections*)

Keith Fudge demonstrated the need for metal detectors at birthday parties.

(*Courtesy California Department of Corrections*)

Stocking Strangler Carlton Gary eluded police for six years by hiding in a South Carolina prison.

(Courtesy Georgia Department of Corrections)

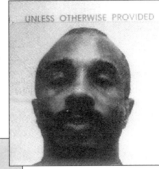

Self-appointed fetal avenger Paul Hill is the guy who shot and killed an abortion doctor and his escort.

(Courtesy Florida Department of Corrections)

Christopher Eric Houston took his grievances back to the hallowed halls of his old alma mater—four killed, ten wounded.

(Courtesy California Department of Corrections)

Randy Kraft, probably the most prolific serial killer in U.S. history.
(*Courtesy California Department of Corrections*)

The affable, one-eyed Henry Lee Lucas. His practical joke on Texas made him a death row legend.
(*Courtesy Texas Department of Corrections*)

Crime looking for a place to happen—James Gregory Marlow.
(*Courtesy California Department of Corrections*)

Night Stalker Richard Ramirez, the man who put the "s" in serial murder.
(*Courtesy California Department of Corrections*)

Overkill is too mild a term for what Larry Robison did to Ricky Bryant. He then wiped out the family next door just to get their car.
(*Courtesy Texas Department of Corrections*)

Danny Rolling, the legendary Gainesville Ripper, visited terror on the University of Florida during a four-day murder binge.
(*Courtesy Florida Department of Corrections*)

In a two-hour lapse of composure, vineyard worker Ramon Salcido killed his wife, her two sisters, their mother, a co-worker, and two of his three daughters.
(*Courtesy California Department of Corrections*)

The purtiest little thang on Texas's death row is ax murderess Karla Faye Tucker.
(*Courtesy Texas Department of Corrections*)

Aileen Wuornos, the Damsel of Death, dispatched six men along north Florida's interstate highways.
(*Courtesy Florida Department of Corrections*)

So why was he surprised? Even though Cabana knew Johnson, he tried to make himself believe that the execution wouldn't be difficult. "I figured all you have to do is give the order to the executioner, and hell, someone else pulls the lever," he said.

In selecting his ten-member execution team from a lengthy list of volunteers, Cabana looked for men who wanted to participate out of a sense of duty, rather than a macabre fascination with the painful ritual. If someone seemed too eager or gave the impression he'd get off on the grisly job, he was rejected. Cabana categorically rejected anyone who worked on death row. Not only would it be bad form, it could create potentially dangerous morale problems after the execution.

Each man on the execution team had a definite job. Because they were working under agonizing pressure, Cabana kept the tasks moron simple. He could have used fewer men and given each man multiple tasks, but that would have been asking for trouble. He didn't want anyone thinking about what he had to do. All each man had to do was perform on cue. The tasks were to maintain a vigil outside the "last night" cell, noting the prisoner's every movement; watch doors leading to the outside yard; stand by the telephone to accept calls from the attorney general's office; supervise witnesses; strap the convict into the chair and monitor his heart on an EKG monitor. Two deputy wardens were assigned to Cabana's side at all times to carry out any last-minute orders.

The only outside person on the team was the paid executioner. His job was to pull the lever, releasing the deadly cyanide pellets. The executioner was appointed by the governor and earned an easy five hundred dollars every time he dropped the lever. An outside executioner was chosen so no one on the execution team would bear the full burden of actually killing the prisoner. (As Cabana saw it, this made no sense.

Technically speaking, every member of the execution team feels like his hand is on the lever. "It's a moot point who actually pulls it," he explained.)

Once the team was assembled, the rehearsals began. The gas chamber had to be inspected and readied for the event. since 1955, thirty-six have died in the chamber. Painted black and made of steel, it looks like an enormous diving bell with windows on six sides. The thick, worn leather straps restrain the prisoner's arms, legs, and chest while the head is secured by a headrest so it doesn't bob, weave, and thrash about when the body goes into wild seizures as the gas does its dirty work.

First, Cabana tested the chamber with rabbits to make sure the chemicals, sodium chloride and sulfuric acid, were mixed properly to produce the lethal gas when the cyanide pellets were dropped into it. It's a good thing animal activists didn't witness this pathetic spectacle. Two plump black rabbits—the cuddly kind you give to kids at Easter—were placed individual cages that were set on top of one another and placed on the chair. This allowed them to be observed when the pellets were dropped into the acid.

The terrified animals went bonkers as soon as the gas began filling the chamber. "Once the cyanide hit them, you could tell their sensory systems were panicking something awful," said Cabana. They charged the bars at breakneck speed, trying to flee, then flopped over on their backs, writhing in agony on the cage floors for a couple of seconds before dying. The execution team stood in front of the chamber and watched their frenetic death dance. "We thought gas just knocked you out and that was it," Cabana said. "But that's not what happens." Horrified by the grisly spectacle, one of Cabana's associate wardens wondered, "If that contraption does that to rabbits, imagine what it will do to a human being."

To make doubly sure everything proceeded according to protocol, Cabana ran another test, this time a cold run using a guard of about the same height and weight as Johnson. They attached the EKG monitor to his chest and strapped him to the chair to make sure the straps worked. They ran through the execution drill, from start to finish, feeling good that everything ran like clockwork. Finally, the rubber seals around the chamber and its large observation window were plied with Vaseline to make sure there were no gas leaks. By then, all members of the execution team knew their parts. The execution would be a piece of cake.

As it turned out, Johnson's execution ran smoothly, except for what Cabana called a "mistiming problem."

Johnson was escorted into the chamber at five minutes before midnight to be prepped for the execution, which was set for one minute after midnight. Johnson had been a quiet guy who minded his own business, but now his reticence and compliance troubled Cabana. He feared all that bottled-up emotion would erupt when it was time to strap him into the chair. But, until the very end, Johnson offered no resistance.

By the time the witnesses were brought into the observation room, he was strapped into the chair. Cabana read him the death warrant, took his last statement, and sealed the chamber. Then he waited for the call from the attorney general and for his men to prepare the cyanide pellets and chemicals. The call came a minute after the chamber was sealed. At this point, the chemicals still weren't ready, and Cabana was beside himself. He stalked into the chemical room and shouted, "Give me the goddamned go-ahead. The poor bastard is just sitting there. This is fucking torture."

Meanwhile Johnson stared into the witness booth and began chanting a gospel hymn at the top of his lungs. He kept on singing, even after the lever was finally thrown and the chamber began filling with gas. When the pungent gas hit his nostrils, he abruptly stopped.

If Cabana thought it was torture waiting to begin, watching Johnson die was much worse. He had seen plenty of men die in Vietnam, but not like this. Johnson was a pathetic sight when he was strapped into the enormous chair, his feet dangling above the floor and his small body seeming to be swallowed up by the massive chair. When the gas struck his nostrils, he tensed, squirmed, and, like the trapped rabbits, instinctively tried to tear himself free. Hardly thirty seconds later, he fell unconscious, his head flopped to the side, his eyes rolled around in the back of his head. He gritted his teeth, drooled, and slobbered while a thick yellowish liquid oozed from his nostrils. Finally, his slight frame slumped forward. Before his body went rigid, a guttural sound bellowed forth from the bottom of his stomach, horrifying the witnesses. The doctors in attendance assured everyone the sound was caused by the autonomic nervous system and that Johnson was already dead.

At a press conference after the execution, Cabana reported the exact time of death as 12:06 A.M. It took Johnson six minutes to die, but he was unconscious less than sixty seconds after the gas hit him. Everything went according to protocol. Cabana met with witnesses and consoled the family. Except for one reporter who actually seemed to be turned on by what he saw, everyone was visibly upset. Many of the witnesses looked ashen.

Cabana and his men were equally shaken by the event. Cabana was angry as well, but he didn't know why. He spent the rest of the night sitting on his porch with his wife smoking cigarettes, drinking coffee, and replaying the day's events. He couldn't get the executioner out of his mind, especially the way he had stared at Cabana while waiting for the signal, gripping the lever so hard his knuckles turned white. Cabana remembered feeling trapped and mustering the courage to say, "Do it." But as hard as he tried, he couldn't make any sense out of the experience. There was no question that Johnson had committed a terrible crime. But why kill him when there were at least nineteen far more dangerous guys who deserved to die before him?

The worst was yet to come. Just when Cabana was beginning to recover from the execution, he got a call from Attorney General Pittman telling him another execution had been scheduled for July 8, 1987, only three and a half weeks later. This time it was Connie Ray Evans, who had been on death row since 1982. Cabana felt like he had been hit by a twelve-gauge shotgun shell at point-blank range. Suddenly his neat little world of good guys/bad guys had been blown to smithereens. All that crap about duty and detachment was meaningless.

It took him almost a day to digest the news. He remembered flopping back in his chair, lighting a cigarette, and thinking about what lay ahead. His career had been going great before the executions began. He ran the show at Parchman and kept the bad guys in line. He had thought he understood how his world worked. He knew all the guys on death row on a first-name basis, but Evans was his favorite. "I remember thinking to myself," he recalled, "Johnson was an unlikely candidate, but executing Evans seemed even more ridiculous. Why the fuck did it have to be him?"

It's not like Evans was this notorious mass murderer. He was no menacing predator. Of medium height and build, he had a soft face and sad eyes. Like most death row inmates, he minded his own business. Unlike Johnson and so many others, he never denied his crime. He admitted to being the triggerman in an armed robbery. Evans had a partner in the crime who beat a hot path to the prosecutor and got a twenty-year manslaughter sentence that was reduced to fifteen years; he was out on the street before Evans was executed. Evans never understood why he never got a second chance in life.

Cabana was Evans's warden for five of his seven and a half years on death row. One of the first inmates Cabana met upon coming to Parchman, Evans figured he'd test him out by hitting him up for a favor. He was hardly on the job a week when Evans asked him if the death row convicts could receive Christmas packages like the other cons. Cabana laughed and said, "Damn, you work fast." Evans returned a big grin, saying, "I gotta break you in early, warden."

Cabana told him to put his request in writing. He was barely halfway down the cell block when Evans shouted, "Hey, what's my name?"

Cabana surprised him by calling back, "Evans," then adding, "And what's my name?"

"Warden," screamed Evans.

"That's close enough. I'll holla atcha later."

Although there was nothing unusual about the exchange, the seeds of friendship had been planted. Cabana and Evans had nothing in common. They were a generation apart. Evans was twenty and Cabana was forty-one. Cabana was white, Evans was black. Evans grew up poor, in Jackson, Mississippi, during the civil-rights demonstrations. Cabana came from a lower-middle-class home in Boston.

There was nothing remarkable about Evans or his story. One of eight kids, he was raised by his mother and stepfather, and never knew his biological father. He fell in with the wrong crowd and discovered smoking pot and snorting cocaine was more fun than going to school or work. Yet over the years, Cabana watched Evans change. He came to prison angry and streetwise, another drug-abusing high-school dropout who thought he had all the answers. Five years later, he was a soft, reflective man who was no threat to anyone. Yet from the beginning, there had been something genuinely likable about Evans.

Even Evans's crime didn't raise any eyebrows. He wasn't a serial killer, child molester, torturer, or even a professional crook. He was just another petty crook who thought he could rob a store to get some money to buy dope. And he made the stupid mistake of botching the only serious crime he ever committed. When the store owner refused to turn over the few dollars in his cash register and fought back, Evans panicked and shot him. The killing wasn't premeditated, just an act of fear. He wasn't even high on drugs when he pulled the trigger. Chances are it was the first and only time Evans ever fired a gun. Nevertheless, he wound up paying for the mistake with his life.

During Cabana's weekly tour of death row, Evans often talked about this ill-fated day. He mused about how he'd do things differently if he had another shot. He spoke of staying in school and getting a degree so he could get involved in some kind of program working with kids who, like him, had screwed up their lives. All that hindsight didn't do him much good, but it did make him feel better to talk about it. What made it worthwhile was knowing Cabana would sit in his cell and listen without judging him. If anyone understood how a stroke of fate could change a person's life, it was Cabana. On other occasions, Evans talked about his mother and how he felt he let her down. He often spoke about his two brothers, one of whom was doing time on a county farm, while the other was serving in the military police.

It wasn't a one-way relationship either. Evans constantly plied the warden with questions, which Cabana willingly answered. The death-bound convict wanted to know everything about his keeper's childhood, especially information about his real mother and father and how his adoptive folks had raised him to be a God-fearing Catholic.

Often, when Cabana had nothing pressing to do, he'd wander down to the death row cell block, hang out with Evans, and shoot the breeze. When they weren't talking about life-and-death issues, they argued about sports, particularly basketball, Evans's passion. When Cabana was so busy that weeks would shoot by before he could get to the cell block, Evans would scold him for abandoning him. "I thought you didn't love me, warden," he'd say. Then they'd strike up another conversation. By the time of Evans's execution, the thin veneer of titles and assigned roles had been stripped away between the two men. "We were just two human beings caught up in a vortex of emotions that neither of us could control and that neither of us could avoid," Cabana said.

The week before the execution, each man went through his own private hell. Evans grew increasingly tense and frightened. Cabana, looking tired, frayed, and constantly wired from too much coffee, cigarettes, and little sleep, was like a hand grenade a hair away from detonation.

Once again, Cabana had to run through the execution protocol to make sure everyone knew their parts. But this time, he was even more fanatical about details. He was determined to do everything humanly possible to make sure Evans suffered as little as possible.

As the execution date approached, the tension level increased as morale sank to an all-time low. Cabana not only had to deal with his own ambivalence, but with Evans's escalating rage, especially when he had learned they were again testing the gas chamber with rabbits. By then, the execution was only twenty-four hours away.

Cabana remembered going down to the row the morning after the chamber had been tested. His men had warned him Evans was bouncing off the walls. Evans's eyes were bloodshot from not having slept in days. He was furious at Cabana. "I can't believe you really tested that son-of-a-bitch," he screamed. "I still have appeals left and you're making plans to fuckin' kill me."

Understanding his panic, Cabana tried to snap him out of his rage. "Knock off the bullshit, Connie," he said. "Stop feeling sorry for yourself. You're a big boy. If you think I'm anxious to do this, you don't fuckin' know me at all."

Evans had flopped down on his cot while Cabana explained that he had tested the chamber to eliminate human error—thereby avoiding a repeat performance of the 1983 Jimmy Lee Gray execution, when a sublethal dose of gas caused the prisoner horrendous suffering. He didn't tell Evans that Gray's execution was a butcher job and how they had to clear the witness room while Gray nearly cracked his skull against the back post, writhed in agony, and drooled all over himself.

Cabana could barely keep his composure. "Don't ask me not to practice," he said. "You know it's not because I'm anxious to kill you. I just don't want any screw-ups."

Even though tempers flared and emotions ran high, Evans knew Cabana was an unwilling participant. At calmer moments, he wanted to know about every step of the execution process. Like all death row inmates, his greatest fear was of losing control of his bodily functions. Cabana was amazed at how classic and irrational this was. Perry Smith, one of the protagonists in Truman Capote's riveting novel *In Cold Blood*, was also concerned about soiling himself. Cabana assured Evans it wasn't a problem and not to worry about it. After he thought about it, Evans responded, "Well, it don't matter anyhow."

The eight hours preceding the execution were the most difficult. By now, inmates were locked down and the prison was in a heightened security state with limited access. The last thing Cabana wanted to deal with was a riot or demonstration.

Everyone who knew Evans, from inmates to guards, was struggling with their emotions. In those last torturous hours, there were no jailers and prisoners. They were just a bunch of men who knew each other well. It wasn't about crime and punishment or right and wrong anymore. The hardest part was knowing there was no way out. Connie Ray Evans had to die and no one wanted to kill him.

Cabana remembered Evans's reaction when he was asked what he wanted for his last meal. Again, he exploded. Evans chuckled cynically and said, "What the fuck difference does it make? Here son, have a steak and baked potato because in two fucking hours we're going to gas your fucking ass into oblivion." Knowing Evans had to let off steam, Cabana backed off. Evans's last meal consisted of a plain omelette and buttered toast, which he hardly ate.

The execution proceeded without any hitches. Forty-five minutes before it began, Cabana escorted the prisoner to the last-night cell next to the gas chamber. Evans exchanged good-byes with other inmates and staff. The last minutes of his life were spent with the prison chaplain and Cabana.

Five minutes before the execution, he turned to Cabana and asked why executions were always conducted at the ominous midnight hour. Not surprised by his question, Cabana gave him the standard bureaucratic answer. In case there's a last-minute stay, the state still has twenty-four hours to rush through legal maneuvers to do the deed before midnight of the next day. Rather than getting angry, Evans said to Cabana, "How ironic for the state. They think they're killing me at midnight. For me it's a new beginning, a midnight sunrise on the rest of my life rather than an end."

Then he smiled at Cabana and asked him if it would be embarrassing to allow an inmate to hug his warden good-bye. As they embraced, Cabana stared into infinity. Moments later, Evans was strapped into the chair. Cabana asked him if he'd like to make a final statement, and Evans said he wanted to say his last words to Cabana privately. He whispered in Cabana's ear that he loved him. As awkward as that last moment was, Cabana put his arm around Evans's shoulder and said he loved him, too.

This time, Cabana made sure there were no fuckups. He wanted to get it over with as quickly as possible. He backed out of the chamber, yet didn't seal it until he got the dreaded phone call from the attorney general's office.

By now, Cabana could barely focus on the drama. He didn't even hear the phone when it rang. It was Dwight Presley, his deputy warden, who picked up the receiver and handed it to Cabana. Not taking his eyes off Evans the whole time, he pressed the receiver to his ear. His heart sank as Attorney General Pittman told him to proceed. All the while the executioner's and the inmate's eyes were locked in a tight stare, both men praying futilely for a miracle.

As soon as Cabana hung up, he nodded at Evans. The prisoner's eyes welled up with tears and he nodded back, his signal to Cabana to get on with it. The chamber was sealed. Cabana turned to the executioner and muttered, "Let's do it." As he spoke it, he looked at Evans, sitting there bound to the chair, tears streaming down his face, and hoped Evans remembered his advice. He had told him, "Son, ya gonna be able to hear the lever when it drops. When it does, start taking deep breaths. I promise you it will be over quick."

Cabana even made a point of telling the two men assigned to strapping Evans into the chair to remind him not to hold his breath. As he watched Evans, he mumbled to himself, "For Christ sake, Connie, breathe! Don't hold your breath!"

But Evans had forgotten. He clung to the last precious moments of his life by holding his breath until the deadly fumes knocked him unconscious. "He suffered a minute longer than he had to," Cabana remembered.

After waiting ten minutes for all the lethal gas to be vented out by exhaust fans, the chamber was opened. When Cabana noticed a big wet spot on Evans's orange jumpsuit, he did all he could do to hold back his tears. "I know it sounds nuts, but I felt real bad he did that," he said.

Wearing gas masks, protective suits, and rubber gloves, the cleanup team cautiously entered the chamber. First, they thoroughly washed Evans's body with a garden hose while it was still strapped in the chair. Then the body was unstrapped and placed on the floor so the jumpsuit could be removed and thrown away and a clean one put on. In a last bit of protocol, the coroner entered the room and offically pronounced Evans dead.

Three hours later, following the cleanup and press conference, an exhausted Cabana dragged himself home. As he drove, he took long drags on a cigarette while his overloaded mind reviewed the hardest day of his career. "I tried, but I couldn't make sense of any of it," he said. "I couldn't get Connie out of my mind, especially those last few minutes of his life. Here is a kid who committed a terrible crime and murdered a man in cold blood. Yet he probably got into heaven. He had forgiven himself, he had forgiven me. If there was anything or anyone in the world he was bitter about, he didn't show it. The topper was he told his executioner he loved him. How many people can do that? I was dumbfounded."

By the time he arrived home, Cabana had made his decision. As soon as he walked in the door he told his wife he couldn't do it anymore. He intended to quit. He had already died once; he couldn't do it again.

A year later, Cabana left Parchman to take another warden's job in a small medium-security state prison in Leekville, Mississippi. Three years after that, he retired.

Don Cabana is now working on a doctoral degree and teaching criminal justice at the University of Southern Mississippi.

PART 2

Who's Who on Death Row

NAME: MUMIA ABU-JAMAL
JURISDICTION: Pennsylvania
GENDER: Male
RACE: Black
DATE OF BIRTH:
PLACE OF BIRTH: Philadelphia, PA
ALIASES/NICKNAMES/MONIKERS: born Wesley Cooke
FATHER:
MOTHER:
YEARS OF SCHOOL:
OCCUPATION: Journalist
DISTINGUISHING MARKS: Waist-length dreadlocks

It is not the fear of death that drives Mumia Abu-Jamal's unique approach to life on death row; it is his outrage over some very real injustices that he has seen and experienced in his lifetime. He genuinely considers himself a political prisoner, and his case, if not perfect, is at least solid enough to have attracted worldwide attention from both critics of and apologists for the American system.

Usually, when a police officer is killed in the line of duty, somebody is going to pay. In the case of Philadelphia officer Daniel Faulkner, Abu-Jamal has been chosen, and there is substantial evidence that Mumia did indeed shoot Officer Faulkner. Although Abu-Jamal disclaims shooting Officer Faulkner, that doesn't mean he thinks what happened was wrong.

Here's what happened. In the early-morning hours—

approximately 4:00 A.M.—of December 9, 1981, Faulkner pulled over William Cooke's Volkswagen. Why Cooke was stopped is not known. According to one account, he was traveling the wrong way down a one-way street. When Abu-Jamal, who was driving a cab to supplement his income, saw his brother being questioned, he asserted himself into the fray. At this point, things get muddled and theories clash. When the smoke cleared, Faulkner was dead, with five bullet wounds to the head and torso. Abu-Jamal had taken a bullet in the chest. A .38-caliber revolver was found next to Mumia, and it was his, and although ballistics tests could not prove Faulkner died from .38-caliber slugs, there were five spent shells in the .38.

But not everyone who kills a cop ends up on death row. There have been plenty of trials less fair than Mumia's, but a few things bear repeating. Between the mid-seventies and 1981, when the murder occurred, Mumia was evolving from a casual observer to an impassioned advocate and follower of the radical black group MOVE, whose standoff with Philadelphia police ended with the disastrous 1985 firebombing of their headquarters. The jury's five-white-to-one-black ratio hardly constitutes a jury of Abu-Jamal's peers. And the presiding judge, Albert Sabo, is known in Pennsylvania as a hanging judge, the "King of Death Row." Granted, Mumia was not a model of mainstream decorum. He dismissed his court-appointed lawyer and tried to replace him with MOVE founder John Africa. He insulted the jury. None of this, however, has anything to do with the facts of the case.

These irregularities would have opened the door to any attorney seeking to demonstrate prejudice. For a person as politicized and as charismatic as Abu-Jamal, they became fuel for a movement. Abu-Jamal is not your standard-issue thug. He was a bookworm in his youth. He turned Black Panther at age thirteen as a result of a brutality episode with police. He worked for several years as a reporter for radio WHYY-FM, covering local political and social events. He served as president of the Philadelphia Chapter of the National Association of Black Journalists. While imprisoned, Jamal has published a book and articles in the *Yale Law Journal, The Nation,* and the *Philadelphia Inquirer,* and he continues to provide inspiration for a worldwide Free Mumia movement, complete with sales of T-shirts, audiotapes, and polemic from his death row cell.

On August 7, 1995, Mumia fought off Pennsylvania's most recent attempt to kill him. Sabo, the judge who sentenced him, granted a stay on the grounds that a higher court would not have time to review the case before execution. So Abu-Jamal's life still hangs by a thread.

TRIAL SUMMARY:
Judge: Albert F. Sabo
Prosecutor: Assistant District Attorney Joseph J. McGill
Defense:
Beginning Date: June 1982
Conviction: July 2, 1982
Appeals: 1989—Pennsylvania Supreme Court turned
  down appeal; 1992—U.S. Supreme Court rejected
  appeal

For additional details on Mumia Abu-Jamal, check out:
Abu-Jamal, Mumia: *Live from Death Row,* New York,
  Addison-Wesley, 1995.
Leonard, Devin: "Presumed Innocent," *Philadelphia
  Magazine,* 84, December 1993, p. 53.

NAME: LAWRENCE SIGMOND BITTAKER
JURISDICTION: California
GENDER: Male
RACE: White
DATE OF BIRTH: September 27, 1940
PLACE OF BIRTH: Pittsburgh, PA
ALIASES/NICKNAMES/MONIKERS: Pliers
MOTHER:
FATHER: George Bittaker
YEARS OF SCHOOL: 11
OCCUPATION: Machinist
DISTINGUISHING MARKS:

On March 30, 1996 Lawrence Sigmond Bittaker cele-
brates the fifteenth anniversary of his sentencing to
California's death row. Plenty of death row prisoners have
killed more people, but none killed with greater cruelty
than Bittaker. His specialty was torture.

The spree began June 24, 1979, when Bittaker and
Ray Norris, his partner in perversion, abducted
Lucinda Schaeffer, sixteen, in Redondo Beach. Bittaker
did Schaeffer in by twisting a coat hanger around her
throat with pliers, crushing her windpipe. He and
Norris dumped her body in the San Dimas Mountains.

Next came Andrea Hall, eighteen. This time,
Bittaker shoved an icepick through Hall's ear before
strangling her, adding to his repertoire of sick deeds.

In September 1979, Bittaker and Norris picked up
Leah Lamp, thirteen, and Jackie Gilliam, sixteen, hitchhiking on the Pacific Coast Highway. After over a day
of terror and torture with vise clamps and pliers,
Gilliam was given the same send-off as Hall. Bittaker
led Lamp to believe he was releasing her and then
smashed her head with a sledgehammer.

The following Halloween night, our murder duo

offered Shirley Lynette Ledford a lift home from a gas station where she had been deposited after refusing to help pay for gas for the car she was riding in. By the time Norris was given his turn at rape, Bittaker had mutilated Ledford to within an inch of her life. Norris finished the job with twenty excruciating minutes of sledgehammer blows. Ledford's pleas and screams throughout these gruesome proceedings were all recorded on tape for Bittaker's twisted pleasure as he cruised Southern California's highways in search of more victims.

Fortunately, Ledford was the last. Two occurrences a week apart finally brought the sick spree to its conclusion. Norris invited Joseph Jackson, a prison acquaintance and an accomplished rapist in his own right, to join the fun, but Norris's description of the enterprise made even this hardened con ill at ease. Ultimately Jackson decided he wanted no part of it. However, now that he knew of it, his only choice was to tell police or risk retaliation. It took Jackson days to convince police to move on his tip. Only when a Hermosa woman reported an assault and robbery did they apprehend Bittaker and Norris.

Hermosa Beach detective Paul Bynum broke the case. He suspected Bittaker and Norris were responsible for the sudden epidemic of death and was trying to assemble enough evidence to make a charge, any charge, stick until he could gain more time. The assault report bought Bynum, fellow detective Tom Cray, and deputy DA Stephen Kay the time they needed. They used it to pit the two culprits against each other. Norris cracked first and struck a bargain to testify against Bittaker.

Convicted on five counts of murder on February 1, 1981, "Pliers" Bittaker was sentenced to die in California's gas chamber .

TRIAL SUMMARY:

Judge: Thomas W. Fredericks
Prosecutor: Deputy District Attorney Stephen Kay
Defense: Albert Barber
Beginning Date: January 1981
Conviction: February 1, 1981
Sentencing: March 22, 1981
Appeals: September 1985—California Supreme Court
   denied Bittaker's motion to "immediately impose exe-
   cution of judgment; July 1989—California Supreme
   Court upheld conviction; U.S. Supreme Court denied
   appeal in May 1991; stay of execution granted July 9,
   1991

For additional details on Lawrence Bittaker, check out:
Markman, Ronald, and Bosco, Dominic: *Alone with the
   Devil,* New York, Doubleday, 1989.

NAME: WILLIAM GEORGE BONIN

JURISDICTION: California

GENDER: Male

RACE: White

DATE OF BIRTH: January 8, 1947

PLACE OF BIRTH:

ALIASES/NICKNAMES/MONIKERS: The Freeway Killer

MOTHER: Alice Benton

FATHER:

YEARS OF SCHOOL: GED

OCCUPATION: Truck driver

DISTINGUISHING MARKS:

Between 1972 and 1980, the bodies of forty-four adolescent males were found dumped along the freeways of Southern California.

It's the most amazing thing. A guy goes to absurd lengths to avoid detection—reincarceration. He kills twelve, possibly more than twenty, young men, allegedly to eliminate witnesses. He says he'll never be taken alive. And when the cops take him in, he spills his guts in toto, first opportunity. William Bonin is the infamous Freeway Killer, one of the most notorious serial murderers in history—and one of the most derivative.

Just reading casual accounts of Bonin's behavior, a brain surgeon or neurologist would have to wonder: What's the chemistry of this? Bonin must have been working on testosterone overload. He targeted teenagers exclusively—"little boys," he called them. But he cruised the Hollywood vicinity to pick them up. We know what that means. With only one or two exceptions, they may have been young, but mostly they were not little boys.

Bonin did his cruising in a van. Hell, Lawrence

Bittaker had a van. It even had a name, "Murder Mac." *Annie had a steamboat.* . . . Bonin allegedly stuck a screwdriver through one of his victim's ears. Bittaker practically invented that one. Bonin liked your homosexual encounter that segued into sadism. Randy Kraft was the virtuoso practitioner of this black art. Kraft may even have invented the freeway dump.

When they questioned Bonin in connection with the so-called Freeway Murders, he is reputed to have protested, "I don't mutilate little boys." Well, that may not be true. Somebody emancipated Thomas Lundgren's "possessions." Bittaker's victims were all female—no evidence of homosexuality there. Kraft was queer, but he specialized in soldiers and barflies. There are, no doubt, legions of perverts, murderous ones, stalking L.A.'s streets nightly, but all indicators point to William Bonin as one sadistic, ear-piercing, castrating, freeway-dumping, serial madman.

Now the number of people willing to testify against Bonin is worthy of note. Two of them, James Michael Munro and Gregory Matthew Miley, were borderline mental defectives whom Bonin drew into his orbit to aid in his endeavors. They starred at his trial and covered three to four of the twelve murders Bonin was charged with. Another accomplice, a certain Vernon Butts, had been implicated in six of the murders, but he hanged himself in his Orange County jail cell just six months before Bonin's trial. William Pugh is the fourth and last of Bonin's accomplices to help put him away. Besides this, Bonin confessed to police. He confessed to the media. In fact, one of the major sideshows of his trial was the testimony of KNXT Channel 2 news reporter David Lopez, who caused a ruckus in the journalism community. Apparently,

Bonin had given Lopez the equivalent of a confession, in considerable detail, very soon after his arrest, and Lopez refused to divulge any of the sources behind his stories until the prosecution had already finished its arguments.

Another sideshow happened a few days into the trial when one of two other inmates in a holding cell gave Bonin a dose of the kind of abuse he gave his victims. It was probably Aryan Brother John W. Stinson who gave the Freeway Killer a broken nose, two black eyes, and possibly a concussion. The other cellmate was Hillside Strangler Angelo Buono. Bonin told officials he fell, but he respectfully requested a cell with a less slippery floor.

He cruised the streets of Hollywood—Mulholland, Normandie, Santa Monica Boulevard—and picked up hitchhikers, runaways, young male prostitutes, desperadoes. If they were willing, they engaged in consensual homosex. Consensual or forced, after the sex, Bonin went for the kill—usually strangulation with the victim's T-shirt. But somebody stabbed German tourist Marcus Grabs, maybe because he resisted. The others:

Stephen Jay Wells, 18	Sean King, 14
Charles Miranda, 15	Steven Wood, 16
James Michael McCabe, 12	Harry Todd Turner, 14
Donald Hyden, 15	Darrin Kendrick, 19
David Murillo, 19	

Counting Grabs and two John Does, these are the murders Los Angeles County would charge him with. Orange County followed with another trial for the murders of four others: Lawrence Sharp, eighteen; Frank Dennis Fox, eighteen; Glen Norman Barker, fourteen; and Russell Duane Rugh, fifteen.

TRIAL SUMMARY:
Judge: William B. Keene
Prosecutor: Sterling Norris
Defense: William Charvet
Beginning Date: November 3, 1981
Conviction: January 5, 1982
Sentence: March 12, 1982

NAME: ROBERT BRETON, SR.

JURISDICTION: Connecticut

GENDER: Male

RACE: White

DATE OF BIRTH: December 10, 1946

PLACE OF BIRTH:

ALIASES/NICKNAMES/MONIKERS:

MOTHER: Lois Breton

FATHER: Roland Breton

YEARS OF SCHOOL:

OCCUPATION:

DISTINGUISHING MARKS:

It was Mother's Day 1986 when Joanne left for good. Bobby Sr. couldn't take it. Married for just two years, she was the only person, save Grandma Eva, who'd ever understood him.

Three generations of Breton men have already come to a violent end. Robert Breton, Sr., is responsible for two—his father and his son. His grandfather was a suicide. If Breton's death sentence is carried out, that'll be four wasted generations. Toss his ex-wife, Joanne Chaisson, into the hopper and it all amounts to a pretty disturbed lifetime.

Where do you start with a guy like Breton? He stabbed his father to death in December 1966, for which he received a manslaughter charge and a suspended sentence. But by the time you're nineteen, doing away with an abusive parent—well, sometimes it's just too late. Grandma Eva Breton gently removed the knife from Robert's hand. She was the only one who ever really loved him.

Breton didn't take a lot of pains to cover his tracks as he departed his second murder scene. Every step he took and everything he touched bore bloody testimony to the murders of his son and former wife. Stab wounds in the neck, both of them. Bobby Jr. at the bottom of the stairs of Apartment 23, 75 Midfield Drive, Waterbury, Connecticut. The blood that squirted from his carotid decorated the length of the staircase as he tumbled down. Joanne lay in the upstairs bedroom. Benjamin Rosado, an eyewitness, told the jury he saw Breton leave the scene that night of December 12, 1987. He swore Breton looked straight at him, but kept on his way.

Breton rejected psychiatric testimony in the guilt portion of his trial, but in the penalty phase, his little sister, Cathy, told quite a story.

Once, when their mother was very drunk, she grabbed one of the many cats she kept and brought it to her bed. "Does this cat die, or does another cat have to die?" "Why does any cat have to die?" Cathy Breton asked. "One cat has to die," her mother insisted, and with that, placed the cat in a bucket, stabbed it repeatedly, and then cut it up. The next morning, a paw was resting on the top of a bureau. Another paw was in a drawer. Well into Robert's adolescence, Lois Breton would force him to strip and belabor his butt and privates with a belt. Cool, Beavis, but she created a monster.

The day Robert killed Roland, his father had been on a rampage because he couldn't find his son. Daddy Roland liked to strap a hunting knife to his thigh when he was angry, just as Robert had the night he wasted his family. Sometimes we're just hell-bent to relive the sins of our fathers.

TRIAL SUMMARY:
Judge: Maxwell Heiman
Prosecutor: John A. Connelly
Defense: Richard Kelly and Alan McWhirter
Arrest: December 15, 1987
Conviction: April 1989
Sentence: October 3, 1989

NAME: JUDIAS BUENOANO
JURISDICTION: Florida
GENDER: Female
RACE: Native American
DATE OF BIRTH: April 4, 1943
PLACE OF BIRTH: Quahana, TX
ALIASES/NICKNAMES/MONIKERS: The Black Widow
MOTHER: Mary Welty
FATHER: Jesse Welty
YEARS OF SCHOOL: 12+
OCCUPATION: Nurse's aide; businesswoman
DISTINGUISHING MARKS:

Judi Buenoano has balls. She "just did it." Among those for whom the value of human life is not an issue, she went for the gusto, she shot the moon. She went for the enchilada toto, and she ended up with the penalté de morte. *C'est la vie.*

Affectionately known among investigators as the Black Widow, Buenoano evolved into a high roller. She drove a Corvette. She owned her own salon, Fingers and Faces. She took her entire staff on a cruise. She bragged about all her degrees, but it turns out she was something of a compulsive liar.

Throughout her life, Buenoano had a habit of consorting with military or ex-military types, insuring them generously, and then seeing how much arsenic or paraformaldehyde they were capable of ingesting before "cashing in." Aside from a limited fling that resulted in the birth of her first son, Michael, Buenoano's first relationship, and the only one that resulted in marriage, was with James Goodyear. Note for intellectuals: Buenoano is Goodyear spelled backward. A navy pilot, Goodyear managed to survive the ordeal that was Vietnam. He returned stateside in May

1971 in the peak of health and in September he was dead. . . . A pilot. Whether one was pro- or anti-Vietnam, a pilot who survived that fray deserves a little respect. What would have been wrong with divorce? Ah; no insurance payoff.

Judi lived well on the proceeds from James's death. Maybe that's why she dignified her dead husband by doting on her two Goodyear kids and killing the non-Goodyear. Arthur Michael Schultz—her firstborn—died during a strange fishing trip. An army something-or-other himself, Michael "Buenoano" came home from the Mayo Clinic in leg braces, a virtual paraplegic. Tests showed a high concentration of arsenic in his system, but police never successfully pinned that on Judi. Michael was game, if not swift of mind. He must have actually trusted his untrustworthy mother. She would insure this bastard child as she had insured James Goodyear, and take his life heedlessly, and live high on the take.

Judi, James, her second son, and Michael went to the river to fish. Michael loved to fish, Judi maintained. Michael never fished in his miserable life, the prosecution countered. We lovingly strapped Michael in the canoe, Judi would assert. A sitting duck, says the prosecution. We paddled up about a half mile and drifted downstream. A snake fell in the canoe from an over-hanging limb. Panic. Confusion. We hit a submerged log. The canoe tipped . . . Michael in braces . . . couldn't swim. I saw my other son struggling, went to his aid, struggled with him to the bank, picked up by a lonesome stranger. We couldn't save Michael. Michael in braces and a lawn chair. Michael at the bottom of the river. Michael dead.

It was the death of Michael Goodyear that sealed Judi Buenoano's fate. Without it, James Goodyear would not likely have been exhumed. John Gentry's near miss when his car exploded, coupled with his near miss from arsenic poisoning a few months earlier, might have been seen as isolated incidents. Michael's death cemented the incidents. A third mysterious death, that of her boyfriend Bobby Joe Morris, though never investigated as a homicide, provided backup "insurance" for the prosecution.

It's so difficult to believe—that a mother would engineer the death of her firstborn. But so much would not add up. What snake? An experienced fisherman testified he'd never seen a snake in a tree on that river. What submerged log? Divers found the riverbed clean. A paraplegic in a lawn chair in a canoe? And the explosion of John Gentry's Ford Fairlane. And the paraformaldehyde-laced vitamin capsules. And the arsenic found when they exhumed James Goodyear's body. And the insurance policies, multiple policies on one and all. Too much. Too much. Maybe it did add up, after all.

The jury thought it did. Judi Buenoano was convicted of capital murder and sentenced to die in Florida's electric chair on November 26, 1985. She was the first woman to face death in Florida after resumption of capital punishment in the U.S. in 1976.

TRIAL SUMMARY:
Judge: Emerson R. Thompson
Prosecutor: Belvin Perry
Defense: James Johnston
Beginning Date: October 21, 1985

For additional details on Judias Buenoano, check out:
Anderson, Chris, and McGehee, Sharon: *Bodies of Evidence,* New York, St. Martin's Press, 1991.

NAME: PETER ANTHONY CANTU
JURISDICTION: Texas
GENDER: Male
RACE: Hispanic
DATE OF BIRTH: May 27, 1975
PLACE OF BIRTH:
ALIASES/NICKNAMES/MONIKERS:
MOTHER:
FATHER:
YEARS OF SCHOOL: GED
OCCUPATION: Laborer
DISTINGUISHING MARKS:

Is a father's rage any match for a hoodlum's cold-blooded viciousness? In a unique ending to the otherwise expeditious proceeding that was Peter Cantu's trial, Judge Bill Harmon gave Randy Ertman the floor. Ertman managed a frothing suggestion that the defendant fell somewhere below the amoeba on the chain of being. A new Texas law allowed families of victims this one last chance to heap abuse, or forgiveness perhaps, upon the convicted.

Peter Anthony Cantu was only seventeen when he gave his gang members a guided tour through the process of murder. The unwitting guests of honor into what had turned into Raul Villareal's gang initiation ceremony into the Black & Whites were Jennifer Ertman, fourteen, and Elizabeth Pena, sixteen, whose only transgression was their unfortunate choice of a shortcut.

This murder is a case study in (1) juveniles on death row, and (2) "same crime" participants getting the death sentence—five of six participants now reside at Huntsville's Ellis Unit, home to fully 13 percent of the nation's condemned and more than 33 percent of those actually executed. As the seal on a Texas Department of Corrections correspondence proclaims: "Don't mess with Texas." Vinnie Medellin alone escaped a death assignment, only because his age, fifteen, bars eligibility. None of the other perpetrators was yet eighteen.

The Ertman/Pena murders evolved like the "house that Jack built." It all started with Raul Villareal's chance meeting with Ephrain Perez. Perez brought Villareal over to José Medellin's house. A few beers later, Peter Cantu appeared and the trash talk started. More gang members arrived. Things rapidly escalated into an offer by newcomer Villareal to kick each gang member's ass in exchange for membership. The tournament moved outdoors and Villareal had bested three Black & Whites when the fourth ended his streak. They inducted him nevertheless for a fine performance and the tone swung toward celebration. That's when Ertman and Pena happened upon the scene, and the tone suddenly shifted again, this time toward blood lust. The gang members raped the girls and beat them unmercifully. They then strangled them. Cantu administered the final disgrace by kicking the lifeless bodies. It took four days to locate the dead girls. Houston police soon picked up the gang members. Typical teenagers, they were unable to contain their secret. It was Cantu's older brother, whose conscience was still intact, who finally blew the whistle on one of Houston's worst nightmares.

TRIAL SUMMARY:
Judge: Bill Harmon
Prosecutor: Don Smyth
Defense: Donald Davis; Robert Morrow

NAME: DAVID JOSEPH CARPENTER
JURISDICTION: California
GENDER: Male
RACE: White
DATE OF BIRTH: May 6, 1930
PLACE OF BIRTH: San Francisco, CA
ALIASES/NICKNAMES/MONIKERS: The Trailside Killer;
   Stuttering Dave
MOTHER: Francis Elizabeth (Hart) Carpenter
FATHER: Elwood Ashley Carpenter
YEARS OF SCHOOL:
OCCUPATION: Printer
DISTINGUISHING MARKS:

Capital murder is pretty much a "man thing." Of the prisoners executed since 1976, women represent only 0.38 percent, while they represent a little over 45 percent of the victims of death row murderers. Statistics like that owe much to guys like David Carpenter. Carpenter hates women and has killed women well in excess of the statistics. Whereas the average person would be incapable of committing murder, Carpenter is incapable of restraining himself from killing.

David Carpenter came to be known as the Trailside Killer. Anyone hiking the mountain trails of Marin County in and around Santa Cruz during the twenty-two months from August 1979 to May 1981 was literally taking her life into her hands. The following table provides a grisly victimology of Carpenter's work.

VICTIM	DATE FOUND
Edda Kane	08–19–1979 *
Frances Bennett	10–21–1979 *
Barbara Schwartz	03–08–1980 *

Cynthia Moreland	10–11–1980
Richard Stowers	10–11–1980
Anne Alderson	10–13–1980
Shauna May	11–28–1980
Diane O'Connell	11–28–1980
Kelly Menjivar	12–28–1980 *
Ellen Marie Hansen	03–29–1981
Heather Scaggs	05–01–1981

*Although there is substantial evidence implicating Carpenter in these deaths, he was never formally charged with them.

Carpenter's criminal history dates from his childhood, but he didn't do any hard time until 1960, when he was convicted for a vicious assault against Lois DeAndrade, a family acquaintance. Released after eight years—about 1968—Carpenter stayed clean for a little more than a year before embarking on another rape-and-assault binge in early 1970. For this, he spent the next nine years behind bars, winning his freedom again on May 21, 1979. Within three months, Carpenter was at it again. Given his history, it's remarkable that he eluded detection for almost two years. The unfortunate reason is that Carpenter had learned from experience that the best way to get away with rape is to kill the victim.

Ironically, Carpenter is a model inmate, manipulative perhaps, but he thrives in prison culture. With an IQ of 125, he is smarter than most of the other inmates. He enrolls in classes and performs well in them, and has even earned college-level credit. He's a paragon of efficiency in his work assignments. He participates in activities like the Investment Club, the Gavel Club, Alcoholics Anonymous, and the Dale Carnegie course. And he immerses himself in group therapy sessions. Carpenter's dedication to his therapy is what convinced Dr. Carl Swedenburg that he had progressed enough to warrant release in 1979.

Carpenter's childhood story is not that uncommon. His mother is said to have been domineering. In fact, many concur that she was a class-A bitch, but that alone is not enough to explain such uncontrollable urges as Carpenter's.*

For additional details on David Carpenter, check out:
Graysmith, Robert: *The Sleeping Lady,* New York, Dutton, 1991.

*Henry Lee Lucas served ten years for killing his mother, and Henry Moormann sits on Arizona's death row for eliminating mom during a short furlough visit right across the street from the prison.

NAME: DOUGLAS DANIEL CLARK

JURISDICTION: California

GENDER: Male

RACE: White

DATE OF BIRTH: March 10, 1948

PLACE OF BIRTH:

ALIASES/NICKNAMES/MONIKERS: The Sunset Strip
  Killer

MOTHER: FATHER:

YEARS OF SCHOOL:

OCCUPATION: Factory boiler tender

DISTINGUISHING MARKS:

California place names are so poetic: Bouquet Canyon
Road, in Antelope Valley. So peaceful . . . that's where they
found the skeletal remains of one of the Jane Doe victims
of Sunset Strip slayer, Douglas Clark.

Since he was defending himself, Clark could show
us more of the cynical, smart aleck, antisocial behaviors so common to his serial-killing cohorts, which usually get concealed from view when a lawyer is calling
the shots. During the penalty phase of a trial already
filled with snide, condescending provocation of Judge
Ricardo Torres, Clark would turn his baiting on the
jury in his closing argument. Clark insisted he be given
the death penalty. He was innocent, he maintained, but
he implied he was the victim of a conformist, tight-
assed, antidiversity society bent on repressing individual self-expression. You may as well kill me, he
chimed. You don't want a guy like me corrupting
things for all the rest.

Clark expressed his individualism in a most unsa-
vory way that sets him apart from us other "cowboys."
Working in partnership with girlfriend Carol Bundy, a
licensed vocational nurse with a knowledge and a

knack for surgical procedures, Clark's MO involved picking up prostitutes along Hollywood's Sunset Strip. He would negotiate the price of a blow job, and as the hooker was performing the act, he would shoot her in the back of the head. He must have known what he was doing, because he never once shot his penis off. Presumably, any acts of necrophilia subsequent to the shooting were on the house. No wait. If the girl's dead, Clark gets to keep all his money, so both the head job and the necrophilia were free. Clark didn't just kill willy-nilly. When Bundy testified against him at his trial, she described his criteria for murder:

"If they were rude, crude, or vulgar, or did not commit the sex act in the way she had agreed to do it . . . he would kill her." The ones who apparently violated one or more elements of Clark's quality code were: Cindy Chandler, sixteen, and Gina Marano, fifteen, half sisters from Huntington Beach; Exxie Lee Wilson, twenty, and Karen Jones, twenty-four, both prostitutes from Little Rock, Arkansas; Marnette Comer, seventeen, of Sacramento; and an unidentified Jane Doe

"How about the severed head of Exxie Lee Wilson that was kept in their freezer?" the prosecutor asked Bundy. She never thought Clark would follow up on her suggestion, Bundy replied, but then he decided it would be "a great trick to play on the police department . . . make them think that they've got a freako out there."

At first, she was "moderately repulsed by the head," Bundy said, but she "learned to have a lot of fun with it." There you go. If at first you don't succeed . . .

Bundy didn't get off scot-free for the light she shed on the dark side of human nature. Actually, her main objective was to sidestep the death penalty herself. Tried separately for another murder, the silencing of a former lover who had figured out Clark was the Sunset

Strip Slayer. John Robert Murray's headless corpse was found shot and stabbed in a van near his Van Nuys home.

TRIAL SUMMARY:
Judge: Ricardo Torres
Prosecutor: Robert N. Jorgensen
Defense: Self; Maxwell Keith; Penelope Watson
Conviction: January 28, 1983
Sentence: March 15, 1983

For additional details on Douglas Clark, check out:
Farr, Louise: *The Sunset Murders,* New York, Pocket Books, 1992.

NAME: ALTON COLEMAN
JURISDICTION: Ohio/Indiana/Illinois
GENDER: Male
RACE: Black
DATE OF BIRTH: November 6, 1955
PLACE OF BIRTH: Waukegan, IL
ALIASES/NICKNAMES/MONIKERS: Al Bates, Alton Bates, Elton Bates, Alton D. Coleman, Alton Eugene Coleman, Elton D. Coleman, Pissy Coleman, Al Harris, Alphonso Harris, Robert Knight, Tony Peterson, Paul Fisher
MOTHER:
FATHER:
YEARS OF SCHOOL:
OCCUPATION:
DISTINGUISHING MARKS:

Anybody who has a beef with Alton Coleman had better just take a number. Coleman should be in *The Guinness Book of Records.* He is the only person in the history of crime in the United States to be sentenced to death in three states.

Coleman has never been a model citizen. He was already charged in the rape of a minor and was out on bail when he and girlfriend Debra Denise Brown were charged with kidnapping. Coleman and Brown took to the road, but rather than lie low until the heat died down, they undertook a seven-week spree that covered six states, left at least eight dead, and put them at the top of the FBI's Most Wanted list.

Coleman preferred victims who wouldn't offer much resistance. The Kenosha, Wisconsin, girl that they kidnapped turned up dead in Waukesha, Illinois, three weeks after the couple became fugitives. Her name was Vernita Wheat and she was only nine years old. On

June 19, 1984, in Gary, Indiana, Coleman raped and killed Tamika Turks. Turks was seven. Her cousin, also raped, narrowly escaped death. She was nine. Next came ten-year-old Rochelle Temple and her mother, Virginia, thirty, found in the crawl space of their home in Toledo, Ohio. Add to the list Tonnie Stewart, fifteen, and Indianapolis resident Eugene Scott, seventy-seven. The only exceptions to Coleman's rule of preying on the most vulnerable were Marlene Waters of Cincinnati and Donna Williams of Gary, forty-four and twenty-five respectively. These are just the murders. The list of kidnapping, assault, and robbery victims who got away with their lives is longer still.

Coleman and Brown fit the classic description of "killer couples." Coleman was clearly the dominant personality and the instigator, but Brown played a critical and possibly indispensable role. Together, the couple could create scenarios and situations that they would not have been able to pull off working alone. Most notably, a woman can lure children into a trap much more convincingly than a man.

Remarkably, the spree had pretty much run its course before the two fugitives were listed among the FBI's Most Wanted on October 24, 1984. Even then, it took authorities another three months to capture Coleman and Brown. The killers had come full circle, and in a rather anticlimactic conclusion to eight months of carnage, they were collared without a word of resistance in a park in Evanston, Illinois.

The trials and their resulting death sentences unfolded in reverse sequence to the atrocities that made them necessary. Ohio got first shot and, in May and June of 1985, gave Coleman two death sentences, one for the murder of Marlene Waters and one for Tonnie Stewart. Indiana followed in April 1986 and sentenced Coleman to death for killing Tamika Turks.

Illinois, where it all began, convicted Coleman for the murder of Vernita Wheat in January 1987.

Coleman and Brown are in custody in Ohio.

For additional details on Alton Coleman, check out:

Lane, Brian, and Gregg, Wilfred: *The Encyclopedia of Serial Killers,* Diamond Books, New York, 1992.

Sabljak, Mark, and Greenberg, Martin H.: *Most Wanted—A History of the FBI's Ten Most Wanted List,* New York, Bonanza Books, 1990, p. 262.

NAME: FAYE COPELAND
JURISDICTION: Missouri
GENDER: Female
RACE: White
DATE OF BIRTH:
PLACE OF BIRTH:
ALIASES/NICKNAMES/MONIKERS:
MOTHER:
FATHER:
YEARS OF SCHOOL:
OCCUPATION: Motel housekeeper
DISTINGUISHING MARKS:

Somebody has to be the oldest person on death row. It's surprising that it would be one of only forty-eight women condemned. It's also surprising that Faye ended up on death row, since the scheme that landed her there was the brainchild of her farmer/husband/partner-in-crime Ray. The Copelands are one of the most unusual cases of serial murder. Residing as they did in the isolated upper reaches of northern Missouri, they literally had to import their victims.

The scam went something like this: Ray, on occasion accompanied by Faye, would recruit transients from shelters in the larger towns near Mooresville, Missouri, their home base. They'd bring them back to the farm and soon open a post office box and a bank account in a nearby town. Once the bank sent personalized checks, Ray and the victim-to-be would go to a cattle sale where the employee would bid on and purchase a load of cattle, paying with one of his checks. Before the check could clear, Copeland would resell the cattle, eliminate the drifter with his .22 rifle, bury the body in some out-of-the-way spot close by, and repeat the cycle.

This was Ray's best scheme yet, and things continued working quite well until the Copelands recruited Jack McCormick. Nobody knows a con artist better than another con artist, and McCormick was more than a match for the old farm couple. On a trip into town after opening his checking account, McCormick went car shopping. He test-drove one of the cars all the way to Washington State and paid for his vacation with his new checks. He also saw to the Copeland's undoing by calling Crimestoppers as he passed through Nebraska and exposing their operation. He mentioned something about a human skull.

This provided county deputy Gary Calvert with the break he needed. Calvert had been wondering about the rash of bad checks that had recently hit area banks. He figured Copeland was involved somehow; Ray's history with bad checks went back a half century. McCormick's report of foul play provided the grounds for a search of the Copeland property. Although authorities found nothing major for weeks, other evidence led them to keep looking. Ultimately, they unearthed the remains of five men, and the Copelands were charged with capital murder. Even homeless drifters leave trails. Among the victims were:

Paul Cowart, 21	Dardanelle, AR
John William Freeman, 27	Tulsa, OK
Jimmy Dale Harvey, 27	Springfield, MO
Wayne Robert Warner, 40	Bloomington, IL
Dennis K. Murphy, 27	Normal, IL

There may have been more.

Faye seems not to have understood how she could get the death penalty if Ray was the triggerman. The Copeland children don't understand this either, although Faye did refuse to testify against Ray. One reason may have been Missouri attorney general Bill Webster's ambition to be governor. To save the county money and unnecessary turmoil, prosecuting attorney Doug Roberts sought a plea bargain that would have given both Copelands life in prison. Roberts was dismissed from the case for his efforts, reinforcing the notion that state politics was a factor in the Copelands's sentence.

Since the 1990 trial of the Copelands, Ray died in prison. Faye still resides at Fulton Reception Diagnostic Center.

TRIAL SUMMARY:

Judge: E. Richard Webber
Prosecutor: Doug Roberts; Ken Hulsof
Defense: David Miller; Barbara Scheckenberg

For additional details on Faye Copeland, check out:
Kunel, Tom: *Death Row Women,* Pocket Books (Simon and Schuster), New York, 1994.

NAME: DANIEL LEE CORWIN
JURISDICTION: Texas
GENDER: Male
RACE: White
DATE OF BIRTH: September 13, 1958
PLACE OF BIRTH: Orange Co., CA
ALIASES/NICKNAMES/MONIKERS:
MOTHER: FATHER:
YEARS OF SCHOOL: 15 ½ years
OCCUPATION: Cabinetmaker
DISTINGUISHING MARKS:

Montgomery County, Texas, authorities weren't even sure they had a serial killer, much less who he was. Daniel Corwin solved their problem for them. While in prison for the rape and attempted murder of a Texas A&M coed, Corwin confessed to the prison psychiatrist three murders he had committed two years prior.

It was October 22, 1988, when Corwin confronted the student in a parking lot on the Texas A&M College Station campus. They drove in her Chevy Suburban to Lick Creek Park. Corwin raped her, tied her to a tree, stabbed her, and left her for dead. He underestimated her will to live. She freed herself and walked to a nearby road, where she collapsed. Passersby found her, however, took her to the hospital, and she survived to identify Daniel Lee Corwin. They were also able to lift some of his fingerprints from the Suburban.

Sentenced to ninety-nine years in a trial that ended March 1, 1989, this was not Corwin's first stint in Texas's prison system. At the tender age of sixteen, Corwin had pulled off a creepily similar stunt. He abducted a girl from Temple High School, raped her, stabbed her in the chest, and left her to die underneath a pile of rubbish. She, too, survived. For this, he received forty years in a plea bargain in which he was charged with aggravated sexual assault, but not attempted capital murder. He earned parole on November 20, 1985, after serving a little less than ten years.

Thirty at the time of his 1989 sentence for ninety-nine years, perhaps he figured he would spend the remainder of his natural life behind bars anyway, he may as well clean the slate. More likely, he thought he could strike a deal by coming clean. Corwin told a prison psychiatrist he was responsible for three unsolved murders in and around Huntsville. On July 10, 1987, he raped and knifed to death Debra Lynn Ewing, a twenty-seven-year-old saleswoman working for an optical store in Huntsville. As a cabinetmaker, Corwin had helped in the construction of the store. On Halloween night of that same year, Corwin attacked a thirty-six-year-old mother, Mary Risinger, at a Huntsville car wash. Risinger's three-year-old daughter, dressed up for an evening of trick-or-treating, watched her mother die from the front seat of their car. Corwin's other attack had come the previous February 13. His victim, Alice Martin, seventy-two, from Normangee, Texas, was out walking her dog when he accosted her.

Corwin received his death sentence under Texas's new Texas serial killer law.

NAME: ROBERT O. COULSON
JURISDICTION: Texas
GENDER: Male
RACE: White
DATE OF BIRTH: March 11, 1968
PLACE OF BIRTH: Providence, RI
ALIASES/NICKNAMES/MONIKERS:
MOTHER: Mary Coulson *
FATHER: Otis Coulson *
YEARS OF SCHOOL: 14
OCCUPATION: Sales
DISTINGUISHING MARKS:

* Adoptive

The psychology of murder is not difficult to fathom.
Whereas we're most intrigued by the ones that don't
make sense—thrill killing, cannibalism, serial murder—
the overwhelming majority are acts that, however abhor-
rent, are at least understandable. In other words, they're
rationally motivated by things like passion, greed, or
revenge. Matlock, Sherlock, and Jessica would have
assigned this one to a graduate assistant. The Houston
police must have been faking perplexity during the five
days they took to make an arrest. Most likely, they were
just building their case. Clearly, they had Coulson tabbed
within seventy-two hours. Five days after the murders,
they had him on tape and in custody. He hadn't figured
the weak link would be his roommate and accomplice,
Jared Lee Althaus.

Coulson eliminated his entire step-family for mone-
tary gain. It was a good plan. Eliminate all rivals to
the throne. Bind the victims. Asphyxiate them with
trash bags. Remove the bindings. Torch the house. It
will look like they all suffocated from smoke inhala-

tion. Collect the insurance money. Live happily ever after.

Stepfather Otis was easy. He was an invalid. Sarah, Coulson's adoptive sister and the only one to whom he had ever shown any warmth, surrendered without a fight. She thanked him for waiting till her baby was born. He hugged her and told her he loved her. He did not wait for his natural sister, Robin, to deliver her baby, however. He whacked her on the head with a crowbar. Her husband Richard, too. And he suffocated them. As expected, Mary, his mother, went down hardest. Either the stun gun was defective or she was too damn fat to feel it. He had to wrestle her. Gross. Neatnik Coulson must have been mortified at the prospect of messing up his hair.

A couple of flaws: (1) arson investigators have become quite sophisticated in determining the origins of fires; (2) gasoline is a helluva lot more flammable than Coulson thought—it ignited from the pilot light on a heater before he was ready; (3) don't boogaloo on your mama's grave. It sends the wrong message.

But Jared . . . Jared . . . Jared was supposed to be Bob's alibi. The story was that Bob had been fishing all day at a lake near his grandfather's place. Bob would take care of Jared for life. Set him up in a nice apartment. Money for trips, sex, whatever strikes your fancy. But something got to Jared. Might've been guilt. Or maybe he fell for one of the oldest police tricks in the book: float a theory, fabricate a witness who puts *you* at the scene of the crime. You, Jared. We know you were there. Tell us what you know. We'll make it easy on you if you'll make it easy on us. We can make a deal, Jared. You don't have to go down for this. All right! All right! Wire me up. I'm supposed to meet Coulson at Motel 6 Wednesday night. . . . Splendid.

"I'm your alibi, and you're my alibi." "They've got to

prove beyond a reasonable doubt." Said for all the world to hear. No sooner had the words rolled off his tongue than Coulson was nabbed. Jared had cut a deal: not more than twenty years. He could have done much, much better.

NAME: ROBERT RUBANE DIAZ
JURISDICTION: California
GENDER: Male
RACE: Mexican-American
DATE OF BIRTH: March 23, 1938
PLACE OF BIRTH:
ALIASES/NICKNAMES/MONIKERS:
MOTHER:
FATHER:
YEARS OF SCHOOL: 12+
OCCUPATION: Nurse
DISTINGUISHING MARKS:

Robert Diaz is what crimologists sometimes call an angel of death. Others would label him a standard-issue thrill killer who just coincidentally chose hospitals as the setting for his mayhem.

Photos of Diaz from the *L.A. Times* coverage of his trial, which ran from October 31, 1983, until the end of March 1984, show a man who bears a striking resemblance to Gabe Kaplan of the seventies TV series *Welcome Back, Kotter* and/or Gene Shalit. Diaz completed his nursing studies at the Calumet, Indiana, campus of Purdue University in 1977 and moved to Southern California to ply his trade in 1978.

Although he vigorously maintained his innocence, this requires the ability to see every event as totally unrelated to every other event, and to pretty much disregard mathematical probability. The popular TV drama *ER* has shown us the unrelenting climate of chaos that permeates emergency-room culture. It's to be expected that you'll lose the occasional patient. It's even within the realm of believability that you could lose four, five, maybe six. Community Hospital of the Valleys in Perris, California, lost eleven between March

30 and April 2, 1981. San Gorgonio Pass Hospital in nearby Banning lost another on April 25. In all, Los Angeles, Riverside, and San Bernardino counties lost a whopping sixty elderly patients unexpectedly in a matter of months.

The evidence fit Diaz like an Armani suit. Most of the patients died from an overdose of a heart-relaxant drug known as Lidocaine. Investigators found three syringes at Community Hospital that held traces of Lidocaine, and were hand-labeled with the receiving patients' names by none other than Nurse Diaz. They had been placed in a box the hospital was using to collect syringes after the L.A. coroner's office began monitoring the mysterious deaths. That falls somewhere between chutzpah and hubris. Already the past May, six months before Diaz's arrest on November 23, authorities had searched his Apple Valley home. At that time, they found syringes of the type used to administer Lidocaine and a partially filled vial of the drug. According to the testimony of his coworkers, Diaz was the kind of functionary who liked to "play doctor." It gave him a sense of power and importance. Indeed, part of his defense strategy involved numerous allegations that doctors on duty just stood around while he undertook heroic measures to save lives. Other coworkers pointed out Diaz's uncanny ability to predict which patients, some of them quite stable, would, as he expressed it, "get in trouble." Finally, there is the matter of the tip that set everything in motion. An anonymous caller contacted the L.A. coroner's office in April 1981 to apprise them of the unusual spate of deaths. Either hospital officials didn't realize or were covering up the trend. There was speculation that Diaz had an accomplice in his little game. If so, it was never proven and Diaz took the full rap himself.

Diaz's trial was a one of a kind in American justice.

It was a nonjury trial, and the first time in California history that the judge who presided over the trial acted as jury, recommended the death penalty, and then formally pronounced the death sentence. In other words, Diaz was tried, convicted, condemned, and sentenced by one person.

TRIAL SUMMARY:

Judge: John H. Barnard
Prosecutor: Patrick F. Magers
Defense: Michael B. Lewis
Beginning Date: October 31, 1983
Verdict: March 29, 1984; recommendation of death penalty April 12, 1984
Sentence: June 10, 1984

Name: DENNIS WAYNE EATON
Jurisdiction: Virginia
Gender: Male
Race: White
Date of Birth:
Place of Birth: Virginia
Aliases/Nicknames/Monikers:
Mother:
Father:
Years of School: 8
Occupation: Laborer
Distinguishing Marks:

However many additional problems a murder may create, we can safely assume that in the mind of the perpetrator, a murder is always a solution to some problem. Dennis Eaton's unique slant on murder is the degree to which he employed it as a problem-solving tool—you make a plan, you execute the plan—in phases, you eliminate anyone who represents an obstacle to successfully executing any given phase of the plan.

Eaton had fallen in love with Judy Ann McDonald. Walter Custer, Jr., was the father of McDonald's child and was living with her when Eaton moved in with them in 1987. Considering the potential rivalry over McDonald's affections, coupled with the fact that Custer might testify against Eaton on burglary charges he was facing, Custer's elimination would accomplish two objectives. So Eaton shot him in one of the orchards where he had worked as an apple picker.

A burglar/murderer on the lam, of course, needs transportation, and time is of the essence. Eaton, again choosing the path of least resistance, targeted his mother's next-door neighbor and twenty-year family friend, Ripley Marston, sixty-eight, as his benefactor.

Eaton was thoughtful enough to take Marston by a local store for a lottery ticket. Back home, Eaton killed Marston and took his wallet and car. Add another murder, armed robbery, and car theft.

On his way out of town, Eaton picked up McDonald and a six-pack. In fact, Virginia state trooper Jerry Hines was thinking that might be an open beer he saw when he pulled over the Ford Fairmont near midnight on February 20, 1989. Bummer . . . barely a hundred miles into their escape to Texas . . . this was not part of the plan, but also not much of a problem for Eaton and McDonald. They killed Hines and drove on. Add a third homicide, this time a respected, well-liked, civic-minded cop; operating a vehicle without a license; leaving the scene; and a possible DUI.

Less than two hours later and about sixty miles farther down I–81, just south of Roanoake, Salem, Virginia, officer Michael Green spotted the Fairmont and gave chase. Eaton and McDonald fled (resisting arrest), and after a pursuit that reached speeds in excess of one hundred miles per hour down Salem's quiet streets (wreckless endangerment), Eaton hit a lightpole. Eaton immediately shot McDonald in the head (homicide #4), and then shot himself, carrying out his and McDonald's death pact. To make a bad day even worse, Eaton survived.

Dennis Eaton's trial represented a state-level test case on the issue of proper interrogation of a suspect. It was a defeat for Eaton and opponents of the death penalty. The issue was who is responsible for taking the initiative in protecting the suspect's right to have an attorney present. The Virginia Supreme Court ruled that since Eaton did not say specifically, "I want an attorney," the interrogation that yielded his confession was legal.

With several steps still to go in his appeals process,

Eaton's death row sojourn at the Mecklenburg
Correctional Center will likely run many more years.

TRIAL SUMMARY:

Judge: George E. Honts III

Prosecutor: Eric Sisler, commonwealth's attorney for
    Rockbridge County

Defense: Anthony Anderson; Thomas Blaylock

Beginning Date: November 28, 1989

Appeals: Execution stayed August 15, 1990; Virginia
    Supreme Court upheld original verdict on September
    21, 1990

NAME: MICHAEL WAYNE ECHOLS

JURISDICTION: Arkansas

GENDER: Male

RACE: White

DATE OF BIRTH: December 11, 1974

PLACE OF BIRTH: Memphis, TN

ALIASES/NICKNAMES/MONIKERS: born Michael Wayne
 Hutchison; Damien Echols

MOTHER: Pam Hutchison Echols

FATHER: Eddie Joe Hutchison

YEARS OF SCHOOL:

OCCUPATION:

DISTINGUISHING MARKS: Egyptian ankh on chest;
 pentagram; cross in webbing of hand;
 letters E-V-I-L on fingers

As the saying goes, "There are no rich men on death row."
If Michael Wayne "Damien" Echols had had O.J.
Simpson's lawyers and money, it is probable he would be
walking around Arkansas a free man. Instead, he resides
among the condemned at the maximum-security facility in
Tucker.

Whether or not a person accepts Echols's guilt
revolves largely around whether or not they believe in
satanic cult worship. Nonbelievers think it's all a
witch-hunt and point to the sparsity of evidence in this
case. Believers wonder who but an organized satanist
group could commit such grisly, unthinkable acts and
leave no evidence.

On May 5, 1993, three West Memphis, Arkansas,
second graders, Michael Moore, Steve Branch, and
Chris Byers, failed to return home. They had ventured
out after school on their bikes to get in a couple hours
of play before dark. After checking all the obvious,
legitimate places they could be, the boys' parents and a

growing search party turned their attention to a
wooded area where the boys liked to go when they
were in a mood for "danger." Robin Hood Hills lies
along Interstate 55 and near the Blue Beacon truck
stop, and had a reputation for attracting drifters, drug
dealers, and practitioners of the black arts.

When the boys' bodies were indeed discovered the
next day in a creek that ran through Robin Hood
Hills, their condition led to unbridled speculation as
to who could have performed such atrocities. They
were found naked and hog-tied. All had been brutally
bludgeoned. Steve Branch's face was laid open from
cheek to jaw. Chris Byers's penis and scrotum had
been cut off.

Speculation soon ran rampant that this was a ritual
satanic "sacrifice of innocents," but because the search
mission had been so disorganized and police had failed
to effectively preserve the crime scene, there was little
physical evidence—none of the usual blood, fingerprints, footprints, or artifacts, not even any overt indi-
cations of witches' activity, like fire circles of a certain
dimension, dead, mutilated animals, or upside-down
crosses or pentagrams etched into trees or in the dirt.
Even the so-called murder weapons introduced as evidence during the trial were highly suspect. Two clubs,
cut from tree limbs, totally overlooked at first, were
retrieved a full two months after the bodies were discovered. A knife found in a lake behind one suspect's
home held no fingerprints or blood and could not be
convincingly linked to any of the accused.

But Damien Echols was not your run-of-the-mill
teenager. Rebellious, with a history of psychological
disorders, he thumbed his nose at society in general
and at law enforcement in particular. In the satanic
hysteria that swept the nation between the late eighties
and early nineties, Echols cultivated the image of a

satanist: pale skin, black clothing and boots, heavy-metal music, tatoos spelling "evil" and depicting satanic signs, an attitude of alienation, and friends who looked and acted similarly. Among this circle of friends were two other teens whose association with Echols implicated them in the crime as well—Jason Baldwin and Jesse Misskelly.

Echols made no attempt to dissuade anyone from believing that he was the embodiment of evil. Therefore he became the focal point of speculation of satanic involvement, and of an investigation that seemed all too inclined to follow the tide of public opinion and hysteria and a growing lynch mentality.

The event that "broke" the case was a "confession" by Misskelly. Tried separately, his lawyers depicted Misskelly as borderline retarded and highly suggestible, and possibly the victim of unscrupulous police interrogation tactics. To his detriment, Misskelly repeated variations of his account on more than one occasion. Ironically, this confession, which formed the basis of the case against Echols and Baldwin, could not be used as evidence during their trial.

The trials were circuslike to say the least—a motley array of experts on satanic cults, psychiatrists, and locals familiar with the defendants, many of them possessing some very imaginative, and conflicting, interpretations of the events. In the end, Misskelly got life in prison, Baldwin life without parole, and Echols alone the ultimate sentence of death.

TRIAL SUMMARY:
Judge: David Burnett
Prosecutor: John N. Fogleman; Brent Davis
Defense: Val Price; Scott Davidson

For additional details on Michael Wayne Echols, check out:
Reel, Guy, Perrusquia, Marc, and Sullivan, Bartholomew:
    The Blood of Innocents, New York, Pinnacle Books,
    1995.

NAME: DONALD LEROY EVANS
JURISDICTION: Mississippi
GENDER: Male
RACE: White
DATE OF BIRTH: July 5, 1957
PLACE OF BIRTH: Watervliet, MI
ALIASES/NICKNAMES/MONIKERS: Joe Williams; Joseph
  Kenzie
MOTHER: Juanita Evans
FATHER: Faye Lawrence Evans
YEARS OF SCHOOL:
OCCUPATION:
DISTINGUISHING MARKS:

*I knew Henry Lee Lucas. Henry Lee Lucas was death
row's consummate joker. You, sir, are no Henry Lee
Lucas.*

There's something about draining the psychic energy of
the collective citizenry, even of the incarcerati, that's even
more despicable than murder itself. Donald Leroy Evans
would have us believe he's some kind of serial killer. He
claims to have reaped sixty souls. Sorry, Donald. Been
there. Done that.

That's not to say Evans deserves to be let off the
hook. There's still that matter of his conduct with
regard to one Beatrice Louise Routh, that little tête-à-
tête with Tami Giles, Beatrice's mother, back in August
1991.

That wasn't his Suzuki Samurai. He stole it from a
guy in his Galveston, Texas, apartment complex. He
was never a teacher. He was never a navy Seal. He is an
imposter, and a child molester, and a child murderer.

Are we to understand that Evans negotiated with Giles to have sex with her ten-year-old daughter? Giles and some friends from Pennsylvania were all staying on the beach at Gulfport, Mississippi, where they made the acquaintance of the suave Mr. Evans. Giles struck a deal with Evans, but then panicked. Too late. She couldn't find him. The police couldn't find him. When they did find him in Amity, Louisiana, he wouldn't talk. When he did talk, Beatrice was already raped, sodomized, and dead from strangulation. When he did talk, and show Mississippi authorities where the body was, he did so only on the condition that he be given the death penalty. We're talking Mississippi. He had to ask?

Evans led them to some weeds off to the side of state road 43 in Pearl River County. There she was, nude and dead. That's all we need to know. Ira Jean Smith, that Fort Lauderdale prostitute whose murder he claimed? Tack her onto the list. Janet Movitch, Florida again? Sure, give him that one, too. If it becomes necessary for Florida to prosecute, they can use it. Let him wear the Klan robes to his trials if he wants. But let's see what Mississippi's going to do first.

Tami Giles got some hard time for her moral degradation. It's called felony child neglect. She also lost custody of her other daughter, Melissa. That sounds about right.

TRIAL SUMMARY:
Judge: Kosta Vlahos
Prosecutor: Cono Caranna
Defense: William Boyd
Beginning Date: September 10, 1993
Conviction: September 16, 1993

NAME: RICHARD WADE FARLEY

JURISDICTION: California

GENDER: Male

RACE: White

DATE OF BIRTH: July 25, 1948

PLACE OF BIRTH: Texas

ALIASES/NICKNAMES/MONIKERS:

MOTHER:

FATHER:

YEARS OF SCHOOL: 13 plus navy training

OCCUPATION: Computer technician

DISTINGUISHING MARKS:

Hell hath no fury like a dweeb scorned. The story of Richard Wade Farley is pretty much like *Fatal Attraction* in reverse, except much, much worse. Laura Black's nightmare began in April 1984. What was wrong with Laura anyway? Why couldn't she love Richard? That first lunch at Eat Your Heart Out café—to him it was the opening chapter of a lifetime of bliss. To Laura it was lunch. Then there was the buttered blueberry bread, lovingly wrapped in foil and left on her desk—for seven straight Monday mornings. She didn't answer a single one of the two hundred love letters he penned during his four-year pursuit. And what girl in her right mind could turn down an invitation to a tractor pull?

Granted, they didn't have much in common. Farley was thirty-six, Black just twenty-two when it all started. He was an avid collector of power tools, guns, and porn. She liked aerobics and tennis. He was a pudgy, out-of-shape couch potato. She was a former gymnast. But hey, sometimes opposites attract.

For sure, Farley didn't understand Black's reticence. When she politely declined his initial overtures, he persisted. Nothing wrong with perseverance, but most

guys would have hung it up when Black told him she
wouldn't go out with him if he were the last person on
earth. Ouch.

Not Farley, though. A computer technician, he
invaded Black's computer files. At lunch, or before or
after work hours, he would rifle through her desk. He
got her home address and phone number from the company's personnel files. He called. She changed her number. It didn't work. He got her date of birth and sent
cards and presents. He stalked her, followed her home,
spied on her dates, joined her health club. Laura moved
three times. Farley always found her. "It's my option to
make your life miserable," he said at one point. When
in May of 1987, ESL, the Sunnyvale, California defense
contractor where they both worked, fired Farley for
harassment, he wrote in a note to Black. "I will not be
pushed around, and I'm beginning to get tired of being
nice." He even copied her house keys and sent them to
her. She got an order of protection.

Unrequited? Yes. Obsessive? Well, yes. Psychotic?
Yes, that, too. Maybe this had more to do with control
than love, with perhaps some unresolved childhood
issues thrown in.

Probably the thing that hurt their relationship most
was the day Farley dressed up like an inflatable
Rambo—complete with bandoliers, headband, and
ninety-eight pounds—not rounds—of ammunition.
Lots of people go through the service without much
impact on their lives afterward. Farley is one of those
pathetic figures who fixates on things military—
weapons, procedures, the whole image. He wallowed
in self-importance. Somehow, while in the navy from
1967 to 1977, he had been given a top-secret security
clearance. He seems to have received some kind of
training that led him to believe he stood above the rest
of us.

It was February 16, 1988. Farley meant to kill himself. That would show her. But in a last-minute change of plans, he decided to turn ESL into a shooting gallery. Every time somebody new popped up, Farley fired. In the end, he killed seven people and injured four others. Four others were injured, including Black.

It took a SWAT team and police negotiator Ruben Grijalva six hours to talk Farley out of the building. The line that finally moved Farley to surrender was, "Let's hurry, we don't want the ice to melt in your Pepsi." That pretty much captures the pathos of this product of postmodern America.

Farley is a study in delusion. The articles about this incident appeared mostly in women's magazines and always contained advice on how best to deal with obsessive, stalker-type behavior. In Farley's particular personality disorder, exerting control over one person—Laura Black, not all women—would consume him. It became more important than his other "real" girlfriend, more important than his job, more important than his freedom, and more important than the lives of seven innocent employees of ESL, Inc.

For additional details on Richard Wade Farley, check out:
Gross, Linda: "Twisted Love—A Deadly Obsession," *Cosmopolitan,* July 1992, p. 190.
Trebilcock, Tim: "I Love You to Death," *Redbook,* March 1992, p. 100.

NAME: PRISCILLA FORD
JURISDICTION: Nevada
GENDER: Female
RACE: Black
DATE OF BIRTH: February 10, 1929
PLACE OF BIRTH: Berrien Springs, MI
ALIASES/NICKNAMES/MONIKERS:
MOTHER: Lucille Lawrence
FATHER:
YEARS OF SCHOOL: 16
OCCUPATION: Teacher
DISTINGUISHING MARKS:

She chose as her murder weapon a black 1974 Lincoln Continental. The setting was downtown Reno, Nevada. It was Thanksgiving Day 1980.

When patrolman Steve Baring reached the vehicle that private citizen Tom Jaffe had taken the initiative to stop, the drunk, diminutive driver identified herself as Priscilla Joyce Ford, and/or Jesus Christ, depending on your perspective. "Jesus" had just wiped out a side-walk full of tourists. "How many did I get?" Ford queried during the sobriety test. "Did I get fifty? I hope I got seventy-five? The more dead, the better. That will keep the mortuaries busy. That's the American way." The final tally was six dead, twenty-three injured.

How do paranoid schizophrenics buy Lincoln Continentals? Ford didn't steal it. How do they get jobs? Ford trained to be a teacher and became a respected one. She even ran for school board. The answer, presumably, is that they are not loony every waking minute.

It was not until 1996 that Ford's condition caught up with her. The episodes of the next fourteen years make

Odysseus look like an accountant. In 1972 Ford and daughter, Wynter Scott, took up residence with Franklin Ford, one of two sons from her first marriage. During the Republican National Convention that year, Ford made Franklin and Wynter go with her down to Florida. She claimed she was scheduled to speak at the convention . . . on the revelations of Ellen G. White (a nineteenth-century prophetess of the Seventh-Day Adventist Church, in which Ford was raised). This came after she had tried to kill herself and trashed Franklin's Illinois home. He went! Security was not amused.

In 1973, Priscilla packed Wynter off to Reno. After three encounters with police, social services caseworkers took charge of Wynter until Ford could prove she had work and shelter for the child.

Ford proceeded to Chicago and wouldn't reestablish contact with her daughter until 1980, by which time Wynter was living with a half brother in Los Angeles. In the intervening seven years, Ford drifted. From Boise, Idaho, in 1978, she filed lawsuits against the Mormon Church and against Joe Califano's Department of Health, Education, and Welfare. In 1979, in Buffalo, she ended up at Buffalo Psychiatric Center, where the schizophrenia was first diagnosed. Then it was on to Maine, where she posed as a successful author.

But it was to retrieve Wynter and exact revenge that Ford returned to Reno in November of 1980. Of course, Ford knew Wynter was in L.A., by now a young woman of eighteen years. Being Jesus, and therefore incapable of wrongdoing, and in obedience to spoken instructions from Joan Kennedy, Ford tanked up . . . herself, cranked up the old Lincoln, and took her grievances to the sidewalks of Reno. It was the fulfillment of a long-held fantasy. She had described it in detail to the folks at Buffalo Psychiatric a couple of years before.

For additional details on Priscilla Joyce Ford, check out:
Kunel, Tom, and Einstein, Paul: *Ladies Who Kill*, New
   York, Pinnacle Books,1985, pp. 70–95.

NAME: LaFONDA FAY FOSTER
JURISDICTION: Kentucky
GENDER: Female
RACE: White
DATE OF BIRTH: 1962
PLACE OF BIRTH: Anderson, IN
ALIASES/NICKNAMES/MONIKERS:
MOTHER: Glenda Adams
FATHER: William T. Foster
YEARS OF SCHOOL: 9 (attempted GED)
OCCUPATION:
DISTINGUISHING MARKS:

Lexington, Kentucky, is the home of America's horse culture. It's not exactly the murder capital of the world. When the occasional unexplained body turns up, the cause of death can usually be assumed to have been accidental. The five people police found scattered all over the city on April 23, 1986, had been stabbed, shot, run over by a car, and in some cases burned. This didn't look like an accident.

It's known locally as the Carlos Kearns murder case, probably because most of the action seems to have occurred in and around Kearns's 1983 Chevrolet. Police answering a call discovered Kearns's car ablaze in a secluded area on the city's eastern outskirts. The bodies of three men were strewn all around the car, one pinned underneath. It wasn't long before the victims were identified as Kearns, who was seventy-one; Theodore Sweet, fifty-three; and Roger Keene, forty-seven. Kearns's wife, Virginia, forty-five, and their live-in housekeeper, Trudy Harrell, fifty-nine, had turned up in separate locations a few hours earlier.

Meanwhile our heroines, Lafonda Foster and Tina Powell, were collared by police at nearby Humana

Hospital on a totally separate call. They said they were trying to telephone for a cab. They were obviously, deliriously inebriated. Powell was carrying a "blood-drenched" knife in her pocket, and Foster resisted officers' attempts to take her into custody. This case was not going to require Sherlock Holmes.

What were three men in their middle years and past doing in the company of a couple of girls in their early twenties? That doesn't take a lot of brainpower either. Both LaFonda Fay and Tina had histories of prostitution and drug-and-alcohol abuse. All the victims had alcohol-related police records as well. The day of the murders, Kearns and company were reportedly driving Foster to the bank to cash a twenty-five-dollar check Kearns had given her. The trial accounts indicate the girls had been on a continuous four-day drinking/cocaine binge. The purpose of the twenty-five dollars was to prolong the fun.

It's not clear what happened. If this was money for sex, why were the two older women along? Had things gotten that kinky? Foster and Powell had a gun and a knife in their possession when they were apprehended. And Foster had been charged previously with kidnapping and robbery. Whether the gun appeared early on at the Kearns's apartment or later in the car on the way to the bank remains a matter of speculation. The coroner did determine that the women were killed first.

At the trial, Powell turned on Foster. Her lawyers were able to present a convincing case that Powell was a follower, and had gone along out of fear that Foster might hurt or kill her if she didn't. More than one jailhouse witness testified that Foster admitted her leadership role and even complained that Powell "wasn't capable of doing the work she felt they had got into." This strategy at least succeeded in keeping Powell off death row. As for Foster, her lawyers could do little more than enumerate a laundry list of mitigating factors—lesbian partnership, dysfunctional family life, borderline intellectual capability, abuse, sexual and otherwise—and appeal to the humanity of the jury, which was composed of eight women and four men.

Now, eight years later, Foster is still the only woman on Kentucky's death row. She is incarcerated at the Kentucky Correctional Institute for Women in Pee Wee Valley, near Louisville.

TRIAL SUMMARY:
Judge: James E. Keeler
Defense: Kevin McNally and Russell Baldwin
Beginning Date: November 3, 1986
Conviction: March 10, 1987
Sentencing: April 25, 1987

Name: KEITH TYRONE FUDGE
Jurisdiction: California
Gender: Male
Race: Black
Date of Birth: May 4, 1966
Place of Birth: Los Angeles, CA
Aliases/Nicknames/Monikers: Ace Capone
Mother: Peggy Sue Fudge
Father: not known
Years of School: 10–11
Occupation: Odd jobs; handyman
Distinguishing Marks:

Gang violence has been with us for a while now. Mafia hits date from the days of Capone, even before. The drive-by shooting, carried out by teenage toughs, is an innovation of very recent vintage, and no coverage of death row would be complete without an example.

South Central L.A. is the land of Rodney King, Watts, Bloods, and Crips—and what area birthday celebration would be complete without some drive-by fireworks and a few fatalities, compliments of a rival gang. Keith Tyrone Fudge, the protagonist in this particular drive-by, doesn't give us much to go on. L.A. street gang members don't talk much, except perhaps among themselves, and even then it's a staccato patter like a rap song and complicated handshakes denoting brotherhood and unity.

Those of us in the general populace will have to content ourselves with isolated bits and pieces. It was a very simple act: the perps pulled up in a car, got out, confronted their target on a sidewalk in front of the house where the party was occurring in the 800 block of West Fifty-fourth Street, and visited destruction upon everyone unlucky enough to be in the vicinity.

The motive seems to have been retaliation against Percy "Buddha" Brewer for stealing Fudge's car a few hours prior. The dead were Brewer, who was seventeen at the time; Shannon Cannon, fourteen; Daryl Coleman, seventeen; Philip Westbrook, eighteen; and Diane Rasberry, seventeen—all children by bourgeois standards, but given the dwindling life expectancy statistics of inner-city youth, they were approaching middle age.

Fudge didn't work alone. "Fat Fred" Knight, twenty, killed two of the victims. We know this because the piercing effect of Fudge's M-1 rifle contrasted with the carnage type of wound Knight produced with his shotgun blasts. Arrival and getaway were provided courtesy of Harold Hall, twenty.

Before Rodney King brought him national acclaim, Fudge and company provided a good photo op for L.A. police chief, Darryl Gates, and a good opportunity to spotlight the new get-tough CRASH program (Community Resources Against Street Hoodlums), whose personnel made the arrest. They apprehended Fudge in a raid on a "rock house," street slang for a fortified residence where crack is sold. "We will be seeking the death penalty," Gates vowed, but in the name of witness protection, he held back on further disclosures. Probably wise.

It took two trials for Gates to get his wish. Florence Bennett, the jury forewoman in the first one, could not bring herself to agree with her eleven cojurors. They deadlocked eleven to one in favor of convicting Fudge. Fellow juror Eliza Au, dismayed but not surprised, declared she knew that if they deadlocked, it would be because of Bennett. She seemed to be mining the evidence not for support of an objective decision, but for mitigating factors. Not to be thwarted, Deputy DA Patrick R. Dixon announced an immediate retrial, and by August 1987, new jury foreman Paul Taylor delivered the jury's decision for conviction and recommendation for the death penalty.

At his sentencing in December, the prisoner showed up in traditional jail togs, boldly accessorized with snappy red shoelaces. Those educated to street wear would immediately recognize these as a "Bloods" trademark. And when deputy probation officer Alexander Peace tried to penetrate Fudge's unrepentant hide, the youth retorted laconically, "My people told me not to talk to you. Adios." Well, adios to you, Mr. Fudge. The judge sentenced him to death on the eleventh day of December 1987.

TRIAL SUMMARY:
Judge: Ronald E. Cappai
Prosecutor: Deputy District Attorney Patrick R. Dixon
Defense: Gerald Lenoir
Conviction: August 27, 1987
Sentencing: December 11, 1987

Name: GERALD ARMAND GALLEGO
Jurisdiction: Nevada/California
Gender: Male
Race: White
Date of Birth: July 17, 1946
Place of Birth: Sacramento, CA
Aliases/Nicknames/Monikers: Sex Slave Killer
Mother:
Father: Gerald Albert Gallego
Years of School:
Occupation: Bartender
Distinguishing Marks:

Gerald Gallego cannot boast the greatest number of simultaneous death row assignments. That honor belongs to Alton Coleman, who's technically on death row in three states. Gallego has only two, Nevada and California, which puts him in the company of seven other death row prisoners. But Gallego has something no one else has. His father, Gerald Albert Gallego, lived on Mississippi's death row, and on March 5, 1955, was the first man to die in that state's gas chamber. The Gallegos are the closest thing we have to a "death row dynasty."

Gallego's forte was sexual assault and the murder of young women in their teens and early twenties. Charlene Williams-Gallego, his spouse at the time, aided him in his exploits. She also helped Gerry get to death row by turning state's evidence against him. Apparently, we have here yet another "killer couple," similar to Alton Coleman/Debra Denise Brown and Alvin and Judith Ann Neelley. These relationships resemble the typical pimp/prostitute arrangement, except instead of bringing back cash, the women procured sex partners as victims.

Gallego engaged in some extravagant sexual fantasies, but one of the problems with an active fantasy life is that reality doesn't always measure up. After his first abduction/rape/murder of Kippi Vaught, sixteen, and Rhonda Scheffler, seventeen, near Sacramento, he complained to Charlene that the girls were older than he had in mind. For her Reno encore, therefore, she would bring back fourteen-year-old Brenda Judd and thirteen-year-old Sandra Colley. They must have been more satisfactory. Gallego didn't complain this time. But this fantasy thing kept developing little twists, little subfantasies. The next pair the Gallegos picked up, back in Sacramento again, were both seventeen, so the rape part may have fallen short of expectations. However, Gallego added a flourish to the murder part by cracking the girls' heads with a hammer. For his next feats, Gallego demonstrated the awesome range of his abilities with two solo moves, first a twenty-one-year-old pregnant hitchhiker, followed by a working woman of thirty-four. Most impressive. For his grand finale, Gallego tackled the gender variable by zeroing in on an engaged couple, Craig Miller, twenty-one, and Mary Elizabeth Sowers, twenty-two, also in Sacramento.

That's ten, and that's where it ended. Someone had witnessed the last outrage and furnished police with the Gallegos's license plate number.

An unusual footnote to the Gallego story bears witness to society's contempt for the couple. California had tried the Gallegos first, but Nevada has a greater reputation for carrying out death sentences. Pershing County, where the Judd/Colley murders occurred, was chosen for the Nevada trials. But Pershing is very sparsely populated, so the expense of a capital trial represented a greater burden on its citizenry. In a macabre version of generosity, a columnist for one Sacramento paper called on interested Californians to send donations to Pershing. Californians responded to the tune of $26,000 to help with trial costs.

Name: CARLTON GARY

Jurisdiction: Georgia

Gender: Male

Race: Black

Date of Birth:

Place of Birth: Columbus, GA

Aliases/Nicknames/Monikers: Carl Michaels; the Stocking Strangler

Mother: Carolyn David

Father:

Years of School:

Occupation:

Distinguishing Marks:

Between September 1977 and April 1978, Columbus, Georgia, a small, complacent Deep-South city, was shocked into the twentieth century by a series of murders worthy of a Hollywood whodunit. Then, without explanation, as suddenly as it had started, the epidemic of death ceased. Who was this monster? What happened? Where'd he go? The case would remain a mystery for the next six years, until May 3, 1984, when an escapee from a South Carolina prison was arrested at an Albany, Georgia, motel.

All the murders fit a distinct pattern. In the dead of night, the perpetrator would enter the homes of middle-aged or elderly women who lived alone. The ages of the seven victims ranged from fifty-two to eighty-nine. He would rape the victim and then strangle her, usually with her own stocking. There were two exceptions: one strangling was done with a venetian blind cord, another with a scarf. The intruder would then pull the bedclothes over the deceased, burglarize the house, and make his escape.

Little Columbus went into twenty-four-hour panic

mode starting September 16, 1977, when sixty-year-old Ferne Jackson's body was discovered. No one knew until Carlton Gary's indictment years later that another assault victim, Ruth Schwob, had survived an attack just days before. Eight days after Jackson's death, retired Columbus retailer Jean Dimerstein, seventy-one, was found strangled the same way. Florence Schweible and Martha Thurmond followed during the first week in October. Then the Stocking Strangler took a sabbatical until December 29, when he murdered Kathleen Woodruff. Mildred Borom in February 1978 and Janet Cofer that April would round out the Stocking Strangler's dispensation of death. To compound the terror, he had pulled off the last few stranglings in the face of round-the-clock surveillance by law enforcement.

In time, the Wynnton Road section of east Columbus regained a modicum of normalcy, although the sense of security predating autumn 1977 was gone forever.

In May of 1984, Albany, Georgia, police apprehended a man at a local motel. He was wanted for questioning by Columbus authorities on a charge unrelated to the stranglings, Found in possession of a .38-caliber revolver, the man resisted arrest vigorously. He made a play for one of the officers' service pistols, but settled down when another leveled a machine gun at him.

Columbus detectives drove over to retrieve Carlton Gary and, on the return trip, say Michael Sellers and fellow cops, Gary talked them through a veritable diary of burglaries in Columbus's Wynnton Road section, including a reference to a .22 pistol he had liberated from one of the houses. Immediately noting the correspondence in time and place with the stocking stranglings, the detectives probed further. Ultimately, they felt they had enough information to charge Gary on three counts of capital murder.

Totally unprepared for such garrulousness, Sellers and fellow officers had to reconstruct Gary's account the next day from memory and minimal notes. This so-called confession, along with a lot of additional information on Gary's checkered past, became a contested issue in his August 1986 trial. Ultimately, although Gary was being tried for only three of the seven murders—Schweible, Thurmond, and Woodruff—Judge Followill permitted prosecutor Bill Smith to introduce testimony from Ruth Schwob, from Albany, New York, police, where the murder of Nellie Farmer fit the Stocking Strangler pattern, and details of the other four Columbus stranglings. Smith's objective was to establish the stocking strangler's MO, and to show patterns in the selection of victim and method of killing. Followill's consent to use all this information sealed Gary's fate. It allowed the prosecution to detail a life of criminal activity and a record of arrests in New York, Connecticut, South Carolina, and Georgia.

So, why the sudden cessation of activity at Wynnton Road after April 1978? Trial testimony revealed that prior to his escape, Gary had spent five of those years in a South Carolina prison for a robbery committed December 15, 1979.

Gary's trial is considered by many to be a relic of Jim Crow days. Because of the notoriety of the case, to "avoid bias," Judge Followill partially honored a defense motion for change of venue. Instead of Muscogee County, with its black population of 34 percent, the jury was selected from Spalding County, more rural and more white, with a 27 percent black constituency. The trial was still held in Muscogee.

TRIAL SUMMARY:

Judge: Kenneth Followill
Prosecutor: Bill Smith
Defense: August "Bud" Siemon III
Beginning Date: August 11, 1986
Conviction: August 26, 1986
Sentence: August 27, 1986

NAME: DAVID ALAN GORE
JURISDICTION: Florida
GENDER: Male
RACE: White
DATE OF BIRTH:
PLACE OF BIRTH:
ALIASES/NICKNAMES/MONIKERS:
MOTHER: Velma Gore
FATHER: Alva Gore
YEARS OF SCHOOL: 11
OCCUPATION: General labor
DISTINGUISHING MARKS:

Discuss among yourselves. I'll give you a topic: Good Old Boys. They are not particularly good, nor are they necessarily old, nor are they boys—except perhaps with regard to mental age. Case in point: Freddie Waterfield and David Gore are a couple of good old boys from Indian River County, Florida. When they were in their midtwenties, Freddie and David, mostly David, killed six women. That's not good. To better understand these characters, consider that a substantial part of David's defense involved positioning Freddie as the brains behind it all. He, David, was the gullible, too-easily-influenced follower type. Perhaps so. "Brains" Waterfield will only spend the rest of his life behind bars. Gore will be lucky to survive the publication of this book.

It could have been more. We know of five who got away, and their experiences say a lot about the MO of these "killing cousins." On June 23,1976, our boys fell in behind Diane Smalley on Highway 60 after she'd stopped for gas. A few miles down the road, they closed in and shot out her rear tires. Freddie had Diane captive in the backseat of his Chevy when fate sent her a car, an old couple who by sheer chance were traveling the same backroad. Diane eased up the lock, burst from the Chevy, and flagged them down. Miracle of miracles, they stopped. She jumped in and told them to haul ass. They did. Dave and Freddie burned that Chevy up trying to put some distance between themselves and the scene.

Dana Sturgis came from a pretty well-to-do background. One of the things the "haves" can do without fear of calamity is have their way with the law. When auxiliary deputy David Gore of the Indian River County Sheriff's Department pulled Sturgis over for speeding, and then told her she'd have to get in his squad car for a little trip down to the station, the teenager coolly instructed the dimwit deputy to follow *her* to the station, but she wasn't getting in his squad car. No way. A few feet down the road, Gore signaled her over again. He'd decided to let her off this time. Sturgis didn't let him off. She told Daddy and Daddy said call the sheriff, so she called her friend Tracey and Tracey's dad called Sheriff Dobeck. The sheriff gave Gore a choice: he could resign quietly or be fired publicly. Busted. It was the first and only time in his life Gore had felt a sense of importance. Of course, he abused the badge shamelessly, but what's a guy have to do? He's still working on that one.

If it had been a Cadillac, or if he were not the size of a rhinoceros, Gore might have gotten away with his next trick, but trying to conceal his fat, sweaty, smelly body in the back seat of Marilyn Owens's Nova was the final straw. Marilyn told deputy Bill Morgan about the foreign object in her car. He checked it out and they ended up nailing Gore with armed trespass. It cost him a few months at Belle Glade Correctional Center. More important, it shed some light on some unresolved missing persons cases in the area.

The abduction of Lynn Elliott and Robin Marks was

Gore's last venture. He'd been out of Belle Glade since November 1982. On July 26, 1983, David and Freddie picked up the two hitchhiking teens and spirited them to the "Gore compound" in Vero Beach. In the course of events, Elliott freed herself and made a mad dash—naked—for survival. Gore, also naked, caught her at the end of the driveway. He put two bullets in her head and loaded her in the trunk of his car. Michael Wayne Rock saw it all. Thirty minutes later, the place was swarming with cops. They got David. They picked up Freddie at his auto shop. Robin Marks was saved, although not unharmed. And that's when David told them about the others. Before Sturgis, Gore had defiled the Indian River County badge by using it to kidnap Hsiang Hua Ling and her daughter Ying Hua Ling, recent immigrants from Taiwan. He killed the mother and raped and killed Ying Hua. He told them about Judith Kay Daley. She was enjoying an afternoon on the beach, free of the kids. Gore popped her hood and pulled off her coil wire. He was there when her car wouldn't start. Give you a ride? Sure. Out to the orange groves, to the shack where the guys take their "dates" for a quick lay. Then he killed her. Angel Lavallee . . . picked her up hitchhiking with Barbie Byer. Shot them both in the head. Grave digging's hard work, even when you cut the bodies up into small pieces. Byers was little, but Lavallee was a bit hefty. She got thrown to the gators.

Gore did a lot of this on his own. They wanted death for Freddie, too, but didn't have enough on him. There's no way, though, that Florida justice was ever going to let Waterfield see light again. When you put all of Freddie's charges together—a little manslaughter here, a little kidnapping there—it adds up.

Cousins—played together all their lives. Freddie taught David about sex and women, about booze and drugs, and about rape and murder. Gore was an attentive, willing student. Only thing he ever was really good at. Together, they make the guys in *Deliverance* look like prep-school pranksters.

TRIAL SUMMARY:
Judge: L. B. "Buck" Vocelle
Prosecutor: Bob Stone
Defense: Jim Long; Ken Phillips
Jury: six women, six men
Beginning Date: March 6, 1984
Conviction: March 9, 1984
Sentence: March 10, 1984

For additional details on David Alan Gore, check out:
Ward, Bernie: *Innocent Prey,* New York, Pinnacle Books, 1994.

NAME: HARRISON GRAHAM
JURISDICTION: Pennsylvania
GENDER: Male
RACE: Black
DATE OF BIRTH: 1959
PLACE OF BIRTH:
ALIASES/NICKNAMES/MONIKERS: Marty
MOTHER: Lillie Graham
FATHER:
YEARS OF SCHOOL: 10
OCCUPATION: Handyman
DISTINGUISHING MARKS:

"I am Harrison Graham's mother. I have Harrison Graham. Come meet me at Eighth and Cecil B. Moore Avenue."

In compliance with that request, a 911 operator would dispatch a police wagon and, within two minutes, end the manhunt for the perpetrator of one of the City of Brotherly Love's most lurid serial murders. If Graham had not turned himself in, he might still be roaming the streets of north Philadelphia, under the noses of Philly police.

Something stinks about the Harrison Graham case, namely the six decomposing bodies discovered in his two-room, ninety-dollar-a-month, third-floor apartment at 1631 North Nineteenth Street on Sunday, August 10, 1987. Evicted just days before the unsettling revelation, Graham had nailed shut the door to an apartment known throughout the neighborhood as a "shooting gallery," a "bay station," a "hit house." Despite waist-high piles of garbage, old mattresses, and buckets of human waste, police could see well enough through the keyhole to confirm reports of bodies and parts of bodies decaying in the boiling Philadelphia summer heat. Authorities would spend the entire next week removing bodies, trying to positively identify the victims, and, more pressing, trying to locate "Marty" Graham.

Emotionally disabled, functionally illiterate, and drug-addicted, Graham, who one reporter described as having the physique of a tight end—six feet, 170 pounds—eluded detection until the following Sunday without straying far from his north Philly neighborhood. The Sunday after the corpses were found, Lillie Graham received a phone call from her distraught, demented son. He was confused and scared, and hadn't eaten in a week. She picked up three hot dogs, an orange soda, and a Tastykake, caught a train and then a bus, and met him on Cecil B. Moore Avenue.

"You see a stray dog? That's what he reminded me of," she remarked.

Graham told his mother he didn't see the bodies in the house. He told her they were already there when he moved in two and a half years ago. Mama told Marty to turn himself in, and tell the truth. Hence the 911 call. Graham confessed all the killings. They were all addicts. Graham supplied them with Ritalin and Talwin. He would trade drugs for sex, and one day during sex, he just started strangling them.

One was his girlfriend, Robin DeShazor, thirty. Her mother said she hadn't heard from Robin for three years. Mary Jeter Mathis was identified by a T-shirt her estranged husband had given her. It had a picture of a rose and the words *Pour toi* on it. Mathis's graduation picture was shown in the *Philadelphia Inquirer*, a beautiful black woman in cap and gown. She had even continued her education to become a licensed practical nurse, but the streets took her back. It makes you wonder what she looked like at thirty-six, ravaged by drugs. The other victims, all black women, were: Cynthia

Brooks, twenty-seven; Barbara Mahoney, twenty-two; Patricia Franklin, twenty-four; and Sandra Garvin, thirty-four.

Remains of a possible seventh body were found in an apartment building three doors down from 1613.

Psychologist Albert Levitt and psychiatrist Robert Stanton were directed to do an evaluation of Graham. They declared him incompetent to stand trial. There was a trial, though; just no jury. Judge Robert Latrone found Graham guilty and gave him multiple death sentences, but in a peculiar ruling, no doubt taking into account Graham's pathetic condition, he also gave him life for one of the murders, that sentence to be served first. The death sentences were to be invoked only in the event of commutation or parole.

TRIAL SUMMARY:
Judge: Robert A. Latrone
Defense: Joel Moldovsky
Conviction: April 27, 1988

NAME: GARY MICHAEL HEIDNIK
JURISDICTION: Pennsylvania
GENDER: Male
RACE: White
DATE OF BIRTH: 1944
PLACE OF BIRTH: Cleveland, OH
ALIASES/NICKNAMES/MONIKERS:
MOTHER: Ellen Rutledge
FATHER: Michael Heidnik
YEARS OF SCHOOL:
OCCUPATION: Minister
DISTINGUISHING MARKS:

One of the problems faced by the unusually intelligent is getting justice. Gary Heidnik has an IQ of 130, possibly higher. Where are you going to find a jury of his peers? He's in about the ninety-eighth percentile when it comes to intellect. He's also schizophrenic. Now how many schizophrenics were on his jury? There is no jury of Gary Heidnik's peers.

Let's face it. We don't know how to deal with a guy like Heidnik. Socrates drank his hemlock willingly. Heidnik just gave up on society. Psychiatrists said he had a need to exert authority—damn right. Is he supposed to take instructions from his intellectual inferiors? They also said, the believable ones, that he was insane. The court simply wouldn't allow that defense.

The experts pointed out how Heidnik surrounded himself with the "dregs of society"—retards, mental cases, prostitutes, people he'd met and befriended at the various institutions he'd been in over the years—twenty-one in all. When they arrested him, he had hundreds of thousands of dollars in a Merrill Lynch account, yet he lived in one of Philly's most downtrodden neighborhoods. He's still getting his two-thousand-dollars-a-month, 100 percent disability from the government. The prosecutor said the insane act was all a ruse, malingering so he could keep getting his pension.

Heidnik's plan was to set up a breeding station in his basement. It was more than a plan. He did it. He wanted children, and how he got them or who he got them with was of little consequence. Starting in November 26, 1986, Heidnik kidnapped six women, some prostitutes he picked up on the streets, some mentally handicapped acquaintances. They were, in order of capture: Josefina Rivera, Sandra Lindsay, Lisa Thomas, Deborah Dudley, Jacquelyn Askins, and Agnes Adams. The goal was to accumulate ten women so he could have ten babies. The health of these partners apparently was of no consequence to Heidnik either, which may explain why, in five months, not a single one conceived.

He bound their ankles and chained them to an overhead pipe in the dank, cold basement of his house at 3520 North Marshall Street. He kept them naked from the waist down. He fed them bread, water, crackers, dog food, human flesh, not much. He beat them with a shovel handle, and sometimes made them beat each other. If they "misbehaved," he administered extra punishment in the hole. Heidnik had broken the concrete floor and dug a shallow pit in the dirt underneath. He would cram one or more of his captives into the hole, pull sheets of plywood over it, and weigh it all down so they couldn't get out—dark, virtually airless, cramped, cold, dirty, isolated. In time, he refined the torture by filling the hole with water. The crowning touch was adding electricity. He would touch the live end of a lamp cord he'd plugged into a wall socket to something in or near the water. It conducted the current nicely. That's how Deborah Dudley died. Before that, Sandra Lindsay had succumbed. It happened one day when Heidnik got miffed because she wouldn't eat. He tried stuffing bread in her mouth. She died, either by choking or perhaps from the prolonged stress of the ordeal.

It was Lindsay's head he kept simmering in a pot upstairs. After her death, he had dismembered her. He froze part, cooked part, fed some to the dog, some to the other captives.

Remarkably, the same man who did all this was a savvy stock market investor. In 1971 he founded the United Church of the Ministers of God, with himself as bishop. The church had a charter, a constitution, services every Sunday, and most important, a tax exemption. The congregation consisted largely of the same circle of mentally and emotionally challenged individuals whose company Heidnik preferred. He never passed the collection plate. He often took them to McDonald's after Sunday services. What money the church did bring in, and money from his disability pension, he invested. Bishop Heidnik started off with $1,500 in 1975. At the time of his arrest, the church's account held in excess of a half million dollars.

Unbelievable. And that's just what Josefina Rivera's boyfriend told her when she approached him after a five-month disappearing act. Rivera had cultivated Heidnik's confidence. He took her out with him sometimes. He took her with him to dispose of Deborah Dudley's body. Docilely, she came back every time, except the last. On March 24, 1987, Rivera called police and blew the whistle on Gary Heidnik's fantasy world.

TRIAL SUMMARY:
Judge: Lynne Abraham
Prosecutor: Charles Gallagher

Defense: Charles Peruto
Beginning Date: June 20, 1988
Conviction: July 1, 1988
Sentence: July 2, 1988

For additional details on Gary Michael Heidnik, check out:

Englade, Ken: *Cellar of Horror,* New York, St. Martin's Press, 1988.

Name: JOSE MARTINEZ HIGH
Jurisdiction: Georgia
Gender: Male
Race: Black
Date of Birth:
Place of Birth:
Aliases/Nicknames/Monikers:
Mother: Father:
Years of School:
Occupation:
Distinguishing Marks:

They blew the head off a guy who'd survived
   the Battle of the Bulge—James C. Gray.

They killed an eleven-year-old child—
   Bonnie Phillips.

They raped and killed Willina Hall and threw
   her body in the Savannah River.

They killed Leroy Linwood.

Why? "Wrong place, wrong time," says Jose High.
Excuse me?
   José Martinez High wanted to be known as the black
Al Capone. Ruthless as he was, there was something to
Capone besides unadorned murder. Not so with High.
There's definitely something not right about this
dude—megalomania, delusions of grandeur, simple
hubris, evil incarnate—something. Law enforcement
officers in Richmond County, Georgia, freely acknowl-
edge that High is a charismatic, born leader. He could

get people to do things, difficult things, things they didn't really want to do, like making Bonnie Phillips lie down on the ground and then shooting him in the back of the head. That was High's shtick, getting people to commit heinous acts. That's how he controlled them. That's how he used his gift for leadership.

High recruited what he called a "family," a group of accomplices to do his bidding. When he was arrested in August 1976, three other guys went down with him: Nathan Brown, Judson Ruffin, and Alphonzo Morgan. It's additional testimony to his charisma that these three were twenty-one, twenty-three, and seventeen respectively. High was only seventeen himself, something that would become a factor in his death row status.

This must have been the Georgia chapter of "Death Struck," as High labeled his enterprise. Police found no evidence of membership beyond these four. High claimed chapters existed also in New Jersey and Philadelphia. National membership probably dropped off a bit when it was learned that the entire Georgia contingent, including its grand high poohbah, had its operations transferred to death row.

Although High claims his objective was to raise the general awareness that blacks had "arrived," so to speak, he didn't discriminate with regard to his victims. He and his group killed whoever was handy. Most of the victims were black. No apparent motive. Just the perverse pleasure of persuading others to commit random acts of unspeakable violence.

High considered it wrong to kill children, but they killed Phillips. They took Hall's life, but let Leon Clay's girlfriend go with just a rape. If there was any one factor that triggered a murder, it was "looking at him." What?

High wanted the whole world to know of his infamy. In one of his last acts of "leadership," he arranged for Richmond County authorities to make a videotape. It was to be in interview format, and he wanted it sent to *60 Minutes.* In it, High laid out his whole warped vision. It could even have been considered a confession of sorts, if not for its pathos, or amusement value, depending on your viewpoint.

Name: PAUL HILL
Jurisdiction: Florida
Gender: Male
Race: White
Date of Birth: 1954
Place of Birth:
Aliases/Nicknames/Monikers:
Mother:
Father:
Years of School:
Occupation: Auto paint detailer
Distinguishing Marks:

Paul Hill testifies to one of the most paradoxical issues of the late twentieth century: is it morally justifiable to kill in order to save the life of an unborn child? Hill says it is, and he has acted on his belief. By taking this stance, Hill also has to come down in favor of the death penalty, because essentially there is no difference between one private citizen executing another and the state doing it. A judge and a jury of Hill's peers decided that's to be his fate. If he does die in Florida's electric chair, Hill can take comfort in another of his beliefs—that dying this way makes him a martyr for his cause.

Heavy stuff. Theologians, leaders of organized religious groups, policy makers, everyone who reads or listens to the news is caught up in the debate.

The facts of Hill's case are very straightforward. At 7:30, Friday morning, July 29, 1994, he pulled from the grass outside a Pensacola abortion clinic the twelve-gauge shotgun he had concealed a few hours earlier. Stepping from behind an eight-foot fence next to the parking lot where abortion doctor John Bayard Britton had just pulled up with his security escort, James H. Barrett, Hill leveled the twelve-gauge and pumped three rounds into the windshield of the pickup. He retreated behind a tree, reloaded, and fired four times more. The bulletproof vest Britton wore as protection against zealots like Hill did him no good. Barrett, a retired air-force officer, was also slain. Mrs. June Barrett was hit but survived the injury to her left arm.

Who is Paul Hill? For one thing, he is a former Presbyterian minister. Not many of them on death row. He was not preaching at the time of the killings, though, because elders had excommunicated him from Trinity Presbyterian Church in Valparaiso, Florida, in June of 1993. Hill is a husband and the father of three children. Up to the time of the killings, he worked as an auto-body detailer. His views against abortion go back years. His belief in violence as a means is more recent, having originated in March 1993 with the slaying of Dr. Britton's predecessor, David Gunn, by Michael Griffin. Hill's advocacy of Griffin's actions won him considerable attention, and he had been interviewed on both *The Phil Donahue Show* and *Nightline.*

For weeks, Hill had been leafleting and demonstrating outside the Ladies Center Clinic in Pensacola. In spite of a citation for disorderly conduct, his tactics were becoming more and more extreme. Britton's death was destiny fulfilled.

Hill represented himself at his trial. The plan was to argue that his action was justifiable homicide, but the trial judge would not permit such a defense. It remains to be seen if appeals judges will show more leniency and give Hill a forum to air his ideology in detail. In the meantime, Paul Hill is the only man on death row for an act that stemmed from deeply held religious beliefs.

For additional details on Paul Hill, check out:

Gleick, Elizabeth: "Crossing the Line—Bad History Repeats Itself As a Second Florida Abortion Doctor Is Murdered," *People Weekly,* August 15, 1994, p. 60.

Vetter, Craig: "The Christian Soldier—A One-on-One Encounter with a Would-Be Martyr," *Playboy,* December 1994, p. 54.

NAME: ERIC CHRISTOPHER HOUSTON
JURISDICTION: California
GENDER: Male
RACE: White
DATE OF BIRTH: June 8, 1971
PLACE OF BIRTH:
ALIASES/NICKNAMES/MONIKERS:
MOTHER:
FATHER:
YEARS OF SCHOOL: 11
OCCUPATION: Computer assembler
DISTINGUISHING MARKS:

Spring 1992 . . . Was it a sign of inflation that Eric Christopher Houston swapped ten of his hostages for a pizza, or did he just lack negotiating skills? Trading another twenty-seven for two bottles of Advil makes more sense. Mass murder, hostage taking, and terrorism make for high-stress business, especially when you're only twenty and you're not real clear on why you're doing it.

Back in '89, Houston was busting his chops just to graduate from Lindhurst High School in Yuba County, California, but he flagged Mr. Brens's history class. Rather than repeat, he dropped out. He took a job as a computer assembler for a while, but he lost that, too, because he didn't have his diploma. He would have it, if not for Mr. Brens. Strike two.

Now out of work, Houston spent his unemployment check on ammunition. According to his sister, every payday, he'd buy bullets and go shooting. By 2:00 P.M., Friday, May 2, 1992, he'd had enough practice. At 2:15, attired in Vietnam-era fatigues and bandoliers, and carrying a twelve-gauge shotgun and a .22 rifle, it was time to move. He spent the next eight and one-half hours holed up in his old alma mater, wandering from class to class, firing indiscriminately at people who were ninth-graders or less when he was last there. Maybe he figured it was justifiable homicide. He had no prior record. He didn't utter a word.

Senior David Spade was one of the first Houston encountered as he entered the school. When Houston put the shotgun to his head, Spade got one with Jesus pronto and requested, respectfully, that Houston not blow him away. Prayer works. Other students adapted skills designed for earthquake emergencies: scrunch up very small underneath your desk.

The outcome was not too good. Damage control seems to have had less to do with the administration's emergency plans and more to do with the natural human impulse for self-preservation. But four did not make it: Robert J. Brens, twenty-eight, Houston's former history teacher; Judy Davis, seventeen; Beamon Anton Hill, sixteen; Jason Edward White, nineteen. Ten more suffered injuries from the gunplay. It wasn't Oklahoma City, but try to imagine the scene—a school of 1,200 students and a gunman you know is there but you're not sure where.

Sheriff Gary Tindel established phone contact around 5:00 P.M. First, Houston wanted a TV. They let him have it, but requested Sacramento TV stations to forgo coverage. The stations complied. Then there was the pizza trade, and the Advil. By 10:30 police negotiators had Houston, his guns, and his ammo, and Houston had a date with death row.

NAME: RANDY STEVEN KRAFT
JURISDICTION: California
GENDER: Male
RACE: White
DATE OF BIRTH: March 19, 1945
PLACE OF BIRTH: Long Beach, CA
ALIASES/NICKNAMES/MONIKERS:
MOTHER: Opal Lee Kraft
FATHER: Harold H. Kraft
YEARS OF SCHOOL: 16
OCCUPATION: Computer analyst
DISTINGUISHING MARKS:

Kraft . . . good name for the man believed to be the most prolific serial killer on record. Randy Kraft was the consummate gamesman. Unlike Ted Bundy, whose trail of murder took him all over the country, Kraft, for the most part, kept it close to home. William Bonin, the Freeway Killer, worked the same territory, but he had the help of a team of accomplices. Kraft worked alone. The killing success of slimy, drug-addicted Richard Ramirez depended largely on luck. Kraft was careful, methodical, calculating. Even the body count of John Wayne Gacy, who buried thirty-some-odd young men in the crawl space of his Illinois home, cannot compare to Kraft. Authorities think the Southern California computer analyst killed more than sixty-five men. And while a guy like Henry Lee Lucas would lay claim, falsely, to murdering hundreds, Kraft has never admitted to a single killing, not even the marine they found in his car the night they caught him.

Kraft is one of the first of what could be called a new generation of murderers. The seventies ushered in the era of the serial killer, and of murderers who grew up in what appears to have been enviable middle-class conditions. Kraft enjoyed the classic nuclear family experience: three older sisters, parents who never divorced, a father well employed. Beaver Cleaver and Rick Nelson had nothing on Randy Kraft. Kraft excelled all through school and demonstrated respectable athletic ability. He graduated high in his class and went on to four years of college. He did a stint in the air force and forged a successful niche in the corporate world. Perhaps the only noteworthy exception was that Kraft was gay and was coming to terms with that before the homosexual lifestyle gained any level of legitimacy. The sixties was a time when homosexuality was lumped together with an array of novel sexual practices branded collectively as perversion. If ever there was anyone who could be considered the embodiment of Emile Durkheim's *anomie*, it was Randy Kraft.

Kraft gave new meaning to the expression *great sex*. For him, the ultimate sexual escapade was one in which his partner ended up dead. He was not above mutilation, although there is no indication Kraft enjoyed the kind of animalistic torture on live victims that distinguishes a Lawrence Bittaker.

Also characteristic of an age of anomie, Kraft specialized. His victim of choice was either a military man or a hitchhiker. A significant percentage of his murder victims came from Fort Pendleton Marine Base, near San Clemente, California.

The ten-woman, two-man jury nailed Kraft with sixteen murder convictions. Kraft's "murder log" contains sixty-one entries, a few of them doubles. Law enforcement officials can convincingly link him to forty murder cases. But in spite of his awesome carnage, there is a quality that separates Kraft from the other personalities profiled in this volume. He was detached, unemotional, and elusive, a thinking man's killer, a fit subject for an Agatha Christie mystery or an episode of TV series *Murder She Wrote*. He is not the model for Hannibal Lechter, but *The Silence of the Lambs* killer had nothing on Randy Kraft.

For additional details on Randy Kraft, check out:

McDougal, Dennis: *Angel of Darkness*, New York, Warner Books, 1991.

NAME: HENRY LEE LUCAS
JURISDICTION: Texas/Florida
GENDER: Male
RACE: White
DATE OF BIRTH: August 23, 1936
PLACE OF BIRTH: Blacksburg, VA
ALIASES/NICKNAMES/MONIKERS:
MOTHER: Viola Lucas
FATHER:
YEARS OF SCHOOL:
OCCUPATION: Roofer; general labor
DISTINGUISHING MARKS: weak left eye

It's hard to hate Henry Lee Lucas. That's not to say we shouldn't hate what he did, but what did he do? For one thing, he lied big time. Henry Lee didn't kill all those people. It's difficult not to feel a certain admiration for a guy who was able to dupe the very state that has elevated exaggeration to an art form.

The beginning of the end for Lucas came on September 16, 1982, with the discovery of the disappearance of Kate Pearl Rich of Ringgold, Texas. A few months before her presumed death, Henry and his "common-law wife," fifteen-year-old Frieda Powell, had been helping Ms. Rich around the house in exchange for room and board. They were introduced to her by Ms. Rich's nephew, Jack Smart, of Hernet, California, who had picked them up hitchhiking.

Few of the other murders Henry Lee confessed to can be pinned on him. Given his cavalier disregard for fact, Lucas's word turned out to be virtually worthless in attempting to solve some of the nation's unsolved killings. One murder we know he committed happened in Tecumseh, Michigan. In 1960, Henry Lee stabbed to death his seventy-four-year-old mother in a bar. For that, he served fifteen years of a twenty-to-forty year sentence in a Michigan prison.

Henry Lee was living in a chicken house in Stoneburg, Texas, when he was apprehended. He had taken up with a group of fundamentalist Christians called the House of Prayer for All People. The group had converted an abandoned chicken brooder building into living quarters. A loner and a drifter, Lucas naturally gravitated to this bizarre setting on the outskirts of a hamlet of four hundred. Although Henry's behavior gave them the creeps, the folks at the House of Prayer felt it their Christian duty to allow him this refuge. Mrs. Faye Munnerlyn began to suspect foul play when Henry left with Powell one day and returned a few days later without her. Powell's body was later found dismembered and scattered over a field a few counties away.

Montague County sheriff, W. F. "Bill" Conway, had suspected Henry of killing Ms. Rich. He had been stalking him for nine months. When Conway and the Texas Rangers caught up with him, it was on a gun charge, a violation of his parole. But while he was in jail, Henry told them he had killed a hundred women. As the media hype built, Lucas's confession grew proportionately outrageous. At one point he is reported to have slain six hundred, and the Texas authorities and media constructed elaborate charts, maps, and time lines in an attempt to confirm his assertions. In the end it turned out to be one of the most celebrated hoaxes in U.S. history. Lucas can be tied to no more than three or four murders.

Ultimately, they found Kate Rich's charred remains in an old woodstove behind Lucas's makeshift living quarters.

TRIAL SUMMARY:

Judge: Frank Douthitt

Prosecutor: Jack McGaughey

Defense: Donald Maxfield

Beginning Date: September 13, 1983

Conviction: April 1984

Appeals: March 1995, Texas Court of Criminal Appeals sent Lucas's case back to trial court just hours before his scheduled execution

For additional details on Henry Lee Lucas, check out:

Cox, Mike: *The Confessions of Henry Lee Lucas,* New York, Pocket Star Books, 1991.

Norris, Joel: *Henry Lee Lucas,* New York, Zebra Books, 1991.

NAME: JEFFREY DON LUNDGREN
JURISDICTION: Ohio
GENDER: Male
RACE: White
DATE OF BIRTH: May 3, 1950
PLACE OF BIRTH: Independence, MO
ALIASES/NICKNAMES/MONIKERS:
MOTHER: Lois (Gadberry) Lundgren
FATHER: Don Lundgren
YEARS OF SCHOOL: 13–14
OCCUPATION: Minister
DISTINGUISHING MARKS:

The crime that put Jeffrey Lundgren on Ohio's death row
was masterminding the extermination of the family of one
of his followers. There was nothing very exceptional in
how the murders were carried out. With the help of other
followers, Lundgren shot Dennis Avery, forty-nine, his
wife Cheryl, forty-two, and their three daughters, Trina,
fifteen, Rebecca, thirteen, and Karen, seven, and buried
them in a mass grave in the barn of a farm the group was
renting.

What's remarkable about the so-called Kirtland
Massacre is the cultish group dynamic Jeff and Alice
Lundgren achieved and the perseverance of group members in their misguided loyalty long after Lundgren's
behavior had obviously lapsed into deviancy.

Lundgren just doesn't fit the description of a cult
leader. Although the Church of Jesus Christ of the
Latter Day Saints (the Mormons) is the fastest-growing
denomination in the nation today, few Americans
know much about the group and many Mormon doctrines are still poorly understood. Lundgren's small following was a splinter of the Reorganized Latter Day
Saints (RLDS), which in turn was a splinter of Joseph

Smith and Brigham Young's original Mormon Church. Lundgren's split occurred over some very fine points of church doctrine, but once he had a following, he gradually insinuated himself into a con game in which he and his wife were in full control and exploited the labor, loyalty, bank accounts, and even the bodies of their flock.

The justification for the eradication of the Averys, lame as it was, was a religious one. Between early 1985 and April 17, 1989, when the murders took place, Lundgren slowly but steadfastly introduced, cultivated, and spread the idea among his followers that they were destined to inherit the RLDS temple in Kirtland, Ohio, a "righteous" undertaking, since church leaders had departed from the true course. Prepared to use force, Lundgren amassed a small arsenal and put his male followers through military maneuvers. For the venture to succeed, it was necessary for the group to be sinless. None of them could enter the kingdom of God as long as any member lived in a state of sin. If necessary, they would have to purge their own ranks. It was Lundgren's arbitrary determination that the Averys were sinners and that some kind of blood sacrifice had to take place. Basically, he just didn't like them.

This message was communicated both formally, through frequent—and lengthy—classes Lungren taught, and casually through everyday conversations with members. Lundgren ensured allegiance by a combination of brainwashing, humiliation, intellectual dominance, and outright terror tactics. Of course, he only recruited people who were vulnerable to these kinds of tactics in the first place.

The following short chronology shows how Lundgren's warped world unraveled during the latter part of 1989, culminating in his arrest in January 1990:

April 17, 1989	The night the Averys were murdered.
April 18, 1989	By sheer coincidence, FBI agents, concerned for months that something was up with the Lundgren group, showed up in force and questioned almost everyone in the group. They didn't know that the Averys were dead.
April 20, 1989	Lundgren and company departed Kirtland. Everyone moved to the "wilderness" of West Virginia, near Wheeling.
September 1989	Inclement weather, a shortage of supplies, and police pressure led to dissension within the group. Jeff sent Alice and his children to Mack's Creek, Missouri.
October 13, 1989	The remaining contingent broke camp and moved to Chilhowee, Missouri. Two key group members jumped ship.
December 1989	Lundgren, his family, and group member Danny Kraft moved to a suburb outside San Diego.
December 31, 1989	Conscience-stricken, and enraged over Lundgren's expropriation of his wife, group member Keith Johnson contacted authorities and told all.
January 3, 1990	Local, state, and federal authorities excavated the alleged

	gravesite and found the five bodies, just as Johnson had told them.
January 7, 1990	Agent Richard Van Haelst of the Bureau of Alcohol, Tobacco and Firearms arrested Jeffrey Don Lundgren, Alice, and their son Damon at a motel in San Diego.

For additional details on Jeffrey Don Lundgren, check out:
Sasse, Cynthia Stalter, and Widder, Peggy Murphy: *The Kirtland Massacre,* New York, Zebra Books, 1991.

NAME: JAMES GREGORY MARLOW
JURISDICTION: California
GENDER: Male
RACE: White
DATE OF BIRTH: May 11, 1956
PLACE OF BIRTH: Cincinnati, OH
ALIASES/NICKNAMES/MONIKERS: The Folsom Wolf
MOTHER: Doris (Walls) Marlow
FATHER: Jeffrey Marlow
YEARS OF SCHOOL: 10
OCCUPATION: General labor
DISTINGUISHING MARKS: A "crouched" wolf on his
   side; a flaming swastika on his chest; bearded
   Vikings on both shoulders; a skull on the left
   shoulder; portrait on right forearm; the name of
   one of his ex-wives on his penis; various and
   sundry other decorations.

Most of the coverage of James Gregory Marlow focuses on
his sidekick, Cynthia Coffman, the first woman sentenced
to death in California in the post-Furman era. Certainly
the story of a typical suburban St. Louis girl run amok is
captivating, but Marlow's entire upbringing adds up to
one big mitigating factor.

The conditions in which Marlow grew up were so
squalid, so bizarre, you wonder how he managed to
survive. His mother, Doris, inclined toward the "high
life," and very early on grew contemptuous of her
small-town beginnings in eastern Kentucky's
Appalachian region. She split with Jeffrey Marlow
when Greg was two. She would absent herself for
weeks at a stretch and leave Greg and his sister with
whomever she could sucker into keeping them.
Marlow, therefore, had no consistent home or family
life, bouncing from relative to relative and later from

foster home to foster home. In February 1963, just four months after Doris's uncle had persuaded Jeffrey Marlow and his second wife to take Greg into their home in Vermilion, Ohio, Mom kidnapped him from his new school and brought him back to Stearns. By May, she was restless again. She stole the wheels off her estranged second husband, Donald Bender's car, transferred them to her car, and the whole Walls family hightailed it to Los Angeles. Doris quickly developed an addiction to heroin and prostituted herself to support it. According to reports from acquaintances, when Greg was thirteen, she initiated an incestuous relationship with him. She also shared her needle with him, and she and her addict friends put him to work stealing for them. It's common practice in cases like this to cite examples of people who rose above hard times or negative influences. But when you start looking for positive handles Greg Marlow could have grasped during the formative years of his life, you won't find enough to count.

Marlow's rap sheet, therefore, reads like an encyclopedia of crime. A dependency case by 1969, Marlow was made a ward of the court. At fifteen, he's listed as a runaway. At sixteen, authorities nailed him for possession of "dangerous drugs for sale." At seventeen, Marlow was booked for petty theft; eighteen, under the influence; nineteen, violation of probation and grand theft. During his twenties, add weapons possession, armed robbery, and kidnapping.

Marlow linked up with Coffman on April 11, 1986. He'd learned about her from Sam Keam, who was sharing a cell with him in a Barstow, California, jail. Coffman was Keam's girlfriend. She was released on the ninth, Marlow on the tenth. He decided to pay this feisty young thang a call. She was intrigued, but soon had to follow Keam, who was extradited to Arizona to straighten out a child-support issue. Back in Barstow about a week later, they looked up Marlow. There was a drug deal. Keam was slow holding up his end. Marlow put him in his place. Cynthia liked that. She dropped Sam and took up with Marlow. By June, their crime spree had commenced, and for practice they would perform the contract snuffing of Greg "Wildman" Hill in Marlow's hometown of Pine Knot, Kentucky.

The killings that put Marlow and Coffman on California's death row occurred in November 1986. On November 7, they abducted Corinna Novis from Redlands Mall in Redlands, California, transported her to the apartment of an acquaintance of Marlow's, robbed and sodomized her, then drove to a nearby vineyard, where she was strangled and buried in a shallow grave. Five days later, they pulled a similar stunt, kidnapping Lynel Murray from her workplace, Prime Cleaners, in Huntington Beach. They took Murray at gunpoint to Huntington Beach Inn, stripped, bound, sodomized, strangled, and then drowned her. Marlow reputedly urinated on the girl's body. This one they just left lying in the tub.

Habitually strung out on methamphetamine, the pair didn't get far into their escape. Two days after Murray's discovery, they were picked up in Big Bear. In subfreezing temperatures, Marlow was wearing a dress shirt, combat boots, and swimming trunks. Coffman had on a bikini and a big sweater. Speed must possess some wondrous warming effects. Of course, when it wears off and you find yourself wandering half-naked in a national forest, the collision with reality has to be a bit depressing.

In custody, for a while, "Wolf" and "Cynful" wrote torrid, X-rated love letters back and forth. At trial, however, the lovebirds turned on each other. If the only alternative to a death sentence is life without parole, amorous considerations can take a backseat to the practical matter of staying alive. Coffman won the battle for sympathy. She received only one death sentence for her role in Novis's murder. She got life for Murray's. Marlow was sentenced to death in both cases.

TRIAL SUMMARY:
Judge: Don Turner
Prosecutor: Chip Haight
Defense: Ray L. Craig; Cheryl Andre
Beginning Date: October 31, 1988
Sentence: June 29,1989

For additional details on James Gregory Marlow, check out:
Lasseter, Don: *Property of the Folsom Wolf,* New York, Pinnacle Books, 1995.

NAME: KENNETH ALLEN MCDUFF
JURISDICTION: Texas
GENDER: Male
RACE: White
DATE OF BIRTH: March 21, 1946
PLACE OF BIRTH: Bell County, TX
ALIASES/NICKNAMES/MONIKERS:
MOTHER: Addie McDuff
FATHER:
YEARS OF SCHOOL: 9 (GED)
OCCUPATION: Machine operator
DISTINGUISHING MARKS:

It's not that unusual for murderers to find themselves with more than one death sentence. Prosecutors often want to make sure if one's overturned, they have backup. Some killers find themselves facing the ultimate penalty in more than one state. Some get sentenced to death and then win a new trial, only to be sentenced to death again. Kenneth McDuff is probably by himself in getting death, having his sentence commuted to life when Furman came down, being paroled, and getting death again for a whole different set of crimes. Released in 1990, he was back on death row by 1993.

McDuff's parole was both the cause and the effect of some high-level political maneuvering. He even has a law named after him—the McDuff Rule—according to which twelve of Texas's eighteen parole board members must agree in order for a capital murderer to be freed. When McDuff received parole, the chairman of the parole board at the time got investigated by the feds on possible influence peddling. The case ultimately led Chairman James Granberry to resign from the board.

It was multiple homicide, with a splash of rape, that

earned McDuff his first death sentence back in 1966.
He killed three Fort Worth teenagers: Edna Sullivan,
sixteen; Robert Brand, seventeen; and Mark Dunnam,
sixteen. McDuff's apprenticeship in violent crime dates
from his school days, which means early, since he only
spent nine years in school. In 1964, at age eighteen, he
was already serving time for burglary. On August 6,
1966, he and buddy Roy Dale Green approached the
three kids at a local ball field in Everman, near Fort
Worth. McDuff had taken a shine to Sullivan. She was
Brand's girlfriend; Dunnam was Brand's cousin.
McDuff flashed a .38 and robbed them, intimidated
them into the trunk of Brand's '55 Ford, and drove out
into the country. There, he transferred the girl to his
car and eliminated Brand and Dunnam with head
shots. A few miles later, he stopped again, dragged
Sullivan from the trunk, raped her, turned her over to
Green, who raped her again. McDuff then killed her
and tossed the body over a fence as if it were some
kind of empty potato chip bag. Disposable people.
Green panicked and told police the next day. Convicted
in 1968 and condemned to die, McDuff beat the reaper
twice, getting two stays during the four years of his
first death sentence. *Furman* v. *Georgia* negated the
Texas capital punishment statute, resulting in a commutation for McDuff and every other death row prisoner in the nation.

Now facing a life sentence, McDuff had a shot at
parole. Of a parole board of only three members, one
already favored letting him out. McDuff's lawyer, Gary
Jackson, kept lobbying James Granberry until he finally
relented and cast the deciding vote to release McDuff,
who had recently had his sentence extended for
attempting to bribe a parole board member.

Let out in December 1990, McDuff managed to
avoid incarceration for a little more than a year. But in

that span, he killed at least three, and probably four, women. He was a prime suspect in three more, and a definite possible in still others, which brings his body count to nine, give or take a couple. Formally charged with the murders of Melissa Northrup, twenty-two, a convenience store clerk; Valencia Kay Joshua, a prostitute from Waco; and Colleen Reed, a twenty-eight-year-old auditor from Austin, he was tried only for Northrup's. He is believed also to have been responsible for the deaths of two other Waco prostitutes, Regina Moore and Brenda Thompson, and several women in the Temple, Texas, vicinity, including Sarafia Parker.

A May '92 segment of *America's Most Wanted* led to McDuff's arrest in Kansas City, Missouri, within three days. He was working on a garbage truck. His second death sentence was handed down in February 1993, just a few months shy of the twenty-fifth anniversary of the first.

Name: ROBERT HENRY MOORMANN
Jurisdiction: Arizona
Gender: Male
Race: White
Date of Birth: June 4, 1948
Place of Birth: Tucson, AZ
Aliases/Nicknames/Monikers:
Mother: Maude Moormann *
Father: Henry Moormann *
Years of School: 12 (GED 1967)
Occupation:
Distinguishing Marks:

* Adoptive: Birth mother died soon after his birth. Birth father gave baby to his parents, who were abusive, so he was put up for adoption at age two.

This is a story about a boy and his mom. Unable, because of a miscarriage, to bear children, Maude Moormann loved her adopted son, Henry. To say she was doting would be an understatement. He could do no wrong. She gave him everything a mother can give, except the chance to develop his own moral compass and take responsibility for his actions.

You have to put your faith in the power of a nurturing environment on the back burner when you're dealing with Henry Moormann. If ever there was a person born to lose, it was he. His birth mother drowned before he was a year old. His father turned custody over to Henry's paternal grandparents, but they lost custody to the state because of abuse. Seven foster homes later, at age two, Henry and Maude found each other. At one point, Henry was thrown through the windshield of a car. His eyes were weak. He was overweight. Maude almost blinded him—accidentally—in the fourth grade.

The school did not exist that he could not flunk out of. He was a liar, a runaway, and a molester. That's what landed him at Valley of the Sun Boarding School for troubled boys when he was thirteen. Home for the holidays, Henry shot Maude in the stomach with a .22. She explained it away as an accident.

Back to Sun Valley, then on to Fort Grant juvenile correctional facility. Finally, at the end of a five-year interlude of Mellaril and minimum wage jobs, Moormann did the dirty deed that would get him some real hard time. In a loser's rendition of *Lolita*, he abducted the eight-year-old daughter of a friend of Maude's and, on a two-day romp through Arizona, molested her in cheap motels in Flagstaff, Ash Ford, and Meadview. He left his mother's Malibu stuck in the mud, and they were on their way to Las Vegas—to get married, he told the girl—when the odyssey finished unraveling. In custody, Moormann was tried, convicted, and sent to Arizona State Prison in Florence.

Now fast-forward seven years. Moormann has won himself a three-day pass for good behavior. Maude, now seventy-four, is on a Greyhound bus to Florence to pay Henry one last visit before she moves back to her home state of Oklahoma. She picks him up at the prison gate and they go back to a room she's taken at the Blue Mist Motel, literally across the road from the prison. They talk. Henry wants her to will him her estate. She insists instead on a trust. He smothers her with a pillow. That's day one.

Now it begins to get bizarre. On day two, Henry bought a buck knife, a box of garbage bags, and some cleaning supplies at a nearby Circle K. He carved up his mother into twelve manageable pieces and wrapped them into tidy packages that he then distributed in Dumpsters around Florence. If Moormann hadn't been so polite, he might have succeeded in his elaborate subterfuge. He asked permission to put some cow guts in the trash bin of George Johnson's pizza parlor. This created a bit of suspicion, but police officers following up found nothing noteworthy. He must have filleted her, because he gave her bones to corrections lieutenant Luther Dammon to feed to the prison dogs. The cow guts, the human body parts found among the dog bones, and Maude's rather conspicuous absence aroused police attention. Booked on murder charges, Henry threw in the towel on the way to the precinct and confessed all.

TRIAL SUMMARY:
Judge: Richard N. Roylston
Prosecutor: W. Allen Stooks
Defense: Tom Kelly
Beginning Date: March 26, 1985
Conviction: April 4, 1985
Sentencing: May 7, 1985

NAME: PERVIS TYRONE PAYNE
JURISDICTION: Tennessee
GENDER: Male
RACE: Black
DATE OF BIRTH:
PLACE OF BIRTH: Munford, TN
ALIASES/NICKNAMES/MONIKERS:
MOTHER: Bernice Payne
FATHER: Carl Payne
YEARS OF SCHOOL: 11
OCCUPATION: Painter, carpenter's helper
DISTINGUISHING MARKS:

You drive south down Highway 51 through the rolling fields of cotton and soybeans, through little country towns like Halls, Ripley, and Covington. At a light about twenty miles this side of Memphis, at the sign that says *Munford*, you turn right. You're headed straight for the Mississippi River, about five miles away. The summer heat is stifling. Another mile down the road, you hit Main Street, Munford. Take a right, then the next left, and three more miles gets you to Drummonds. Pervis Payne's mother and father still live in the modest, well-kept brick house where their son grew up. From here, if you know the back roads, you can cover the twelve miles to Millington in about fifteen minutes. That's where it all happened.

It's hard to imagine that violence would enter the mind of someone raised in such a slow-paced bucolic setting. And that's just it; not a lot of thought went into the bloody crime attributed to Pervis Payne. Was it cocaine? Police say they found some cocaine residue on a little slip of paper in Pervis's pocket when they caught him, and a wadded up sack from Boatright's Drugstore with an empty hypodermic case inside.

Pervis knew Charisse Christopher. She lived right

across the hall from Bobbi Thomas, his girlfriend. White woman, black man, the possibility of drugs— leniency would not come easy in this law-abiding Southern town. Forget acquittal.

She'd been stabbed eighty-four times, forty-two of them defensive wounds. Her little girl, Lacie Jo, only two, had been stabbed to death, too. They found some skin tissue and Type A blood under the fingernails of Christopher's right hand. That was Payne's blood type, and he had scratch marks on his shoulder. They found his fingerprints on the phone, and on a glass in the kitchen, and on the drawer the butcher knife was taken from.

The story that surfaced during the trial has Payne leaving Drummonds early in the day of June 27, 1987. His buddy, Sylvester Robinson, drove him into Millington to make a withdrawal from the bank. They stopped by Bobbi Thomas's, but she still hadn't returned from a trip to visit family in Arkansas. A couple of other people were there, though. Payne made a deposit for Ray Sparks, one of the two, and brought back the receipt.

Thomas still not back. Payne and Robinson returned to Drummonds. Pervis packed some clothes, went by his aunt's to pay back some money he had borrowed, looked for a friend, but couldn't find him. Sylvester drove him back to Millington. They made several more trips to Thomas's. No luck. Finally, Robinson gave up and went home, leaving Payne in Millington.

Payne says he went once more to the Hiwassee Apartments, looking for Thomas. He'd left his bag outside her door. He thought he heard someone crying for help inside the apartment across the hall. He let himself in. He found Christopher and her two kids bleeding on the floor. He pulled a large butcher knife from Christopher's neck. That's how he got all that blood on his pants. He started to phone for help, but then he saw a police cruiser pull up into the parking lot. He panicked and left. The reason he ran when he encountered Officer C. E. Owens on the steps going down was because he was scared the police wouldn't believe him. All things considered, that's a reasonable assumption, and an understandable response.

Christopher's son, three-year-old Nicholas, was the lucky one—or maybe not. He'd been cut to ribbons, too. They rushed him to the hospital and got him stabilized. He spent weeks at Le Bonheur Children's Medical Center in Memphis fighting for his life. He was still recovering seven months later when Payne's trial began in Division 1 of the Criminal Court in Memphis. Nicholas couldn't testify, but prosecutors put him at the center of what was to become a landmark decision in the U.S. Supreme Court. Victims have rights, too, they said, and in an emotion-laden argument for the death penalty, they laid out in graphic detail how Nicholas would carry his scars for the rest of his life, how he would never again receive the hugs and affection of a loving mother. This was new stuff. The defense objected vehemently, but Judge Bernie Weinman allowed it, the jury found Payne guilty and sentenced him to death on February 24, 1988, and in a reversal of *Booth* v. *Maryland* (1987) and *South Carolina* v. *Gathers* (1989), the Supreme Court upheld the decision on June 27, 1991.

TRIAL SUMMARY:

Judge: Bernie Weinman

Prosecutor: Thomas Henderson; Phyllis Gardner

Defense: James Garts

Beginning Date: February 8, 1988

Conviction: February 16, 1988

Sentencing: February 24, 1988

Appeals: June 27, 1991—U.S. Supreme Court upheld conviction

NAME: CLEOPHUS PRINCE, JR.

JURISDICTION: California

GENDER: Male

RACE: Black

DATE OF BIRTH: July 24, 1967

PLACE OF BIRTH:

ALIASES/NICKNAMES/MONIKERS: "Little Pie"; Rodney
  Higgs; Cleophus Brown; The Claremont Killer

MOTHER: Dorothy Prince

FATHER: Cleophus Prince, Sr.

YEARS OF SCHOOL: 12

OCCUPATION:

DISTINGUISHING MARKS:

Jackie Robinson, first black man in the major leagues;
Jesse Jackson, first black man to run for president;
Cleophus Prince, first black man to go against the stereo-
type that serial killers don't kill outside their race. The
fact that Prince's six victims were all white was a compli-
cating factor in the investigation. Given what we know
about serial murder and its perpetrators, police were not
looking for a black male.

Prince liked his women fit and he liked them clean.
He also liked them dead. It was his habit to stalk his
victims from a local health club or an apartment complex pool back to their homes. He had a sixth sense for
which ones would head immediately for the shower
and capitalized on that knowledge. The noise from the
running water and the womblike feeling of warmth and
security one gets when showering gave Prince the window of opportunity he needed to slip a door lock with
a credit card and get familiar with the kitchen cutlery.
His pattern was to stab his victims multiple times in
the breasts. He liked a long, sweeping thrust, and he
liked to position the corpses on their backs, with the

arms and legs just so, very meticulous. He never raped; well, once he did. Maybe there was some kind of sexual release associated with those sweeping knife thrusts. One victim had fifty stab wounds. That doesn't sound like your run-of-the-mill passion killing.

Named after the California town where the murders were occurring, the Claremont Killer made it very difficult for police to obtain leads. It was that one little indiscretion, that one rape of Janene Weinhold, that did Prince in. They nailed him with DNA "fingerprinting." DNA evidence is controversial, and, in fact, the prosecution was forced to dilute its own findings because of a slipup in the Prince case. But in this case, the DNA check was used mainly to pinpoint the suspect, after which additional evidence surfaced. Most incriminating were rings belonging to two of the victims, one found in the possession of Prince's girlfriend, one at his parents' home in Birmingham.

During the investigation and the trial as well, Prince played the "race card," but not even local civil-rights activists were going to touch this one. What about those rings? What about that DNA? And why did he run home to Birmingham?

TRIAL SUMMARY:
Judge: Charles R. Hayes
Prosecutor: Daniel Lamborn

NAME: THOMAS PROVENZANO
JURISDICTION: Florida
GENDER: Male
RACE: White
DATE OF BIRTH: 1950
PLACE OF BIRTH: Chicago, IL
ALIASES/NICKNAMES/MONIKERS:
MOTHER:
FATHER:
YEARS OF SCHOOL:
OCCUPATION: Electrician
DISTINGUISHING MARKS:

Thomas Provenzano should be charged with contempt of court. He shot up the Orange County courtroom where he was about to be tried for disorderly conduct. Now he's on Florida's death row for the murder of a bailiff during that episode.

Provenzano comes across as one of those perennially pissed-off people, like maybe he's suffering from Tourette's. The situation that led to his original disorderly conduct/resisting arrest charge grew out of some rather extravagant, and public, expressions of disdain at the driving prowess of his Orlando roadmates. Why police considered this noteworthy is a matter of question. It's de rigueur behavior in many parts of the country (New York). Maybe Provenzano was paranoid. He did entertain the belief that Orlando police were setting up speed traps, changing lights by remote from yellow to red to trap drivers so they could issue more tickets. Provenzano had collected fifteen of those citations. Frankly, to believe in speed traps in the South hardly qualifies as delusions of persecution.

Between his August 1983 arrest and his trial date, Provenzano bought four guns and hundreds of rounds of ammunition. He took to wearing military garb—combat boots, bandannas. In fact, he decked out that way for his court appearance. Now a pattern is starting to take shape. Clearly, these were the days before metal detectors in courthouses, because Provenzano sallied into his trial carrying a backpack full of surprises. Bailiff Harry Dalton told him the backpack had to go. That annoyed Provenzano. When he returned a few minutes later, sans pack, Dalton said he would have to search him. That annoyed him, too, since he had concealed a Rossi .38 in his pocket. They exchanged words and Provenzano pulled the gun and shot Dalton in the head.

In the confusion that reigned thereafter, another bailiff, Arnie Wilkerson, unleashed a hail of bullets in Provenzano's general direction. They all missed, but one caught corrections officer Mark Parker in the back. This gave Provenzano time to whip out his twelve-gauge and apply a round to Wilkerson's chest. That brought the curtain down on Wilkerson's life at sixty. Officers finally managed to fell Provenzano with a shot to the leg.

Bailiff Dalton survived, but with severe brain damage, until his death in 1991, also at sixty. Parker's injury left him paralyzed from the waist down. Only nineteen when he was shot, he's now thirty.

Certainly not a lot had gone right in Provenzano's thirty-four years. His mother left home when he was just a tot. He fell into some petty criminal activity as a teenager. His first marriage failed. His wife's second husband adopted Provenzano's son from that marriage, significantly limiting his access to the child. He got ejected from the air force because he was a discipline problem. A second child was born dead. A second marriage came and went. Old friends died. He was hurt on the job and had to jump through hoops to get his workers' comp claim accepted.

Most unlucky perhaps is that Provenzano was not blessed with a stoic disposition and a sense of humor to help him weather life's viscissitudes. He distanced himself from family and friends who could have helped temper his very understandable frustration. Psychiatrists at his trial said he was simply insane. Jurors weren't buying it. But in the final analysis, he way overreacted to events and his Florida peers assessed him for what he did, not how he came to do it.

NAME: RICHARD RAMIREZ
JURISDICTION: California
GENDER: Male
RACE: Mexican-American
DATE OF BIRTH: February 28, 1960
PLACE OF BIRTH: El Paso, Texas
ALIASES/NICKNAMES/MONIKERS: The Night Stalker
MOTHER:
FATHER:
YEARS OF SCHOOL: 10
OCCUPATION:
DISTINGUISHING MARKS:

Let's look at the good Richard Ramirez did. He almost single-handedly set off an economic boomlet in Southern California during the spring and summer of 1985. Thanks to Ramirez, sales of car services, dead bolts, handguns, alarm systems, garage door openers, and other security-related services and equipment skyrocketed. Californians dealt with Ramirez the way Floridians deal with hurricanes: stock up, lock out, hunker down. Men came home earlier, spending more time with and gaining a greater appreciation of their families. And he gave the media six quality months to speculate, compete, report, and otherwise generate excitement. Oh yes, Richard Ramirez changed the way America thinks. He is the Night Stalker.

By bringing serial murder into the homes of middle-class Americans, Ramirez offered a level of convenience never before available: rape, robbery, multiple murder, and mutilation, all in one timesaving, cost-effective visit. The apparent randomness maximized everyone's feelings of vulnerability and hysteria. It wasn't until shortly before his capture that authorities began to see any pattern at all in Ramirez's activity. The terror he instilled far exceeded the number of his victims, thirteen killed, far beyond the borders of California.

Ramirez didn't have a college degree. Actually, he didn't have a high-school diploma. He didn't have a job either. In fact, he never had a job. He didn't expend a great deal of effort on personal hygiene. He did consume large quantities of drugs and he listened to a lot of heavy metal, although he devoted a disproportionate share to "Night Prowler," by AC/DC.

A number of "novel" behaviors being practiced separately by rival sickos Ramirez synthesized into one compact bundle. He out-Charlied Manson with his deranged scribblings at murder scenes. Although experts question the genuineness of his devotion to Satan, he did raise our level of awareness of satanic practice through his use of pentangles, pentagrams, witches' circles, and other symbols of evil, sometimes rendered in lipstick, sometimes in his victim's blood. He raped with abandon, shot, sodomized, slashed throats, mutilated, bludgeoned, blew out brains, men, old women, young women, children, from Mission Viejo to San Francisco. He cut out one victim's eyes. The accompanying chart lists a sampling of the Night Stalker's body count and sums up the summer of '85:

Victim	Date Murdered
Dale Okazaki	March 16–17, 1985
Tsai-Lian Yu	March 16–17, 1985
Zazarra murders (husband & wife)	March 26, 1985
William Doi	May 14, 1985
Mary Louise Cannon	July 2, 1985
Joyce Nelson	July 7, 1985
Maxson Kneiding	July 20, 1985
Lela Kneiding	July 20, 1985

The last few hours before Ramirez's capture on August 31, 1985, could have been scripted in Hollywood. Early that morning, a Saturday, he stepped off an arriving Greyhound bus and nonchalantly, obliviously walked right past six cops assigned to that station to monitor departing buses as part of the campaign to apprehend him. He had been to Phoenix to score some coke. Spotted at about 8:30 by a woman in a downtown L.A. liquor store, Ramirez ran the better part of a marathon in a three-hour chase scene that ended with his near lynching at the hands of angry barrio residents in East L.A.

Although his lawyers employed every legal angle available to them, Ramirez's trial was little more than a formality. His fate was sealed the moment he admitted to arresting officer Andres Ramirez (no relation), "Yeah, man, I'm Richard Ramirez. . . . I did it, you know. You guys got me, the Stalker."

TRIAL SUMMARY:
Judge: Michael A. Tynan
Sentencing: November 7, 1989

For additional details on Richard Ramirez, check out:
Linedecker, Clifford L.: *Night Stalker,* New York, St. Martin's Press, 1991.

NAME: LARRY KEITH ROBISON
JURISDICTION: Texas
GENDER: Male
RACE: White
DATE OF BIRTH: August 12, 1957
PLACE OF BIRTH: Abilene, TX
ALIASES/NICKNAMES/MONIKERS: born Larry Keith Epp
MOTHER: Lois (Epp) Robison
FATHER: Lloyd Epp
YEARS OF SCHOOL: 13
OCCUPATION: Carpenter
DISTINGUISHING MARKS:

> *"He built a pyramid out of plywood . . . and put it over his head when he was sleeping; or even during the day, he would lie on the couch with this pyramid over his head. He thought it gave him special powers."*
>
> —LOIS ROBISON

God knows, Lois Robison did all she could to protect society from her firstborn son. For years, she stoically endured his drug abuse, the arrests for petty thievery, the schizophrenic episodes. They finally committed him at age twenty-one when he called one night in a paranoid fit, thinking he had blown up a car with his mind and killed its occupants. Doctors at the hospital quickly diagnosed Robison as someone who needed to be confined and sent him to Fort Worth's John Peter Smith Hospital. He was diagnosed as schizophrenic, and his taste for LSD and PCP duly noted, but they couldn't hold him because he wasn't violent. Next stop, a veterans hospital in Waco, but that didn't last long either. Released into Lois's care, Robison was jailed before she could arrange for another institution to take him. She let him vegetate in jail for a

few months just to keep him out of people's hair.
Ultimately, nothing worked, and on Larry's twenty-fourth
birthday, Lois Robison heard on the radio the reports of
what her son had done.

Troubled as he is, by the time of Larry Robison's
defining deed, August 10, 1982, we had already grown
jaded with the likes of Richard Ramirez, Randy Kraft,
William Bonin, and David Carpenter. Besides, Robison
is no Jeffrey Dahmer. The unfortunate bottom-line
truth is that Larry's a perfectly respectable Peoria–level
cannibal, but he'll never play Broadway.

Robison really only set out to kill Ricky Bryant, and
he did. In fact, he removed Bryant's head—laboriously
sawed it off with a steak knife and placed it in the
crook of his arm. That's bound to have struck Ricky's
mother, Junett, as a cute touch when she discovered
her son later on the afternoon of the tenth. Larry only
killed the Reeds, Georgia Ann and her son, Scott;
Georgia's mother, Mrs. Barker; and boyfriend Bruce
Gardner because he needed their car. It's not as if they
were a tight-knit, nuclear, *Leave It to Beaver* type of
family: just a single mother and child, live-in mother,
and boyfriend. They weren't even married. Robison
shot them all at close range and stabbed them thoroughly and then slashed their throats.

As for Bryant, Robison may have been acting out
some revenge for a homosexual liaison he and Bryant
had had some weeks prior. Having met through a
mutual friend in June 1982, Robison moved in with
Bryant just weeks before the murder. He had been away
for part of that span, in Kansas, trying to get his marriage to Tina Pummill back on track. That explains why
he had a key. He let himself in, went to the bathroom
where Bryant was preparing for some local political
gathering, shot Bryant in the head, stabbed him sixty-
plus times, cut his head off, sexually mutilated him, and

allegedly devoured a portion of him. After smearing the scene with Bryant's blood, as if finger-paintng, Robison turned his attention toward escape.

After wiping out the household next door, the rest is just routine. Robison took no extraordinary measures to cover his tracks. Police in Wichita, Kansas, learned soon after they found him asleep in his car that he was wanted for the Bryant murder in Texas, so they sent him back, and now he lives in Huntsville.

Name: DANNY HAROLD ROLLING

Jurisdiction: Florida

Gender: Male

Race: White

Date of Birth: May 26, 1954

Place of Birth: Shreveport, LA

Aliases/Nicknames/Monikers: Mike Kennedy

Mother: Claudia Beatrice Rolling

Father: James Harold Rolling

Years of School: 12 (GED)

Occupation:

Distinguishing Marks:

Let's not confuse Danny Rolling with Ted Bundy. Bundy ended his career as a serial killer in Gainesville, Florida. Rolling made his career there.

On Sunday, August 26, 1990, parents and local police officers began finding young people—mostly coeds—dead in their new apartments. They had all been basking in the euphoria that always accompanies the start of a new college term, but they were denied the follow-through. Wasn't that a favor to them, a service? Danny Rolling had never been allowed to feel success, or euphoria. Why shouldn't these spoiled rich girls get the chance to experience life as he had? It's true. Danny's abusive father had choked off his self-esteem from day one. Chalk up one mitigating factor. But what of society's outrage?

Rolling is not a typical serial killer. He's not even a typical mutilator. He's a tease, a taunt, a very special kind of liar, and he believes his own lies. Danny Rolling wanted nothing more than recognition—his songs, his writing, the message he taped to send to his parents as he embarked on his murderous mission, the special messages he gave police. . . .

Rolling posed his victims. It's what psychiatrists and students of serial killing call a "signature." Christina Powell and Sonya Larson, killed together in the apartment they were sharing, were positioned nude, spread-eagle, and strategically within the rooms for maximum shock value. He cut off Christa Leigh Hoyt's head and placed it just so, so someone looking in a certain window would see the reflection of the severed head in the mirror. There was a vertical incision the length of her torso. Her nipples had been sliced off and placed carefully beside her on the bed. Christa, only eighteen, was the one exception to the "student rule." She was employed by the county sheriff's department and was pursuing a career in law enforcement.

Tracy Paules, found nude on the hallway floor of the Gatorwood apartment she had just moved into, had her legs spread wide apart, too. Her roommate and long-time friend, Manny Taboada . . . well, Manny probably just got in the way. And he damn near killed the killer. If Manny had just managed to get his huge dying hands around Rolling's throat, Tracy might have been saved. But a knife in the back is a rude way to wake up. And thirty cuts and stab wounds can drain a guy's energy, even someone of Manny's size and strength. He can be forgiven a few moments of befuddlement.

That's it. Only five . . . in Gainesville, that is. It's pretty certain Rolling was responsible for the remarkably similar 1989 slaying, complete with signature, of Julie Grissom in Shreveport, Louisiana. Julie's father, Tom, and his grandson Sean were also killed in that attack. But Rolling created a climate of panic, enough to send thousands of UF students and other Gainesville residents packing. And the Gainesville police—they nailed the wrong guy, a hapless schizophrenic who'd been around town forever. It took George Humphrey years to (a) get out of jail and (b) get any kind of acknowledgment from authorities that they'd done the wrong thing.

Rolling's trial and life in prison are about as twisted as the murder spree that got him there. Prisoner groupie Sondra London took up Rolling's cause during his trial. At one point during the pretrial hearings, the dorkmeister took it home with a corny a cappella courtroom rendition of one of his songs for his new-found sweetheart. Court officials and observers were alternately spellbound and embarrassed by Rolling's saccharine exhibitionism.

But that's Danny Rolling. Recognition is recognition. He was always the gentleman perp, apologizing to his victims, their families, his family, the police, society—always admitting his guilt to arresting officers. It's like, "Oh well, I screwed up again . . . but who expected otherwise?"

Nobody, Danny. Nobody.

TRIAL SUMMARY:
Judge: Stanley J. Morris
Prosecutor: Rodney Smith
Defense: C. Richard Parker
Jury: Nine women, three men
Beginning Date: February 15, 1994
Sentencing: April 20, 1994

For additional details on Danny Harold Rolling, check out:
Ryzuk, Mary S.: *The Gainesville Ripper,* New York, Donald J. Fine, 1994.

NAME: RAMON SALCIDO
JURISDICTION: California
GENDER: Male
RACE: Mexican-American
DATE OF BIRTH: March 6, 1961
PLACE OF BIRTH: Los Mochis, Mexico
ALIASES/NICKNAMES/MONIKERS:
MOTHER:
FATHER:
YEARS OF SCHOOL:
OCCUPATION: Forklift driver; migrant worker
DISTINGUISHING MARKS:

It was a summer of love for Angela Richards. Never before in her bizarre, sheltered life had she felt like this. She was nineteen. Ramon was twenty-three. He was five-eight, easygoing, energetic, earthy. She was five-six, quiet, and reserved. She had been raised that way, and to work hard. Maybe Ramon would change all that. They met at a soccer game in Larson Park. It was about the only entertainment she had known her whole life. Angela was so in love, she would slip out of the house late at night to rendezvous with Ramon. He taught her the facts of life.

Bob Richards was not happy to learn of his daughter's pregnancy in November 1984. Nor was he enchanted with Angela's choice of suitor. But Bob was a firm believer in traditional values: marriage, family, hard work. This Mexican migrant worker would simply have to do the right thing. That's what Tradition, Family, and Property was all about. His sect's interpretation of orthodox Catholicism put it very close to cult status. To describe TFP's mystical, oppressive, ardently anticommunist doctrines as fringe is putting it mildly. The new couple picked up their marriage license at

Santa Rosa courthouse on November 28, and on
December 8, they were married at St. Margaret Mary's
in Oakland.

Free at last. Angela had her baby; a girl, Sophia.
Then another, Carmina. Then another, Teresa. She
started a sewing business. She liked that ruffled, lacy
country-western look, like Grand Ole Opry. Ramon
drove a forklift at Grand Cru, one of Sonoma's winer-
ies. Turns out Ramon was hardly less protective than
Bob Richards and TFP. He didn't like the idea of
Angela working. He was even more dismayed when
someone planted the idea in Angela's head to go to
modeling school—Barbizon. He survived the classes;
he would sit outside in the car, waiting impatiently,
through all of them. Now she needed a photo session.
Why did any woman need to be so glamorous? What
was she going to do with all this? It ran counter to his
macho notions of a woman's place. It aggravated that
streak in him that tended toward booze, drugs, obnox-
iousness, and domestic violence.

Beside that, he had just heard from Debra Whitten.
In fact, he was not really divorced from Debra. If he
were, the DA might not be pressing so hard for child
support for his daughter. On April 11, 1985, the sheriff served papers for him to fork over $511 monthly in
child-support payments. It was the last straw.
Thursday night, Ramon hit the bars and didn't come
home. Early Friday, Angela had gone to a nearby cash
machine when Ramon came home. In a jealous rage,
he took the kids and went searching for her. He drove
to a secluded area and slashed his daughters' throats.
Sophia and Teresa died. Miraculously, Carmina survived. He drove to the Richards' residence and killed
Angela's mother, Louise, and her two sisters, Ruth
and Mary Ann. He took Bob's gun, returned to his
own house, and killed Angela. Then on to Grand Cru,

where he killed Tracy Troovey, and wounded his supervisor, Ken Butti. It was all over by 8:00 A.M.— seven dead, two more wounded—the worst massacre in Sonoma County history.

Ramon fled back to Mexico but was arrested just four days later when his sister turned him in to get the forty-thousand dollar reward. He gave up without a fight and confessed everything on the plane on the way back.

For additional details on Ramon Salcido, check out:

Streshinsky, Shirley: "Angela: A Story of Innocence, Hope, Despair, and Mass Murder," *Glamour,* March 1990, p. 268.

Sanders, Alain L.: "Bringing Them Back to Justice— Extradition Can Be a Breeze, or a Byzantine Business," *Time*, May 1, 1989, p. 42.

NAME: SEAN RICHARD SELLERS
JURISDICTION: Oklahoma
GENDER: Male
RACE: White
DATE OF BIRTH: 1973
PLACE OF BIRTH:
ALIASES/NICKNAMES/MONIKERS:
MOTHER: Vonda Bellofatto
FATHER:
YEARS OF SCHOOL: 11+
OCCUPATION:
DISTINGUISHING MARKS:

None of us will likely ever report back whether Sean Sellers spends eternity in heaven or hell. Certainly he has befriended both Jesus and Satan in his short lifetime.

The ruse must have seemed plausible to Sellers's sixteen-year-old mind: kill the folks, get your ever-loyal best friend to swear to your whereabouts at the time of the crime, discover the scene yourself, and fake tears and sorrow for neighbors and authorities till it all blows over.

Nevertheless, it took detective Ron Mitchell less than a day to dismantle Sellers's story and bring bosom buddy Richard Howard over to the state's side to testify against his best friend. Sean had speculated that it was burglars who broke in his house and killed his parents. Mitchell found no evidence of forced entry nor anything missing. Besides, burglars don't typically shoot people in their sleep.

For people who need a sensible motive for every act, good or evil, the closest one is that Sellers was angered by his mother's objections to the girl he wanted to date. She forbade him to see her. The more captivating theory is that Sellers had entered a pact with Satan.

Because of the secretiveness with which it's exercised, Satan worship is difficult to fathom. That Sellers was dabbling is indisputable. His schoolmates attest to his drinking blood in the cafeteria. Various other friends and acquaintances claim Sellers devoted considerable time, energy, and resources to satanic pursuits.

In fact, his mother and stepfather were not Sean Sellers's first murder victims. Six months earlier, he had gunned down an Oklahoma City convenience store clerk, Robert Paul Bower. There was no motive for that one either, unless the desire to see how murder feels can be considered a motive. Lack of motive kept police baffled until Richard Howard shed light on Bower's murder during the investigation. In the six-month interval, neither Sean's teachers nor his parents nor any other adult detected any change in his behavior or words. He apparently felt no remorse.

Lately, Sellers has become a celebrity of sorts. Oprah Winfrey, Geraldo Rivera, and *48 Hours* all taped and aired interviews with him, and he was written up in *People*. Maybe all his stumping for Jesus will keep him out of hell. Whether it will keep him off the lethal injection gurney at Oklahoma's H-Unit remains in question.

For additional details on Sean Sellers, check out:
Kahaner, Larry: *Cults That Kill*, New York, Warner Books, 1988.

NAME: MITCHELL SIMS
JURISDICTION: South Carolina
GENDER: Male
RACE: White
DATE OF BIRTH:
PLACE OF BIRTH:
ALIASES/NICKNAMES/MONIKERS:
MOTHER: Mildred Cranford
FATHER:
YEARS OF SCHOOL:
OCCUPATION:
DISTINGUISHING MARKS:

Mitchell Sims probably is not the inspiration for the film *Natural Born Killers,* but he could be. Inside Sims thumps a felonious heart, and because of it, he has two states vying for the right to take him out. Currently, South Carolina has him, although California tried him first. Given the Deep South's greater penchant for rough justice, Sims is not likely to see the Golden State again.

Sims's distinction among death row denizens is an uncharacteristic personality mix. He is quite the ladies' man, but unlike many of his death row brethren, he eschews kidnap and rape. The forthrightness of his robberies and murders did not carry over to his relationships with women. He preferred to court and cajole his way into his object's affections. In fact, one of his first stints in jail resulted from trying to frame the husband of a woman he wanted. He actually got a friend to shoot him to make it look like jealous rage at discovering the two of them in bed. It almost worked.

Another girlfriend, Ruby Carolyn Padgett, accompanied Sims on his cross-country flight from justice after knocking off his first Domino's pizza store, and she was on hand for Domino's II, another robbery/murder starring Sims. Law enforcement would label Mitch and Ruby the "Killing Team." Finally, there's Sims's long-suffering wife Theresa. Talk about "till death us do part," Theresa saw Sims through his crime career, through his other women—even counseling him that perhaps Ruby was a bad influence—and finally through his death sentence. She conceived a child by him from death row in South Carolina. Go figure. Oh, let's not forget Sims's mother. During the sentencing phase of Mitch's trial, Mildred Cranford informed jurors of her incestuous relations with her son in his teen years. Is that a mother's love or what?

Another aspect of Sims's "Renaissance" persona was his meticulous attention to detail. He seems to have taken a certain pride of craftsmanship in his heists and other deceits. There was the attempt to set up his lover's husband, already cited. The Domino's jobs were very thoroughly planned. Well, maybe not the first one, but he improved. In the second Domino's hit, he and Ruby went shopping in advance for extra ammunition, rope, duct tape, socks to be used as gags—everything needed for a successful stickup. See the priorities? He probably spent as much on supplies as he netted in the robbery. And the execution—exquisite, a perfect 10—the way he placed that pizza order . . . the hiding behind the motel-room door, the knots around young John Harrigan's wrists and ankles—doubled, tripled, quadrupled . . . the drowning in the tub, no bloody mess, no big bang. And then to don Harrigan's Domino's delivery shirt, what irony, what a sense of humor. The guys back at the Domino's store were sure surprised. Sims took all the money and strung up Ed Sicam and Kory Spiroff by their necks in the cooler. Only the fortuituous arrival of another employee spared them a visit from Mr. Reaper.

Sims's Domino's affinity reveals another interesting

aspect of his thinking. So much of Sims's errant behavior arose from revenge and greed. He had worked at Domino's, was even managing a store, but he got canned. The "official" reason given was poor performance, a generic corporate euphemism for some specific deed or quirk that bosses just don't like. In Sims's case, it meant smoking dope all day in the cooler with one of the girls he had hired. He shouldn't have been surprised at his firing, but it just ate away at him, and he became obsessed with getting even.

Well, it's all over now. After the Glendale, California, Domino's robbery/murder, Sims and Padgett split for Las Vegas and a little R&R preparatory to a third Domino's strike. Determined California law enforcement officials got the word out far and wide, and Domino's put up a reward of $100,000. The discovery of John Harrigan's truck in Las Vegas narrowed the field, and an alert Vegas bartender administered the coup de grâce. Sims and Padgett were collared on Christmas Day 1985.

NAME: KARLA FAYE TUCKER
JURISDICTION: Texas
GENDER: Female
RACE: White
DATE OF BIRTH: November 18, 1959
PLACE OF BIRTH: Houston, TX
ALIASES/NICKNAMES/MONIKERS:
MOTHER: Carolyn Ann Moore
FATHER: Lawrence Earl Tucker
YEARS OF SCHOOL: 7 (GED in prison)
OCCUPATION: Office worker; call girl
DISTINGUISHING MARKS:

In street parlance, Kari Tucker is a snitch. That's Kari, not Karla. Kari is Karla's sister. Douglas Garrett is a snitch, too. He's Danny Garrett's brother. Danny was Karla's boyfriend, and her partner in the pickax murders of Jerry Lynn Dean and Deborah Ruth Thornton. Kari was Doug's girlfriend. They married a little before Karla's trial. Girlfriend and boyfriend testifying against girlfriend and boyfriend. Sister and brother testifying against sister and brother. Hookers, both Kari and Karla, biker brethren, testifying against . . . Something doesn't add up here.

Blood doesn't turn on blood. Karla and Kari were sisters, roommates, coworkers, family. They were two of Carolyn Moore's three daughters, and Mama Carolyn was known to stand by her own—daughters and otherwise—and her daughters loved and respected her. She was a "high-dollar whore" herself, and she taught them the trade. They all did drugs together. Carolyn "knew how to operate." That's how Karla wanted to be. Blood doesn't turn on blood. And since when do hookers cooperate with police? The entire household, and their circle of friends went the extra mile to appear tough. They *were* tough. What happened?

Murder's scary. This murder was . . . spectacular. Karla Faye is not Lizzie Borden. She didn't go to Wal-Mart and purchase a pickax to kill Jerry Lynn Dean. It was Jerry's pick. He used it to cut through Bermuda grass in his job laying cable. Karla was just there to intimidate Jerry Lynn. She thought he was a wuss. They were going to steal the chopper parts he'd been busting ass to accumulate, and to scare the spineless bastard into another dimension.

Mission accomplished. All indicators point to Jerry Lynn having been plenty concerned before somebody clubbed him into oblivion. All the pickax work, Karla says, was to make Jerry stop gurgling—death rattle probably. Deborah Thornton is your real victim, though. She sure as hell didn't know what was going on. She didn't even know Jerry Dean, at whose apartment she was enjoying your proverbial one-night stand. No way did she know Karla Tucker and Danny Garrett.

She almost made it. Karla noticed a quivering lump under a blanket in the corner only after she'd polished off Dean. Honest to God . . . when they got there, as they clubbed Dean senseless and then dead, they didn't know there was anyone else in the apartment—in the room, three or four feet from the brouhaha! But have a witness? No; sorry, Deborah. Bad luck. Really, really sorry. As much as a murderer can empathize with the murdered, Karla seems to have done so with Deborah. Somebody, however, left the pickax buried in Thornton's chest. That flourish, or oversight, or whatever it was, pretty much set the tone for the trials.

The ax was seven inches into Thornton's chest, which is to say it came out the back. S. C. Pilgrim pulled it out. But Karla was not being tried for Thornton's murder. Garrett was. Karla was on trial for Dean's. Hell-bent to get death for Karla, prosecutors tried her for the hard one, and held the easy one in reserve, just in case. They didn't need it.

When Karla hit death row in Gatesville, she was by herself, not the first woman on Texas's death row, though. Pam Perillo was first, but she didn't get to Gatesville till later. Then came Betty Lou Beets, and Frances Newton. They get along swimmingly, kind of a little sorority.

Staying a biker chick on death row didn't make much sense. Karla has forgiven Douglas for wearing that wire, and Kari for her damning testimony. Kari visits. It's all water under the bridge. Karla's a symbol now. She must be. However guilty she may be, she's no guiltier than Danny Garrett, and he's off now. She's a model prisoner—knits, crochets, cooks, makes dolls, plays games, takes courses, reads, writes, walks with Jesus, does aerobics. Deathrowbics. They'll probably keep her there as long as they can, as a message to all of Texas's feisty young women. Do you want to end up like Karla Faye . . . ?

TRIAL SUMMARY:
Judge: Patricia Lykos
Prosecutor: Joe Magliolo
Defense: Mack Arnold; Henry Oncken
Beginning Date: April 11, 1984
Sentence: April 23, 1984

For additional details on Karla Faye Tucker, check out:
Lowry, Beverly: *Crossed Over,* New York, Warner Books, 1992.

Name: ROBERT WAYNE VICKERS
Jurisdiction: Arizona
Gender: Male
Race: White
Date of Birth: April 29, 1958
Place of Birth: Phoenix, AZ
Aliases/Nicknames/Monikers: "Bonzai Bob"
Mother:
Father:
Years of School:
Occupation:
Distinguishing Marks:

Banzai: May you live a thousand years; a battle cry for Japanese kamikaze pilots during World War II.

Bonsai: The cultivation of diminutive plants, intentionally stunted.

The "Bonzai," in Bonzai Bob, then, must be some hybrid of the two: May you live as a stunted plant for a thousand years, with periodic homicidal episodes along the way.

In January 1989 the *St. Louis Post-Dispatch* ran brief profiles of the sixty-nine death row inmates in Missouri's prison system. (That number is now up to ninety-three.) Of those sixty-nine, thirteen received their death sentences for murders they committed while in custody. They killed either another inmate or a corrections officer. That's 19 percent. The murders happened within the most closely guarded, intensely regimented environment in the United States.

For people who think the punishment of going to prison is being doled out by the state authorities, it's an eye-opener to learn that in fact, it's the inmates punishing each other. All officials have to do is lock these guys up together and let nature take its course.

Robert Vickers falls into this class of death row prisoner, and he has distinguished himself even among this incorrigible few. Not only did Vickers get his death sentence for a killing committed while he was in Arizona State Penitentiary in Florence, he killed a second time while on death row itself. That makes Vickers an anomaly, and a poster boy for the failures of America's prison system. Prior to his imprisonment for burglary, Vickers was just a small-time rip-off artist, with occasional bouts of employment as a bricklayer, gas station attendant, cook, and landscaper.

But prison is tough. And Vickers is small. He needed to make a statement, a warning to all the predators to keep a distance. Frank Ponciano was first, and Marshall McLuhan should be proud of the way Vickers proved his theory. Ponciano was strangled with a knotted bedsheet and stabbed multiple times with a sharpened toothbrush. On his back—the "medium"—Vickers used that same toothbrush to carve his moniker, "Bonzai." No mistaking the message. Very clear. Very concise. "I got the idea from Zorro," Vickers explained. Chalk up one "inability to relate positively to cellmate" for Vickers. That's the last time anybody'll drink his Kool-Aid allowance.

So what did nine-hundred-pound Buster Holsinger do to deserve the firebomb he got from Vickers? Where did Vickers get the materials to make a fire-bomb? Bonzai was showing Buster a photo of his niece. Buster insinuated something of a sexual nature regarding the girl, to Vickers's consternation. Later on, Bonzai marinated Buster in a once-popular hair product and tossed in a match. Given Buster's girth, the five-by-eight cell offered few avenues of retreat, and he died of some variation on asphyxiation. By the way, if you're wearing Vitalis, you could be flammable.

TRIAL SUMMARY:
Judge: Robert R. Bean
Prosecutor: Victor Cook
Beginning Date: September 28, 1982
Conviction: September 29, 1982
Sentencing: October 18, 1982

NAME: AILEEN CAROL WUORNOS
JURISDICTION: Florida
GENDER: Female
RACE: White
DATE OF BIRTH: February 29, 1956
PLACE OF BIRTH: Rochester, MI
ALIASES/NICKNAMES/MONIKERS: Lee; Cammie Marsh
    Greene; Susan Lynn Blahovec; Sandra Beatrice
    Kretsch; Lori Kristine Grody; the I–75 Killer; the
    Damsel of Death
MOTHER: Diane Wuornos
FATHER: Leo Dale Pittman
YEARS OF SCHOOL: 9–10
OCCUPATION: Callgirl
DISTINGUISHING MARKS:

Aileen Wuornos got her fifteen minutes of fame in the
face of some stiff competition. Jeffrey Dahmer, the Persian
Gulf War, and "Gainesville Ripper" Danny Rolling were
all front-page news when coverage of Wuornos's trial hit
in January 1992. She's not the first female serial murderer, as many headlines claimed, but she is the most
notorious. Most women guilty of multiple killings do it
quietly, usually by poisoning, and usually in some caregiv-
ing role, the victims children or the elderly. Wuornos, the
Damsel of Death, killed like a man: her seven victims
were all adult males, none of whom she had known previously. She dispatched them with her trusty .22-caliber
"double nine."

There is enough human interest in Wuornos's story
for several books and movies and endless tabloid
exploitation—prostitution, lesbianism, murder, bikers,
dysfunctional families, born-again Christians, politically
ambitious lawyers, and a surprise-a-day investigation.

As a prostitute, Wuornos was a bit long in the tooth.

She saved up her lust for her over-the-edge beer habit. There was a time when she could get it up for Ty Moore—Tyria Jolene Moore—her lesbian friend and lover and Howdy Doody look-alike, whom she met at the Zodiac Bar in 1986. But by the time Wuornos undertook her murder binge, she and Ty were more like sisters, just good, good friends and roommates. Wuornos made her living as a "hitchhiker prostitute." She plied the interstates and secondary highways of north Florida, around Ocala, Gainesville, and Daytona. She would thumb a ride, unload some hard-luck story, work around to a proposition, direct the john to a secluded woodsy area, and shoot him many times. She would usually steal their cars and pawn or store the men's possessions. The unlucky seven,* in order of demise are:

VICTIM	AGE	LINE OF WORK	DATE FOUND
Richard Mallory	51	Electronics repairman	12–13–89
David Spears	43	Heavy-equipment operator	06–01–90
Charles Carskaddon	40	Possible drug trafficker	06–06–90
Peter Siems	65	Christian outreach missionary	06–22–90
Troy Burress	50	Driver, sausage delivery truck	08–04–90
Dick Humphreys	56	Supervisor, protective investigation— abused and injured children	09–12–90
Walter Gino Antonio	60	Reserve policeman	11–19–90

* Although the prosecution believed she was guilty of seven murders, Wuornos admitted to only six.

Detectives finally caught up with Wuornos at the Last Resort, a biker bar in Port Orange, Florida. They apprehended Ty Moore at her parents' home in Ohio at about the same time. Although not implicated in the murders, Ty was the key to wrangling a confession out of Wuornos. Police put her in a motel room and gave telephone access to the jail, while they listened in and taped the conversation. It took three days, but Wuornos's unusual devotion to her more-or-less-innocent sidekick prevailed over her razor-sharp sense of self-preservation. "Your [sic] my left and right arm." Lee declared. "I'd die for you." That was okay with Ty. She testified against her friend at the trial.

The freak show soon hit full tilt with the arrival of legions of opportunists, all looking to cut a lucrative deal. This was tabloid journalism's finest hour. They descended on Marion County like vultures: *Hard Copy, Inside Edition, Nightline, Geraldo.* Instant producer Jackelyn Giroux struck fast, negotiating rights to everything under the sun, from as many people as she could. The detectives who broke the case were approached with movie deals. Perhaps the finest stroke of all came from one Arlene Pralle, a born-again Christian God instructed to take up Lee's cause. She actually adopted Wuornos. The real show, though, lay in the accounts of her exploits Wuornos gave authorities, richly detailed prevarications put forth with lavish doses of profanity. Consistency was not a priority for Lee Wuornos.

As had been the case throughout her life, Lee was on her own at trial, too. She was the sole witness for the defense, and true to form, her perfomance removed most remaining traces of sympathy jurors may have harbored. The seven-woman, five-man jury convicted her with minimal deliberation and were unanimous in recommending death. And what did Lee think of that? She heaped abuse on the cops, the system, the prosecutor,

Ty, her family, her clientele, her lawyers. She told the jury she hoped they got raped. She called them "scumbags of America." At the conclusion of her second trial, she offered her middle finger in one final contemptuous salute to Judge Sawaya, and in an uncharacteristically brief response to his pronouncement of additional death sentences, she called the judge a motherfucker.

TRIAL SUMMARY:

Judge: Uriel "Bunky" Blount, after Gayle Graziano recused

Prosecutor: John Tanner; grunt work by assistants David Damore and Sean Daley

Defense: Tricia Jenkins; Billy Nolas; William Miller; Don Sanchez

Beginning Date: January 13, 1992

Conviction: January 27, 1992

Sentence: January 30, 1992

For additional details on Aileen Carol Wuornos, check out:

Reynolds, Michael: *Dead Ends,* New York, Warner Books, 1992.

BOB WEINSTEIN is a former editor-in-chief of *Prison Life Magazine* Author and journalist, he's written ten books and his articles have appeared in *The Boston Globe, Newsday, The Washington Post, The New York Times, The Daily News, Family Circle* and *McCall's*.

JIM BESSENT is an editor and writer on a wide range of nonfiction subjects. As an editor, he has worked for more than ten years at major publishing houses. As a writer, he specializes in popular culture.